Scott Foresman - Addison Wesley
MIDDLE SCHOOL MATH

Practice Masters

Course 3

Scott Foresman - Addison Wesley

Editorial Offices: Menlo Park, California • Glenview, Illinois
Sales Offices: Reading, Massachusetts • Atlanta, Georgia • Glenview, Illinois
Carrollton, Texas • Menlo Park, California

http://www.sf.aw.com

Overview

Practice Masters provide additional exercises for students who have not mastered key skills and concepts covered in the student text. A Practice Master is provided for each regular lesson in the student text. In addition, a Practice Master is also provided for each Section Review and Cumulative Review lesson.

Lesson worksheets provide exercises similar to those in the Practice and Apply section of the student text.

Section Review worksheets review the student text section and include application problems that review previous material.

Cumulative Review worksheets cover important skills from the chapter at hand and from previous chapters. References to the applicable student text lessons are provided.

ISBN 0–201–31240–9

Contents

Line Plots and Stem-and-Leaf Diagrams

State the range and draw a line plot for each data set.

1. Some students were asked "How many magazines do you subscribe to?" Their answers were 3, 0, 2, 3, 0, 0, 5, 1, 3, and 2.

range _____

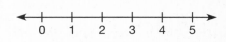

2. Jorge wrote down the number of songs on each of his ten favorite CDs. The numbers he wrote were 8, 10, 14, 11, 7, 10, 9, 10, 12, and 9.

range _____

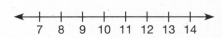

3. Career A real estate agent wrote the number of bedrooms in each of the homes on Cedar Avenue. They were 2, 3, 3, 2, 4, 3, 2, 2, 5, 3, 2, 2, and 1.

range _____

State the range and draw a stem-and-leaf diagram for each data set.

4. The number of pages in the books on Syd's bookshelf are 84, 96, 132, 115, 100, 97, 89, 126, 98, 115, 86, 135, and 92.

range _____

stem	leaf

5. Ms. Trejo's history class took a test last week. The scores were 89, 92, 74, 87, 98, 86, 79, 83, 94, 100, 68, 80, 93, 70, 84, 73, 62, 83, 91, 86, 77, and 87.

range _____

stem	leaf

Measures of Central Tendency

Find the mean, median, and mode(s) of each data set.

1. The number of students in classes at Johnson School are 30, 27, 31, 26, 33, 29, 21, 31, 30, 28, and 26.

   mean _____ median _____ mode(s) _____

2. The number of children in families on Memory Lane are 3, 0, 2, 1, 2, 1, 1, 0, 3, and 4.

   mean _____ median _____ mode(s) _____

3. The daily wages for employees at Burrito Hut are $62, $47, $75, $59, and $49.

   mean _____ median _____ mode(s) _____

Health The table shows the calcium and potassium content of several vegetable foods. Use the table for Exercises 4–7.

Food	1 raw carrot	1 ear corn	1/2 cup lentils	1/2 cup raw mushrooms	1 baked potato	1/2 cup tofu	1 raw tomato
Calcium (mg)	19	2	19	2	20	130	9
Potassium (mg)	233	192	366	130	844	150	255

4. Find the mean, median, and mode(s) for the amount of calcium.

   mean _____ median _____ mode(s) _____

5. Identify the outlier in the calcium data. _____

   Recalculate the mean and median as if the outlier were not in the data set.

   mean _____ median _____

6. Find the mean, median, and mode(s) for the amount of potassium.

   mean _____ median _____ mode(s) _____

7. Is there an outlier in the potassium data? Explain.

   _____

Name _____

Box-and-Whisker Plots

Sketch a box-and-whisker plot for each set of data. Between what range does the middle half of the data fall?

1. Howard counted the number of convenience stores he saw the last six times he went for a drive with his parents. The numbers were 7, 4, 12, 3, 6, and 8.

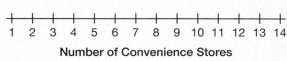
Number of Convenience Stores

_____

2. The last fifteen people to leave the library checked out 1, 5, 3, 0, 4, 1, 2, 0, 3, 6, 12, 6, 4, 8, and 2 books.

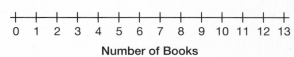
Number of Books

_____

3. From 1980 to 1994, the winning scores in the British Open men's golf championship were 271, 276, 284, 275, 276, 282, 280, 279, 273, 275, 270, 272, 272, 267, and 268.

British Open - Winning Scores

_____

4. The number of faces of regular polyhedra are 6, 4, 8, 20, and 12.

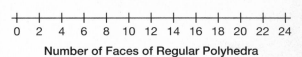
Number of Faces of Regular Polyhedra

_____

The box-and-whisker plot shows the 1990 populations of the 20 largest U.S. metropolitan areas. Use it for Exercises 5–7.

Population of Major U.S. Metropolitan Areas (millions)

5. Give the range, median, and quartiles of the data (in millions).

range _____   median _____

lower quartile _____   upper quartile _____

6. What fraction of the 20 areas have a population between 3.45 million and 5.3 million?   _____

7. What is shown by the whisker right of the median?

_____

_____

Bar Graphs and Line Graphs

1. Create a bar graph to represent the data, showing the five rhythm and blues performers with the most number-one singles since 1965.

Performer	James Brown	Aretha Franklin	Marvin Gaye	The Temptations	Stevie Wonder
#1 singles	16	20	13	14	18

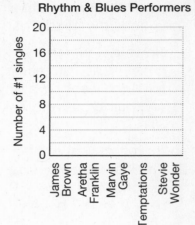

2. Career The data shows the approximate number of civilians (in thousands) working for the military in a given year. Create a line graph to represent the data. Draw a conclusion about the civilian staff in the military from 1985 to 1993.

Year	'85	'86	'87	'88	'89	'90	'91	'92	'93
Civilians	980	960	970	950	960	930	900	890	850

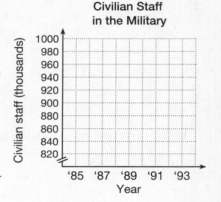

_____

_____

3. The table shows the median age of American men and women at the time of their first marriage. Create a double line graph to represent this data. What conclusions can you draw?

Year	1940	1950	1960	1970	1980	1990
Men	24.3	22.8	22.8	23.2	24.7	26.1
Women	21.5	20.3	20.3	20.8	22.0	23.9

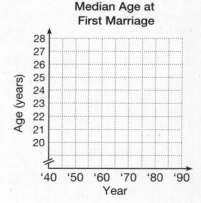

_____

_____

_____

© Scott Foresman • Addison Wesley 8

Name _____

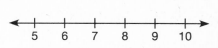
Section 1A Review

1. Edwin counted the number of cars that passed him as he walked to school each day for two weeks. The numbers were 8, 7, 5, 9, 7, 6, 9, 6, 7, and 10. Find the mean, median, and mode(s) of these numbers. Draw a line plot to show the mode(s).

   mean _____ median _____ mode(s) _____

The table shows the number of outlets (in thousands) and the sales (in billions of dollars) of the ten largest American fast-food chains in 1991.

Chain	Arby's	Burger King	Dairy Queen	Domino's Pizza	Hardee's	KFC	McDonald's	Pizza Hut	Taco Bell	Wendy's
Outlets	2.2	6.1	5.2	5.2	3.2	7.9	11.2	7.4	3.1	3.8
Sales	1.3	5.7	2.2	2.5	2.9	5.3	17.3	4.1	2.1	3.0

2. Create a stem-and-leaf diagram for the sales data. (Use the digit after the decimal point for each leaf.)

   stem | leaf

3. Find the mean number of outlets and sales of these fast-food chains.

   mean number of outlets _____

   mean sales _____

4. Create a box-and-whisker plot for the amount of sales, in billions of dollars.

   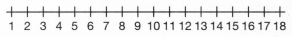

5. Create a box-and-whisker plot and a bar graph for the number of outlets of these fast-food chains.

   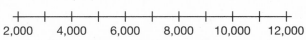

6. Describe a possible relationship between the number of outlets and the amount of sales. Use your results from Exercises 2–5.

   _____

7. On April 30, 1986, Ashrita Furman performed 8341 somersaults in 630 minutes. About how many somersaults did he perform each minute? *[Previous Course]*

   _____

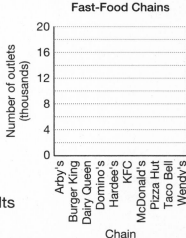

Fast-Food Chains

Understanding Surveys

For Exercises 1–4, state whether or not the sample is random.

1. For the population of popular music fans: a top-40 radio station asks listeners to call in and name their three favorite songs. _____

2. For the population of students in Ellen's history class: Ellen chooses the seven students she feels most comfortable talking to. _____

3. For the population of students at Horton Junior High School: Each student's name is written on a separate card. The cards are mixed in a barrel, and a blindfolded student removes 15 cards from the drum. _____

4. For the population of all residents in a particular area code: A computer is used to select 7-digit numbers at random, and the telephone numbers are dialed until the surveyor is able to contact 25 people who are willing to answer some questions. _____

5. A publisher wants to know whether their new book about rocket science will appeal to high school students. The publisher sends free copies of the book to science clubs at 100 high schools nationwide. The students like the book very much. Can the publisher be reasonably certain that the book will sell well to high school students? Explain.

   _____

   _____

6. A software manufacturer offers a World Wide Web site where users can ask questions about the software. Most of the users who write in report that they are having trouble using the software. Should the manufacturer conclude that most people who buy the software are having problems? Explain.

   _____

   _____

7. A pharmaceutical company distributed 31,600 trial samples of acne soap to high school students. Each sample was packaged with a questionnaire, and 8,350 of the questionnaires were returned.

   a. What is the population of this survey? _____

   b. What is the sample size of this survey? _____

© Scott Foresman • Addison Wesley 8

Recording and Organizing Data

1. Mr. Ishii made a histogram showing his students' performance
on a recent English test.

a. What is the interval
width in this
histogram?

b. How many students
scored between 80
and 89 points?

_____   _____

c. Make a frequency table for the histogram.

Score					
Students					

d. Can you tell how many students scored
73 points? Explain.

_____

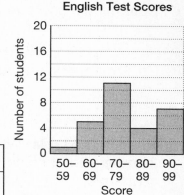

English Test Scores

2. The frequency table shows the ages of U.S. Senators
in the 103rd Congress in 1994. Create a histogram to
represent the data.

Age	under 40	40–49	50–59	60–69	70 or over
Number	1	16	48	22	12

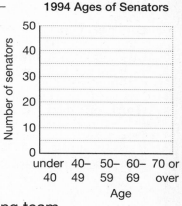

1994 Ages of Senators

3. The data shows the number of points scored by the winning team
of each Super Bowl for the years 1980 to 1994. Create a frequency
table and a histogram to represent the data. Use intervals of 10.

Year	'80	'81	'82	'83	'84	'85	'86	'87
Points	31	27	26	27	38	38	46	39

Year	'88	'89	'90	'91	'92	'93	'94
Points	42	20	55	20	37	52	30

Points				
Number of Years				

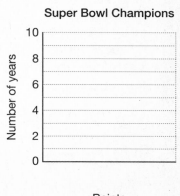

Super Bowl Champions

Name _____

Scatterplots and Trends

1. The data shows the results of the 1994 NBA Eastern Conference Semi-finals. Create a scatterplot for the data. Determine a trend and draw a trend line if possible.

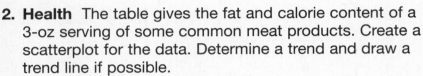

Away	86	91	102	83	86	79	77	96	69	81	86	76	79
Home	90	96	104	95	87	93	87	85	92	101	102	88	98

_____

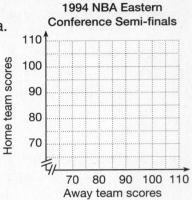

1994 NBA Eastern Conference Semi-finals

2. Health The table gives the fat and calorie content of a 3-oz serving of some common meat products. Create a scatterplot for the data. Determine a trend and draw a trend line if possible.

Food	Fat (g)	Calories
Raw clams	1	63
Fish sticks	10	231
Canned tuna	7	169
Lean ground beef	16	231
Lamb chop	17	252
Ham, canned, roasted	7	140
Fried chicken wings	7	103
Frankfurters, beef and pork	25	274

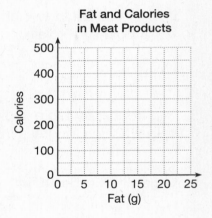

Fat and Calories in Meat Products

3. Health An *outpatient* is someone who receives treatment at a hospital without being confined to the hospital. The table shows the approximate number of every 100 hospital surgeries performed on outpatients from 1982 to 1992. Create a scatterplot for the data. Determine a trend and draw a trend line.

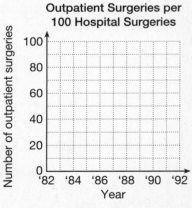

Outpatient Surgeries per 100 Hospital Surgeries

Year	'82	'83	'84	'85	'86	'87	'88	'89	'90	'91	'92
Outpatients	21	28	31	37	40	45	48	50	52	57	60

Name _____

Designing a Survey

1. Provide a possible question that would appear on a survey card that comes with a new book.

   _____

2. Provide a possible question that would appear on a survey card that comes with a frozen dinner.

   _____

3. Provide a possible question that would appear on a survey card that comes with a new calculator.

   _____

4. The organizers of a youth troop in downtown Dallas, Texas, plan to print some brochures to target young people in their community. To find out what images and activities appeal to these young people, they plan to take a survey.

   a. Who is the population of the survey?

   _____

   b. Why do the organizers want to know what images and activities appeal to the target population?

   _____

   _____

   c. The organizers discover that a similar survey has already been taken in a rural Pennsylvania community. Should they use the results of that survey instead of taking a new survey? Explain.

   _____

   _____

   _____

5. The bar graph shows the results of a survey that asked, "On the average, how many minutes do you exercise every day?"

   a. What was the most frequent answer? _____

   b. How many people exercise an hour or more? _____

   c. How many people were surveyed? _____

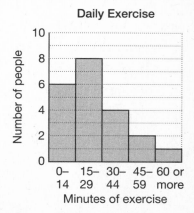

Daily Exercise

Name _____

Section 1B Review

1. Josh is surveying the students in his class. He does not want to bias his results, so he talks only to students he does not know. Is the following survey random or not random? If the sample is not random, state the part of the population that is not represented.

_____

2. The scatterplot shows the price and fuel efficiency of several automobile models. What trend is evident in the data? Why might this be true?

_____

_____

_____

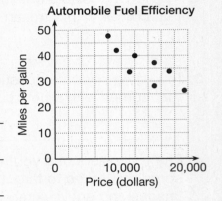

Automobile Fuel Efficiency

3. The table shows the land area of midwestern states (in thousands of square miles). Make a frequency chart of the data, using intervals of 10,000 square miles. Then make a histogram.

State	IA	IL	IN	KS	MI	MN	MO
Area	56.0	55.6	35.9	81.8	57.0	79.5	68.9

State	ND	NE	OH	SD	WI
Area	70.7	76.6	41.0	76.0	54.0

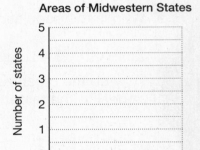

Areas of Midwestern States

Area
(thousands of square miles)

Area						
States						

4. The data gives the number of points scored by each player of the Vancouver Canucks hockey team during the 1993–1994 season. Make a box-and-whisker plot to represent the data. *[Lesson 1-3]*

107, 70, 68, 66, 61, 55, 55, 38, 37, 32, 29, 28, 28, 27, 20, 15, 14, 12, 11, 10, 9, 7, 7, 6, 6, 5

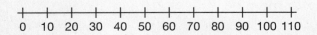

Cumulative Review Chapter 1

Add, subtract, multiply, or divide. *[Previous Course]*

1. 32 + 67   **2.** 91 − 27   **3.** 6 × 7   **4.** 296 ÷ 8

_____   _____   _____   _____

5. 365 + 83   **6.** 38 − 29   **7.** 9 × 28   **8.** 952 ÷ 17

_____   _____   _____   _____

9. 127 + 98   **10.** 183 − 76   **11.** 37 × 24   **12.** 1932 ÷ 23

_____   _____   _____   _____

State the range and draw a stem-and-leaf diagram for each data set.
[Lesson 1-1]

13. 84, 59, 63, 72, 87, 63, 61, 62,
70, 65, 74, 62, 77, 75, 71

range _____

stem	leaf

14. 94, 87, 103, 76, 100, 83, 79, 87,
85, 82, 98, 92, 79, 84, 89, 96

range _____

stem	leaf

Find the mean, median, and mode(s) of each data set. *[Lesson 1-2]*

15. 6.8, 9.3, 15.8, 12.7, 13.7, 22.8

mean _____ median _____

mode(s) _____

16. 3, 8, 7, 6, 8, 11, 8, 2, 9, 6

mean _____ median _____

mode(s) _____

17. Create a scatterplot of the data below.
Draw a trend line. *[Lesson 1-7]*

Price ($)	3.75	8.25	2.50	7.00	4.50	9.00	6.25
Size (oz)	9	23	8	17	12	22	16

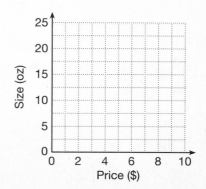

Name _____

Integers and Absolute Value

Name the opposite of each number.

1. 7 _____   **2.** −8 _____   **3.** 11 _____   **4.** −47 _____

5. −15 _____   **6.** 28 _____   **7.** −98 _____   **8.** 638 _____

Describe a situation that could be represented by each integer.

9. 4 _____   **10.** −16 _____

11. −2 hours _____   **12.** −$3 _____

Use >, <, or = to compare each set of numbers.

13. −$4 ◯ −$8   **14.** −7 ◯ |−7| **15.** 6 ◯ −6   **16.** 0 ◯ −8

17. −9 ◯ 3   **18.** −2 ◯ −1   **19.** 15 ◯ |15| **20.** 17 ◯ −35

Find each absolute value.

21. $|-3|$ **22.** $|8|$ **23.** $|635|$ **24.** $|-56|$

_____   _____   _____   _____

25. $|-845|$ **26.** $|12-3|$ **27.** $|35-7|$ **28.** $|-3487|$

_____   _____   _____   _____

29. What integer is described by the following? The absolute
value is 21 and the number is to the right of 0 on a number line. _____

30. Henrietta's business lost $3200 last month. She told
her cousin that her profit for the month was −$3200.
Name a profit amount lower than −$3200.

_____

31. In 1979, Jon Brower Minnoch set a world record for
weight loss by losing 920 pounds in 16 months.
Use an integer to represent the change in his weight. _____

32. What integer is described by the following? The absolute
value is 10 and the number is to the left of 0 on a number line. _____

Name _____

Addition of Integers

Write the addition problem for each model.

1. _____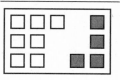

2. _____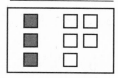

3. _____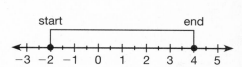

Add.

4. 17 + 12

5. −17 + 12

6. 17 + (−12)

7. −17 + (−12)

_____   _____   _____   _____

8. 81 + (−53)

9. −21 + 32

10. −18 + (−14)

11. 56 + (−16)

_____   _____   _____   _____

12. 3 + (−7) + 12

13. −4 + (−11) + (−5)

14. 18 + 5 + (−24)

_____   _____   _____

15. −14 + 3 + 11

16. 29 + (−8) + (−7)

17. −13 + 41 + (−8)

_____   _____   _____

Decide whether the sum is always, sometimes, or never positive.

18. three positive numbers _____

19. zero and a negative number _____

20. five negative numbers _____

21. a positive number and a negative number _____

22. One night the temperature in Fairbanks, Alaska, was −22°F.
By the next afternoon, the temperature had increased 13°.
What was the new temperature? _____

23. Career A real estate appraiser determined that a home was
worth $127,000 plus adjustments of −2,000 (no fireplace) and
+4,500 (extra bedroom). How much was the home worth? _____

Name _____

Subtraction of Integers

Write each problem as an addition problem. Compute the answer.

1. $16 - 5$ _____ **2.** $-6 - 11$ _____

3. $31 - (-8)$ _____ **4.** $47 - 83$ _____

5. $-12 - (-15)$ _____ **6.** $-38 - (-12)$ _____

Add or subtract.

7. $9 - 15$ **8.** $16 - 7$ **9.** $-32 - (-18)$ **10.** $-38 - 41$

_____   _____   _____   _____

11. $-23 + 57$ **12.** $-41 - 85$ **13.** $-17 - (-4)$ **14.** $-23 - (-47)$

_____   _____   _____   _____

15. $8 - (-63)$ **16.** $12 - (-5)$ **17.** $83 - 184$ **18.** $63 + (-28)$

_____   _____   _____   _____

19. A roller coaster, beginning 24 feet above ground level, goes up 15 feet, down 8 feet, up 23 feet, down 14 feet, up 35 feet, and finally down 75 feet. How far above or below ground level is it at the end of the ride?

_____

20. Consumer A checking account is overdrawn if it has a negative balance. Marc's account is overdrawn by $52. What will his balance be after he deposits $200 and writes a check for $18?

21. The average temperature in Caribou, Maine, is 18°C in July, and −12°C in January. What is the difference between these temperatures?

22. Polyus Nedostupnosti, Antarctica, is the coldest place in the world. Its annual mean temperature is 166° colder than that of Dallol, Ethiopia, the world's hottest place where the annual mean temperature is 94°F. What is the annual mean temperature of Polyus Nedostupnosti? _____

Multiplication and Division of Integers

Multiply or divide.

1. $4 \cdot (-7)$

2. $-2 \cdot 10$

3. $4 \cdot (-18)$

4. $-21 \div 3$

_____ _____ _____ _____

5. $18 \div (-6)$

6. $86 \div 43$

7. $-52 \div (-13)$

8. $(15)(-11)$

_____ _____ _____ _____

9. $-6(7)$

10. -5×18

11. $3 \times (-8)$

12. $-18 \times (-16)$

_____ _____ _____ _____

13. $38 \div (-2)$

14. $-45 \div (-3)$

15. $-164 \div (-4)$

16. $3 \cdot (-2) \cdot (-5)$

_____ _____ _____ _____

17. $-8 \cdot (-9) \cdot 10$

18. $-3 \cdot (-12) \cdot 2$

19. $\dfrac{21}{-7}$

20. $\dfrac{35}{5}$

_____ _____ _____ _____

21. $\dfrac{-90}{-15}$

22. $\dfrac{64}{-16}$

23. $\dfrac{-88}{11}$

24. $\dfrac{-221}{-13}$

_____ _____ _____ _____

Evaluate.

25. $|-4 \times (-3)|$

26. $|-81| \div |9|$

27. $|12 \cdot (-9)|$

28. $|100 \div (-5)|$

_____ _____ _____ _____

29. The value of Jim's telephone calling card decreases 15 cents for every minute he uses it. Yesterday he used the card to make a 6-minute call. How much did the value of the card change? _____

30. One day the temperature in Lone Grove, Oklahoma fell 3 degrees per hour for 5 consecutive hours. Give the total change in temperature. _____

31. The population of New Orleans, Louisiana, decreased from about 558,000 in 1980 to 497,000 in 1990. About how much did the population change each year? _____

Evaluating Expressions Using Integers

Evaluate each pair of expressions.

1. 3 · 4 + 5 _____   **2.** (10 − 3) × 5 _____   **3.** 30 ÷ 2 × 3 _____

3 · (4 + 5) _____   10 − 3 × 5 _____   30 ÷ (2 × 3) _____

Evaluate each expression two different ways.

4. 8(3 + 7)   **5.** −6(12 − 15)   **6.** 7(3 − 5)

_____   _____   _____

_____   _____   _____

7. 6(7 + 5)   **8.** −5(8 + 1)   **9.** 2(−3 − 4)

_____   _____   _____

_____   _____   _____

Evaluate each expression.

10. 8 · 9 + 10 · 11   **11.** −24 ÷ 6 × 2 − (−4)   **12.** 7(11 − 5) + 2

_____   _____   _____

13. −18 + 3 · (−9) + 15   **14.** $12 - \dfrac{7 + 8}{5 - 2}$ **15.** $\dfrac{30}{2(-6 + 9)} - 1$

_____   _____   _____

Insert parentheses to make each sentence true.

16. 12 ÷ 3 − 6 + 5 = 1   **17.** 8 + 16 ÷ 2 + 2 = 14

18. 63 − 9 − 15 − 4 = 65   **19.** 3 − 12 + 4 × 6 = −93

20. 12 − 3 × 5 − 7 = −10   **21.** 5 × 7 × 2 − 8 = 30

22. Stan bought donuts for the Drama Club meeting. He bought
6 regular donuts for 45 cents each and 9 premium donuts for
55 cents each.

a. How much did he spend? _____

b. What was the mean price per donut? _____

Section 2A Review

1. Refer to the number line.

   <-----+---+---+---+---+---+---+---+---+---+---+---+----->
           -8   -6   -4   -2   0   2   4

   a. Which of the labeled numbers are positive? _____

   b. Which of the labeled numbers are negative? _____

   c. Name the pairs of opposites shown. _____

   d. Which labeled number is the greatest? _____

   e. Which labeled number has the greatest absolute value? _____

Use the distributive property to evaluate.

2. $8(-12 + 4)$ _____ **3.** $-5(5 - 9)$ _____ **4.** $7(7 + 13)$ _____

Evaluate the following.

5. $|-8|$ _____ **6.** $|10|$ _____ **7.** $|20 - 6|$ _____

Compute the following.

8. $8 - (-4)$ _____ **9.** $42 \div (-3)$ _____ **10.** $8 + \dfrac{50}{14 - 9}$ _____

11. The data gives the number of runs scored by New York Mets players in 1994. Make a histogram using this data. *[Lesson 1-6]*

    16, 53, 60, 11, 18, 39, 47, 23, 20, 20, 46, 26, 45, 39, 5, 1

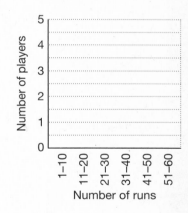

12. A fast-food restaurant chain plans to make a new sandwich intended to appeal to teenagers throughout Ohio, where the restaurants are located. To find out what foods appeal to this age group, the restaurant will take a survey. *[Lesson 1-8]*

    a. Who is the population of the survey? _____

    b. Would a sample of teenagers in downtown Cleveland be a representative sample? Explain.

    _____

    _____

Name _____

Integers in the Coordinate System

Plot and label each point on the coordinate grid at the right.

1. A(2, 0)   **2.** B(1, 4)

3. C(0, −4)   **4.** D(−4, −1)

5. E(−3, 2)   **6.** F(3, −1)

Find the coordinates of each point.

7. G _____   **8.** I _____

9. L _____   **10.** M _____

11. P _____   **12.** Q _____

Name the point for each ordered pair.

13. (4, −2) _____   **14.** (0, 1) _____

15. (−2, 2) _____   **16.** (1, 3) _____

17. (−2, −1) _____ **18.** (3, 1) _____

19. Geometry Name the ordered pairs for the vertices of the figures.

_____

_____

Geography Using the map, estimate the approximate coordinates of the following capitol cities.

20. Daker, Senegal

latitude _____

longitude _____

21. Abidjan, Ivory Coast

latitude _____

longitude _____

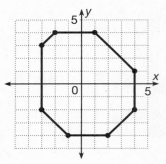

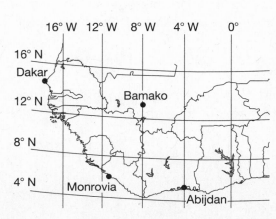

Name _____

Powers and Exponents

Geometry A shortcut to finding the area of a square is to square the length of a side. Find each area.

1. _____
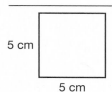
5 cm
5 cm

2. _____
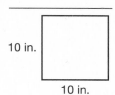
10 in.
10 in.

3. _____
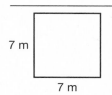
7 m
7 m

4. _____
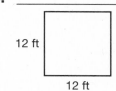
12 ft
12 ft

Geometry A shortcut to finding the volume of a cube is to cube the length of a side. Find each volume.

5. _____
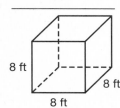
8 ft   8 ft
8 ft

6. _____
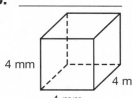
4 mm   4 mm
4 mm

7. _____
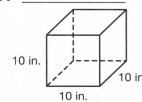
10 in.   10 in.
10 in.

8. _____
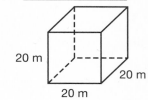
20 m   20 m
20 m

Evaluate.

9. 3^5

10. -2^4

11. $(-2)^4$

12. $(-2)^5$

_____ _____ _____ _____

13. -2^5

14. 7^3

15. 15^2

16. $(-8)^2$

_____ _____ _____ _____

17. $(-7)^0$

18. 4^5

19. $(-17)^1$

20. -25^2

_____ _____ _____ _____

21. $3^4 + 5^6$

22. $8^2 - 3^3$

23. $15 + 3^7$

24. $1^5 - 2^4$

_____ _____ _____ _____

25. $(3^3 + 4^4 + 5^5) \div 4^2$

26. $3(5 - 7)^5 + 8^0$

27. $(8 + 4)^2 \times (8 - 3)^3$

_____ _____ _____

28. A gray whale can weigh more than 3^{10} pounds. Write 3^{10} in standard form.

_____

Scientific Notation Using Positive Exponents

Social Science Exercises 1–6 give approximate 1993 populations.

Write each population in scientific notation.

1. California: 31 million

2. N. Dakota: 635 thousand

3. Rhode Island: 1.0 million

_____

_____

_____

Write each population in standard notation.

4. Utah: 1.9×10^6

5. Alaska: 5.99×10^5

6. Pennsylvania: 1.2×10^7

_____

_____

_____

Write each calculator display in standard notation.

7. | 8.375   E 14 |

8. | −3.4   E 8 |

_____

_____

9. | 9.0207   12 |

10. | −7.23   11 |

_____

_____

Without actually calculating, tell which number in each pair is greater. Explain.

11. 3.87×10^{12} or 3.9×10^{12}

_____

12. 2.1×10^{11} or 8.9×10^{10}

_____

13. Two of the wealthiest American families are the DuPont family, with assets estimated at $\$1.5 \times 10^{11}$, and the Walton retailing family, with assets estimated at $\$2.35 \times 10^{10}$. Find the combined net worth of the two families. Show how you found this.

_____

_____

Name _____

Scientific Notation Using Negative Exponents

Write each number in scientific notation.

1. five billionths

2. forty-seven thousandths

3. eighteen hundredths

4. two hundred thirty-seven millionths

5. eighty-two billionths

6. five hundred three thousandths

Science These are the approximate masses or weights of atoms.
Write each in scientific notation.

7. bismuth: 0.00000000000000000347 mg _____

8. hydrogen: 0.00000000000000000000000000394 lb _____

9. oxygen: 0.0000000000000000000000266 g _____

Measurement Write these very small amounts in standard notation.

10. second: 3.17×10^{-8} year

11. angstrom: 10^{-10} meter

12. centimeter: 6.214×10^{-6} mile

13. mile: 1.701×10^{-13} light-year

Write each of these calculator displays in standard notation.

14. | 3.47   −9 |

15. | −8.62   −11 |

16. | 1.003   E −5 |

17. In 1926, Alfred McEwen set a world record for small writing. He wrote 56 words in a space of area 0.00000128 square inches. Write 0.00000128 in scientific notation. _____

Name _____

Section 2B Review

Plot and label the following points. What quadrant is each point in?

1. $A(0, -2)$; quadrant _____
2. $B(-3, 4)$; quadrant _____

3. $C(2, -3)$; quadrant _____
4. $D(1, 3)$; quadrant _____

Geography Using the map, locate the approximate latitude and longitude of these cities.

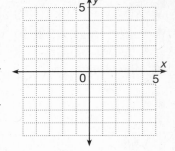

5. Pittsburgh, PA
6. Baltimore, MD

latitude _____
latitude _____

longitude _____
longitude _____

Find the area or volume of the following.

7.  area _____
8. 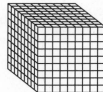 volume _____

Write each number in scientific notation.

9. In 1990, about 64,000 Native Americans lived in Texas. _____

10. One ounce is equal to 0.00003125 ton. _____

Write each of these calculator displays in standard notation.

11. | 4.25   E −8 |
12. | −3.8   14 |
13. | 6.25   −10 |

_____
_____
_____

14. Put these numbers in order from smallest to largest. _____

a. 4.23×10^4
b. 9.37×10^{-4}
c. 38,000
d. 4.23×10^5

15. The Carson family has three dogs and two cats. Each dog weighs 46 pounds and each cat weighs 16 pounds. Write an expression for the mean weight of the five animals. Evaluate the expression to find the mean weight. *[Lesson 2-5]*

_____

Cumulative Review Chapters 1–2

1. State the range and draw a line plot for the data set. *[Lesson 1-1]*

Jose asked passengers on his bus how many hours they worked that day. Their answers were 8, 9, 8, 6, 8, 4, 8, 7, 2, 0, 8, and 6

_____

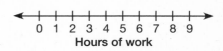

Hours of work

Find the mean, median, and mode(s) for each data set. *[Lesson 1-2]*

2. 12, 18, 16, 14, 13, 20, 15, 16, 19

mean _____

median _____

mode(s) _____

3. 83, 77, 128, 63, 92, 77, 101, 118

mean _____

median _____

mode(s) _____

Add or subtract. *[Lessons 2-2, 2-3]*

4. $7 + (-8)$ _____

5. $8 - (-3)$ _____

6. $7 + (-18)$ _____

7. $-15 - 3$ _____

8. $24 + (-8)$ _____

9. $35 - (-21)$ _____

10. $-21 - (-5)$ _____

11. $16 + (-18)$ _____

12. $38 + (-18)$ _____

Evaluate each expression two different ways. *[Lesson 2-5]*

13. $5(3 + 7)$

14. $6(-8 - 4)$

15. $-3(5 + 3)$

_____   _____   _____

_____   _____   _____

Plot and label each point. *[Lesson 2-6]*

16. $A(-3, -1)$

17. $B(0, -2)$

18. $C(1, 4)$

19. $D(4, 2)$

20. $E(-4, 1)$

21. $F(3, -3)$

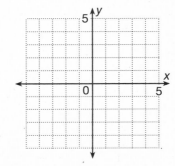

Formulas and Variables

Solve each formula for the values given. The purpose of the formula is given.

1. $d = rt$, for $r = 25$ and $t = 3$ (*Distance*, given *rate* and *time*) $d =$ _____

2. $P = 4s$, for $s = 11$ (*Perimeter* of a square, given *side length*) $P =$ _____

3. $K = C + 273$, for $C = 37$
(*Kelvin* temperature, given *Celsius* temperature) $K =$ _____

4. $S = 180(n - 2)$, for $n = 7$
(*Sum* of the angles, given *number* of sides) $S =$ _____

5. $m = \frac{a + b + c}{3}$, for $a = 11.2$, $b = 12.3$, and $c = 11.9$
(*Mean*, given *three values*) $m =$ _____

6. $A = \pi r^2$, for $r = 8.5$; use 3.14 for π
(*Area* of a circle, given *radius*) $A =$ _____

7. $P = 2b + 2h$, for $b = 3\frac{1}{8}$ and $h = 4\frac{1}{2}$
(*Perimeter* of a rectangle, given *base* and *height*) $P =$ _____

8. $V = \frac{1}{3}Bh$, for $B = 17$ and $h = 12$
(*Volume* of a pyramid, given *base area* and *height*) $V =$ _____

9. $A = 2(\ell w + wh + \ell h)$, for $\ell = 8$, $w = 5$, and $h = 3$ (*Surface*
area of a rectangular prism, given *length*, *width*, and *height*) $A =$ _____

10. $C = \frac{5}{9}(F - 32)$, for $F = 77$
(*Celsius* temperature, given *Fahrenheit* temperature) $C =$ _____

11. $T = 0.0825p$, for $p = \$160.00$ (*Tax*, given *price*) $T =$ _____

12. $F = ma$, for $m = 12$ and $a = 9.8$
(*Force*, given *mass* and *acceleration*) $F =$ _____

13. In 1989, Dutch ice skater Dries van Wijhe skated 200 km at
an average speed of 35.27 km/hr. How long was he skating?   _____

14. Career A roofer calculates his bid price using the formula
$P = 1.85s + 4.2f$, where s is the area of the roof in square
feet and f is the length of the fascia in feet. Find the price
for a roof with area 1800 square feet and 190 feet of fascia.   _____

Algebraic Expressions and Equations

Evaluate each expression. Remember that operations within parentheses should be done first.

1. $5y + 3x$, for $x = 7$ and $y = 6$ **2.** $10(x - 5)$, for $x = 3$

_____   _____

3. $2y - 17$, for $y = 21$ **4.** $20 - \frac{3}{4}x$, for $x = 16$

_____   _____

5. $(3x - 2)y$, for $x = -8$ and $y = -5$ **6.** $(3x + 4y) \cdot 8$, for $x = 10$ and $y = -2$

_____   _____

Solve each equation.

7. $3 + z = 18$ **8.** $k - 7 = 10$ **9.** $3d = 12$ **10.** $j = 9(-8 + 3)$

$z =$ _____ $k =$ _____ $d =$ _____ $j =$ _____

11. $p = \frac{2 + 7}{-3}$ **12.** $y + 8 = 30$ **13.** $-2g = 6$ **14.** $u = 4(-15)$

$p =$ _____ $y =$ _____ $g =$ _____ $u =$ _____

15. $5t = 35$ **16.** $h = 3(8 + 3)$ **17.** $w - 5 = -10$ **18.** $s = \frac{8 + (-4)}{2}$

$t =$ _____ $h =$ _____ $w =$ _____ $s =$ _____

19. Geometry Each angle of a regular polygon can be found using the expression $\frac{180(n - 2)}{n}$, where n is the number of sides. A nonagon has 9 sides. Find the measure of each angle in a regular nonagon.   _____

20. Technology Complete the table showing the rents collected in an apartment complex. Entries in column D are obtained by multiplying columns B and C.

	A	B	C	D
1	Unit Type	Number of Units	Unit Rent	Total Rent
2	Efficiency	14	$520	
3	1-bedroom	28	$595	
4	2-bedroom	18	$695	

Writing Algebraic Expressions

Write an expression for each situation.

1. the number of corners on *c* cubes   _____

2. the number of gallons in *h* half-gallon containers   _____

3. the number of cans in *s* six-packs of soda   _____

4. the number of fingers on *p* people   _____

5. To square a number ending with 5, multiply 5 less than the number by 5 more than the number, and then add 25. Write an expression or equation for this situation.

_____

Write a formula for each situation. Then solve for two values and explain the solution in terms of the problem situation.

6. Science To find the force on a certain spring, multiply the displacement by 12.

_____

7. Consumer To find the cost of ordering shirts by mail, multiply the number of shirts by $22.50 and then add $6.75 for shipping and handling.

_____

8. Geometry To find the approximate surface area of a sphere, find the square of the radius and multiply by 12.57.

_____

9. Accounting To find the 1995 federal income tax of a single person earning between $23,350 and $56,550, multiply 0.28 times the amount of income over $23,350, and then add $3502.50.

_____

_____

Section 3A Review

Evaluate each formula for the values given.

1. $V = \ell wh$, for $\ell = 11$, $w = 8$, and $h = 9$ $V =$ _____

2. $F = 1.8C + 32$, for $C = 27$ $F =$ _____

3. The speed limit on many freeways is 55 mi/hr. How far can you travel in 4 hours at this speed? _____

Evaluate each expression.

4. $15x - 4y$ for $x = 8$ and $y = 12$ **5.** $10y(x + 7)$ for $x = 4$ and $y = 2$

_____   _____

Solve each equation. Use number sense or "guess and check."

6. $x + 2 = 20$ **7.** $y - 5 = 10$ **8.** $u = 4(3 + 2)$ **9.** $c = -5 \cdot 11$

$x =$ _____ $y =$ _____ $u =$ _____ $c =$ _____

10. $3a = 21$ **11.** $n = \dfrac{42}{-7}$ **12.** $\dfrac{t}{5} = 8$ **13.** $p = \dfrac{100}{18 + 2}$

$a =$ _____ $n =$ _____ $t =$ _____ $p =$ _____

Write an expression for each situation.

14. the number of wings on b birds   _____

15. the number of centimeters in m meters   _____

16. A mountain climber started one morning at an altitude of 6380 ft and began to climb to higher altitudes at a rate of 1500 ft per hour.

a. Write an expression to find her height after t hours.   _____

b. What was her height after $3\frac{1}{2}$ hours?   _____

17. Suppose you wanted to draw a graph showing the ages of all people living on your street. Which would be better, a line plot or a histogram? Explain. *[Lesson 1-6]*

_____

_____

Name _____

Solving Equations by Adding or Subtracting

What is the next step in solving each equation?

1. $x + 7 = 39$

2. $x - 4 = 13$

_____

_____

3. $-4 = x + 17$

4. $3 = x - 12$

_____

_____

Solve each equation. Check your solution.

5. $t - 4 = 17$

$t =$ _____

6. $-14 = r - 5$

$r =$ _____

7. $s + 9 = -13$

$s =$ _____

8. $7 = w - 15$

$w =$ _____

9. $11 = k + 25$

$k =$ _____

10. $e - 5 = -13$

$e =$ _____

11. $b + 17 = 31$

$b =$ _____

12. $y - 21 = -4$

$y =$ _____

13. $8.3 = j + 2.7$

$j =$ _____

14. $a - 8.1 = 3.6$

$a =$ _____

15. $8 = n - 4.9$

$n =$ _____

16. $3.8 = m + 9.7$

$m =$ _____

17. $v - 18.4 = 3.9$

$v =$ _____

18. $f + 8.7 = 9.3$

$f =$ _____

19. $z - 4.6 = 12.7$

$z =$ _____

20. $c + 21.9 = 8.4$

$c =$ _____

21. $10 = q - 4\frac{1}{2}$

$q =$ _____

22. $u - \frac{2}{3} = 21$

$u =$ _____

23. $h + \frac{1}{2} = 5\frac{1}{4}$

$h =$ _____

24. $x - 3\frac{1}{8} = 21$

$x =$ _____

25. $d + 17 = 4$

$d =$ _____

26. $g - 2\frac{1}{2} = 7$

$g =$ _____

27. $8 = p + \frac{1}{3}$

$p =$ _____

28. $w - 8\frac{1}{2} = 23$

$w =$ _____

29. Consumer In 1996, Pacific Gas and Electric offered customers a $150 rebate on the purchase of an efficient washing machine. If the machine cost $849 with the rebate, how much would it cost without the rebate? _____

30. The formula $K = C + 273$ relates Kelvin temperature, K, to Celsius temperature, C. What Celsius temperature is equivalent to 287° Kelvin? _____

Solving Equations by Multiplying or Dividing

Solve each equation.

1. $5n = 40$

$n =$ _____

2. $10c = 120$

$c =$ _____

3. $7g = 28$

$g =$ _____

4. $15x = 180$

$x =$ _____

5. $6f = 84$

$f =$ _____

6. $\frac{1}{2}s = 21$

$s =$ _____

7. $4r = 12$

$r =$ _____

8. $9k = 63$

$k =$ _____

9. $\frac{1}{5}u = 17$

$u =$ _____

10. $\frac{h}{3} = 17$

$h =$ _____

11. $\frac{b}{17} = 7$

$b =$ _____

12. $\frac{s}{20} = 11$

$s =$ _____

13. $\frac{3}{4}t = 81$

$t =$ _____

14. $3a = 33$

$a =$ _____

15. $13q = 78$

$q =$ _____

16. $\frac{2}{3}m = 42$

$m =$ _____

17. $\frac{x}{4} = 35$

$x =$ _____

18. $\frac{d}{7} = 15$

$d =$ _____

19. $\frac{1}{4}z = 21$

$z =$ _____

20. $\frac{u}{8} = 13$

$u =$ _____

21. $7r = 91$

$r =$ _____

22. $11e = 99$

$e =$ _____

23. $8w = 40$

$w =$ _____

24. $16d = 144$

$d =$ _____

25. $12d = 180$

$d =$ _____

26. $\frac{1}{3}n = 24$

$n =$ _____

27. $\frac{3}{5}h = 45$

$h =$ _____

28. $20k = 150$

$k =$ _____

29. $\frac{1}{6}x = 7$

$x =$ _____

30. $\frac{a}{5} = 24$

$a =$ _____

31. $\frac{u}{7} = 12$

$u =$ _____

32. $\frac{m}{10} = 6.1$

$m =$ _____

33. Accounting In 1995, the federal income tax for married couples earning less than $39,000 was 0.15 times the taxable income. If the Jacksons paid $4054 in federal income tax, what was their taxable income?

_____

34. A box of oatmeal has instructions to use $\frac{1}{3}$ cup of oats for each serving. Han used 4 cups of oats. How many servings did he make?

_____

Name _____

Solving Two-Step Equations

Solve each equation.

1. $6x + 5 = -19$ **2.** $2x + 12 = 24$ **3.** $15x - 9 = 21$ **4.** $5x - 11 = -36$

$x =$ _____ $x =$ _____ $x =$ _____ $x =$ _____

5. $18x - 6 = 84$ **6.** $9x + 2.3 = -10.3$ **7.** $11x + 4 = -29$ **8.** $8x + 15 = 71$

$x =$ _____ $x =$ _____ $x =$ _____ $x =$ _____

9. $\frac{1}{2}x + 3 = 5$ **10.** $\frac{x}{6} - 7 = 3$ **11.** $\frac{1}{4}x + 10 = -7$ **12.** $\frac{x}{9} - 15 = 5$

$x =$ _____ $x =$ _____ $x =$ _____ $x =$ _____

13. $12x + 7 = 139$ **14.** $3x - 8 = 55$ **15.** $7x - 5.8 = 13.1$ **16.** $4x + 13 = 61$

$x =$ _____ $x =$ _____ $x =$ _____ $x =$ _____

17. $\frac{x}{8} - 7 = -12$ **18.** $\frac{1}{5}x + 8 = -2$ **19.** $\frac{n}{11} + 2 = 6$ **20.** $\frac{x}{7} - 9 = -4$

$x =$ _____ $x =$ _____ $n =$ _____ $x =$ _____

21. $20n - 2 = 138$ **22.** $10x - 3 = -83$ **23.** $8x - 3.2 = 37.6$ **24.** $12x - 10 = -130$

$n =$ _____ $x =$ _____ $x =$ _____ $x =$ _____

25. $\frac{w}{10} - 11 = 6$ **26.** $\frac{1}{3}x + 3 = -9$ **27.** $\frac{u}{12} + 4 = 8$ **28.** $\frac{x}{25} - 8 = -3$

$w =$ _____ $x =$ _____ $u =$ _____ $x =$ _____

29. The Drama Club's production of "Oklahoma!" is going to cost
$1250 to produce. How many tickets will they need to sell for
$8 each in order to make a profit of $830? _____

30. Consumer In 1995, the monthly cost to use America Online
was $9.95 (including the first 5 hours of usage), plus $2.95
for each additional hour. Phil paid $30.60 in March.

   a. Let x be the number of "additional" hours that Phil used.
      Write and solve an equation to find x.

_____

   b. How many hours did Phil use America Online in March? _____

© Scott Foresman • Addison Wesley 8

Solving Inequalities

Write an inequality for each graph.

1. _____

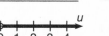
-4 -3 -2 -1 0 1 2 3 4   u

2. _____

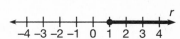
-4 -3 -2 -1 0 1 2 3 4   x

3. _____

-4 -3 -2 -1 0 1 2 3 4   r

4. _____

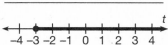
-4 -3 -2 -1 0 1 2 3 4   t

5. _____

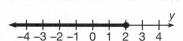
-4 -3 -2 -1 0 1 2 3 4   y

6. _____

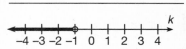
-4 -3 -2 -1 0 1 2 3 4   k

Determine whether -3 is a solution for each inequality.

7. $x + 3 \geq 0$ **8.** $2x < -4$ **9.** $-3x < 9$ **10.** $x - 5 \geq 8$

_____   _____   _____   _____

Solve each inequality. Graph the solution.

11. $x + 8 \leq 10$ _____   **12.** $y - 5 > -6$_____   **13.** $8h < 16$_____

-4 -3 -2 -1 0 1 2 3 4   x   -4 -3 -2 -1 0 1 2 3 4   y   -4 -3 -2 -1 0 1 2 3 4   h

14. $7f \geq 21$ _____   **15.** $6n > 6$_____   **16.** $3r + 5 > 5$ _____

-4 -3 -2 -1 0 1 2 3 4   f   -4 -3 -2 -1 0 1 2 3 4   n   -4 -3 -2 -1 0 1 2 3 4   r

17. $2t - 3 \leq 5$ _____   **18.** $3k + 5 < 10$ _____   **19.** $4c + 20 \geq 9$ _____

-4 -3 -2 -1 0 1 2 3 4   t   -4 -3 -2 -1 0 1 2 3 4   k   -4 -3 -2 -1 0 1 2 3 4   c

20. A rental car costs $25.00 per day, plus $0.30 per mile. Dan
wants to know how far he can drive each day and still keep
his cost under $85.00 per day. Help him by solving
$0.3x + 25 < 85$.   _____

21. The volume of a pyramid is given by $\frac{1}{3}Bh$, where B is the area
of the base and h is the height. Zelda is making a solid pyramid
out of modeling clay. The base is to be a 5 in. by 5 in. square,
and she has 50 in^3 of clay available. Solve $\frac{1}{3} \cdot 5^2 \cdot h < 50$ to
find the possible heights of her pyramid.   _____

Name _____

Section 3B Review

Solve each equation.

1. $y + 7 = 24$ **2.** $g - 10 = -3$ **3.** $x + 5.7 = 8.3$ **4.** $t - 7\frac{3}{8} = 2\frac{1}{4}$

$y =$ _____ $g =$ _____ $x =$ _____ $t =$ _____

5. $18c = 90$ **6.** $\frac{u}{12} = 7$ **7.** $1.3k = 7.93$ **8.** $\frac{s}{7.81} = 11$

$c =$ _____ $u =$ _____ $k =$ _____ $s =$ _____

9. $5n - 8 = -18$ **10.** $3p + 15 = 36$ **11.** $\frac{3}{5}z - 14 = 25$ **12.** $20r - 5 = 9$

$n =$ _____ $p =$ _____ $z =$ _____ $r =$ _____

13. Blazin' Bakery has a jar of cookie samples on the counter. Each cookie sample weighs 0.75 oz, and the jar weighs 27 oz. If the total weight is 45.75 oz, how many cookie samples are in the jar? _____

Solve and graph each inequality.

14. $m - 5 < -4$ **15.** $g + 7 \geq 10$ **16.** $8d > -24$

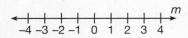   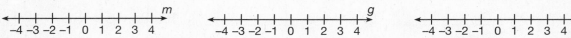   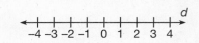

17. $5t \leq 12$ **18.** $3a + 4 > 13$ **19.** $4u - 7 < 3$

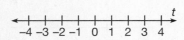   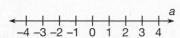   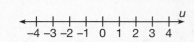

20. Tien's library allows her to check out a maximum of 10 books at a time. She has selected 3 history books and 4 science fiction novels she wants to read. Solve $3 + 4 + x \leq 10$ to find how many additional books she might check out. _____

21. Ardeshir bought 4 pints of ice cream for $1.65 each and 2 cans of baked beans for $0.83 each. He also redeemed 3 coupons for $0.20 each. How much did he spend? *[Lesson 2-5]* _____

22. The area of a typical postage stamp is about 0.00000000022 mi^2. Write this number in scientific notation. *[Lesson 2-9]* _____

Cumulative Review Chapters 1–3

1. The data gives the number of dogs and cats in animal shelters in Roverton. Create a scatterplot and draw a trend line. *[Lesson 1-7]*

Dogs	13	27	41	35	21
Cats	7	10	28	23	16

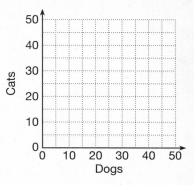

Multiply or divide. *[Lesson 2-4]*

2. $-3 \cdot 4$

3. $52 \div (-4)$

4. $-8(-5)$

5. $126 \div (-18)$

_____   _____   _____   _____

6. $-135 \div 9$

7. $11 \cdot (-4)$

8. $-96 \div 8$

9. $-7 \cdot 8$

_____   _____   _____   _____

Write each number using an exponent. *[Lesson 2-7]*

10. $8 \cdot 8 \cdot 8 \cdot 8$

11. $-2 \cdot (-2)$

12. $7 \cdot 7 \cdot 7$

13. $-13 \cdot (-13)$

_____   _____   _____   _____

Write an expression for each situation. *[Lesson 3-3]*

14. the number of sides in k rectangles   _____

15. the number of legs on d dogs   _____

16. the number of weeks in x days   _____

Solve each inequality. Graph the solution. *[Lesson 3-7]*

17. $3x > -6$

18. $2p - 4 \leq 3$

19. $8w - 5 < -13$

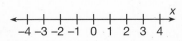

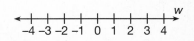

Name _____

Understanding Two-Variable Relationships

Find the value of y when x = 7 in each of the following equations.

1. $y = 10x$ **2.** $y = x - 4$ **3.** $y = 14x$ **4.** $y = x + 23$

_____   _____   _____   _____

Complete each table of values.

5.

x	0	1	2	3	4	5
y = x + 5						

6.

x	0	1	2	3	4	5
y = 4x						

7.

x	0	1	2	3	4	5
y = x − 7						

8.

x	0	1	2	3	4	5
y = −8x						

Make a table of values for each equation. Use 0, 1, 2, 3, 4, and 5.

9. $y = x + 10$

10. $y = -3x$

Find a rule that relates x and y in each table. Then find y when x = 25.

11. rule: _____

    y = _____

12. rule: _____

    y = _____

13. rule: _____

    y = _____

x	y
0	0
1	−7
2	−14
3	−21
4	−28
5	−35

x	y
0	7
1	8
2	9
3	10
4	11
5	12

x	y
0	0
1	11
2	22
3	33
4	44
5	55

14. Science Every spider has 8 legs. Make a table relating the number of spiders to the number of legs.

Solutions of Two-Variable Equations

Determine whether each ordered pair is a solution of the equation.

1. $y = x + 9$ **a.** (4, 13)   **b.** (5, −4)   **c.** (−8, 1)

_____ _____ _____

2. $y = 4x$ **a.** (3, 12)   **b.** (16, 4)   **c.** (6, 10)

_____ _____ _____

3. $y = -\dfrac{1}{3}x$ **a.** (−3, 9)   **b.** (6, −2)   **c.** (−15, −5)

_____ _____ _____

4. $x = y + 4$ **a.** (−2, 2)   **b.** (−2, −6)   **c.** (12, 8)

_____ _____ _____

5. $x + 2y = 10$ **a.** (2, 8)   **b.** (4, 3)   **c.** (3, 4)

_____ _____ _____

Give two solution pairs for each equation.

6. $y = x + 8$ **7.** $y = x - 3$ **8.** $y = 7x$

_____ _____ _____

9. $y = 3x - 2$ **10.** $y = \dfrac{1}{4}x + 8$ **11.** $y = -3x + 7$

_____ _____ _____

12. $x - y = 5$ **13.** $2x + y = 11$ **14.** $x - 4y = 10$

_____ _____ _____

15. The equation $y = 0.23x + 0.09$ gives the cost, in dollars, of mailing a letter weighing x ounces, where x is a positive integer. Make a table showing the number of ounces and the price, for letters weighing 1 to 6 ounces.

Name _____

Graphing Two-Variable Relationships

Graph each equation. Use 0, 1, 2, and 3 as *x*-values.

1. $y = x - 2$

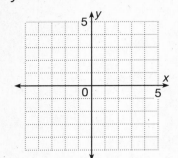

2. $y = -\frac{1}{3}x$

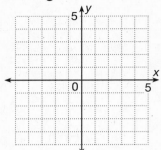

3. $y = -x + 1$

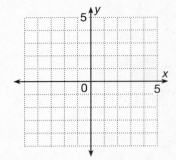

4. $y = \frac{1}{2}x + \frac{3}{2}$

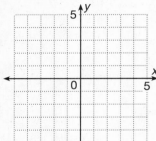

5. $y = 3x - 4$

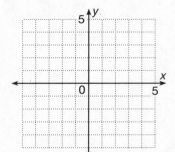

6. $y = -2x + 3$

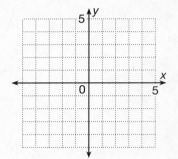

Graph the ordered pairs in each table. Connect the points to determine if the graphs are linear. Write linear or not linear.

7. _____

x	y
−3	3
−1	2
1	1
4	0

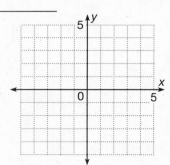

8. _____

x	y
−6	2
−4	3
0	5
6	8

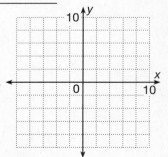

9. Consumer Adeshima plans to order some fabric from a mail-order catalog. The price is $0.75 per yard, plus $2.00 for shipping. Use *x* for the number of yards, and *y* for the price she will pay. Graph the price that she will pay.

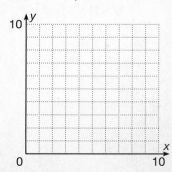

Name _____

Section 4A Review

Find the value of y for $x = -4$ in each equation.

1. $y = x + 21$ **2.** $y = x - 5$ **3.** $y = -\frac{3}{4}x$ **4.** $y - x = 5$

_____   _____   _____   _____

5. Make a table of values for the equation $y = -1.5x + 3$. Use 0, 1, 2, 3, and 4 as x-values.

Determine whether each ordered pair is a solution of the equation.

6. $y = x - 3$ **a.** (2, 5) _____   **b.** (−4, −7) _____

7. $y = -10x$ **a.** (30, −3) _____   **b.** (−4, 40) _____

8. a. Find a rule that relates x and y in the table. _____

     b. Find the value of y when $x = 32$. _____

x	0	1	2	3	4	5
y	−8	−7	−6	−5	−4	−3

Graph each equation.

9. $y = -x - 2$ **10.** $y = 3x + 2$ **11.** $y = \frac{1}{2}x - 1$

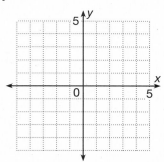 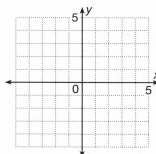 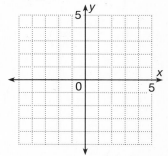

12. In 1994, the top ten best selling prerecorded videos sold 27.0, 21.5, 12.0, 11.5, 9.1, 8.2, 7.5, 5.2, 5.1, and 4.2 million copies, respectively. Make a box-and-whisker plot showing the number of millions of videos sold. *[Lesson 1-3]*

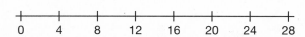

13. The sum of the natural numbers 1 through n is given by $\frac{1}{2}n(n + 1)$. Find the sum of the natural numbers 1 through 85. *[Lesson 3-2]* _____

Name _____

Understanding Slope

Give the slope of each of these items.

1. _____ **2.** _____ **3.** _____

 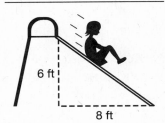 

Find the slope of each line on the graph.

4. Line through *A* and *B* _____

5. Line through *B* and *C* _____

6. Line through *B* and *D* _____

7. Line through *A* and *E* _____

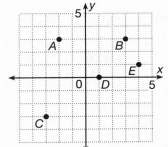

Draw a line through the origin with each of the given slopes.

8. −1

9. $\frac{2}{3}$

10. 4

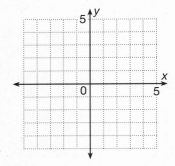 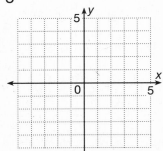 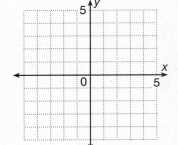

11. The steepest street in the world is Baldwin St. in Dunedin, New Zealand, which rises 1 m in a horizontal distance of 1.266 m. Find the slope of Baldwin St. Round to the nearest hundredth if necessary.

_____

12. Industry A roofing manufacturer says its product is suitable for roofs that rise at least $2\frac{1}{2}$ in. for every 12 horizontal in. What is the minimum positive slope of a roof that can use this product?

_____

Patterns in Linear Equations and Graphs

For each line, find the slope, the *x*-intercept, and the *y*-intercept.

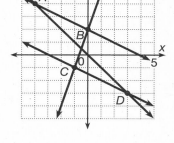

1. Line through *A* and *B*

slope: _____

x-intercept: _____

y-intercept: _____

2. Line through *B* and *C*

slope: _____

x-intercept: _____

y-intercept: _____

3. Line through *C* and *D*

slope: _____

x-intercept: _____

y-intercept: _____

4. Line through *A* and *D*

slope: _____

x-intercept: _____

y-intercept: _____

5. Which lines in Exercises 1–4 are parallel? Explain.

_____

_____

_____

Graph each equation. Find the slope, the *x*-intercept, and the *y*-intercept.

6. $y = -x + 2$

slope: _____

x-intercept: _____

y-intercept: _____

7. $y = \frac{1}{2}x + 3$

slope: _____

x-intercept: _____

y-intercept: _____

8. $y = 2x - 4$

slope: _____

x-intercept: _____

y-intercept: _____

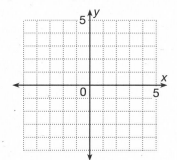

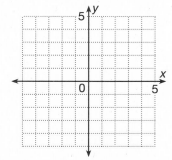

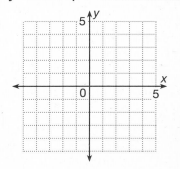

9. Which lines in Exercises 6–8 are parallel? Explain.

_____

Name _____

Pairs of Linear Equations

Solve each system of equations by graphing.

1. $y = x + 2$

$y = 2x + 1$

Solution: _____

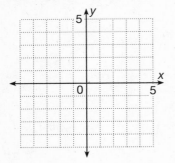

2. $y = -2x + 2$

$y = 3x + 2$

Solution: _____

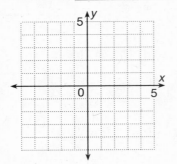

3. $y = -\frac{1}{2}x - 1$

$y = x - 4$

Solution: _____

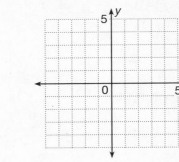

4. $y = 2x + 3$

$y = \frac{1}{2}x$

Solution: _____

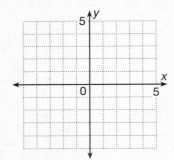

5. $y = -\frac{3}{2}x + 2$

$y = \frac{1}{2}x - 2$

Solution: _____

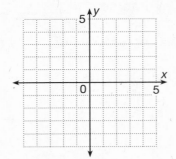

6. $y = 2x - 5$

$y = \frac{1}{4}x + 2$

Solution: _____

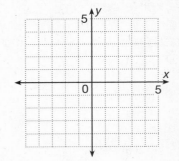

7. Tomatoes are $0.80 per pound at Rob's Market, and $1.20 per pound at Sal's Produce. You have a coupon for $1.40 off at Sal's. (Assume that you buy at least $1.40 worth of tomatoes.)

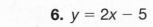

   a. Write an equation relating the cost, y, to the number of pounds, x, at each market.

   Rob's: _____   Sal's: _____

   b. Use a graph to estimate the number of pounds for which the cost is the same at either store.

_____

Name _____

Linear Inequalities

Test whether each point is a solution of the inequality.

1. $y \geq -2x + 5$ **a.** $(2, -1)$ _____   **b.** $(3, -1)$ _____   **c.** $(4, -1)$_____

2. $y < 3x - 4$ **a.** $(2, 1)$ _____   **b.** $(2, 2)$ _____   **c.** $(3, 2)$ _____

Graph each inequality.

3. $y \leq \frac{1}{2}x + 2$ **4.** $y > -x + 3$ **5.** $y \geq 2x$

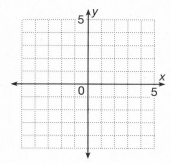 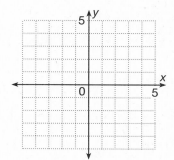 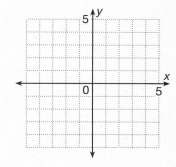

6. $y < x - 2$ **7.** $y \leq \frac{2}{3}x - 1$ **8.** $y > -\frac{1}{2}x$

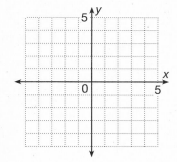 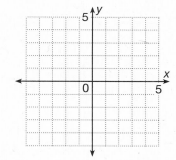 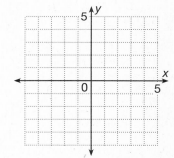

9. "The number of women is at least half the number of men." Express this statement as an inequality, using x for the number of men.

_____

10. Harold is making soup. He wants the soup to have at least twice as many ounces of broccoli as ounces of carrots. Graph the number of ounces of broccoli, y, for x ounces of carrots.

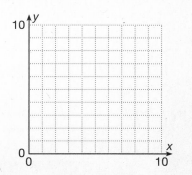

Name _____

Section 4B Review

Find the slope of each line. Then find the *x*-intercept and the *y*-intercept for each line.

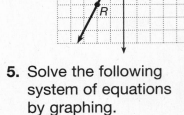

1. Line through *R* and *S*

slope: _____

x-intercept: _____

y-intercept: _____

2. Line through *S* and *T*

slope: _____

x-intercept: _____

y-intercept: _____

3. Graph a line through the origin having a a slope of $-\frac{4}{3}$.

4. Graph $y = \frac{2}{3}x + 2$. Find the following:

slope: _____

x-intercept: _____

y-intercept: _____

5. Solve the following system of equations by graphing.

$y = \frac{1}{2}x + 3$

$y = -\frac{3}{2}x - 1$

Solution: _____

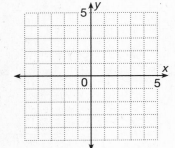

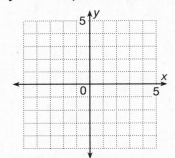

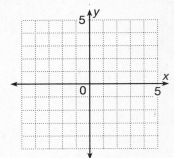

Graph each inequality.

6. $y \le 2x + 3$

7. $y > x - 3$

8. $y < -\frac{1}{3}x + 2$

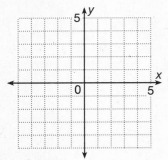

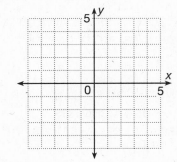

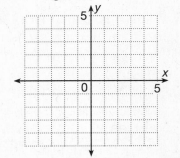

9. Geography Mt. McKinley in Alaska is 5,826 ft taller than Mt. Whitney in California. If Mt. McKinley is 20,320 ft tall, how tall is Mt. Whitney? *[Lesson 3-4]*

_____

Practice

Cumulative Review Chapters 1–4

State the range and draw a stem-and-leaf diagram for each data set. *[Lesson 1-1]*

1. 38, 51, 42, 23, 40, 23, 31, 53, 47, 33, 41, 27, 36, 41, 29, 30, 58

Range: _____

stem	leaf

2. 107, 91, 83, 110, 87, 86, 91, 95, 104, 83, 113, 83, 96, 89, 90, 106, 112, 91

Range: _____

stem	leaf

Evaluate. *[Lesson 2-7]*

3. 3^5 _____ **4.** $(-2)^6$ _____ **5.** 17^1 _____ **6.** $(-4)^3$ _____

Solve each equation. *[Lesson 3-6]*

7. $7x - 4 = 73$ **8.** $-53 = 5c + 7$ **9.** $\frac{u}{3} + 8 = 5$ **10.** $23 = -3m + 2$

$x =$ _____ $c =$ _____ $u =$ _____ $m =$ _____

Determine whether each ordered pair is a solution of the equation. *[Lesson 4-2]*

11. $y = -2x + 5$ **a.** (2, 1)_____ **b** (−3, 11)_____ **c.** (1, 2)_____

12. $y = -x + 3$ **a.** (2, 5)_____ **b.** (−1, 4)_____ **c.** (4, −1)_____

Graph each inequality. *[Lesson 4-7]*

13. $y \geq x + 1$ **14.** $y < \frac{3}{4}x - 2$ **15.** $y \leq 3x + 2$

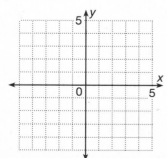 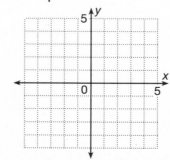 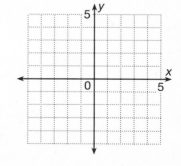

Use with page 217. **43**

Exploring and Estimating Ratios and Rates

Write each ratio or rate as a fraction.

1. 8 : 7

2. 5 to 21

3. 120 beats per second

_____   _____   _____

Draw a picture to show each ratio.

4. squares to circles 3 : 5   _____

5. circles to stars 1 : 4   _____

Write all the ratios that can be made using the figure.

6.

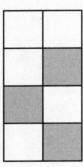

_____
_____
_____
_____
_____
_____

Language Arts Write a ratio comparing the number of vowels to the number of consonants in each word.

7. algebra

8. calculator

9. literature

_____   _____   _____

_____   _____   _____

10. Yesterday the fax machine at Shambles Realty handled 38 incoming faxes and 49 outgoing faxes. Estimate each ratio:

a. incoming faxes to outgoing faxes   _____

b. total faxes to incoming faxes   _____

© Scott Foresman • Addison Wesley 8

Proportions and Equal Ratios

Complete each table to create ratios equal to the given ratio.

1.

3	6	9	12	15
5				

2.

1				
2	4	6	8	10

3.

7	14	21	28	35
3				

4.

8				
7	14	21	28	35

5.

4				
9	18	27	36	45

6.

11	22	33	44	55
5				

Check each pair of ratios to see if a proportion is formed. Use = or ≠ .

7. $\frac{13}{20} \bigcirc \frac{3}{5}$

8. $\frac{9}{11} \bigcirc \frac{17}{20}$

9. $\frac{2}{1} \bigcirc \frac{4}{2}$

10. $\frac{12}{9} \bigcirc \frac{8}{6}$

11. $\frac{11}{7} \bigcirc \frac{5}{3}$

12. $\frac{3}{19} \bigcirc \frac{1}{8}$

13. $\frac{45}{40} \bigcirc \frac{18}{16}$

14. $\frac{10}{2} \bigcirc \frac{25}{5}$

15. $\frac{1.8}{0.5} \bigcirc \frac{7.2}{2.0}$

16. $\frac{1.6}{1.4} \bigcirc \frac{1.3}{1.1}$

17. $\frac{30}{1.5} \bigcirc \frac{20}{1.0}$

18. $\frac{2.4}{1.5} \bigcirc \frac{3.2}{2.0}$

19. $\frac{\left(\frac{2}{3}\right)}{10} \bigcirc \frac{1}{15}$

20. $\frac{\left(\frac{1}{2}\right)}{6} \bigcirc \frac{4}{24}$

21. $\frac{\left(\frac{4}{7}\right)}{9} \bigcirc \frac{4}{63}$

22. $\frac{\left(\frac{3}{4}\right)}{5} \bigcirc \frac{6}{40}$

23. Measurement Fill in the table of equal rates.

Gallons		4	6	8	
Pints	16		48		80

24. Social Science In 1990, Wyoming had about 7,650 foreign-born residents and a total population of about 454,000. North Carolina had about 115,000 foreign-born residents and a total population of about 6,630,000. Did these states have about the same ratio of foreign-born residents to total residents? Explain.

_____

_____

25. Career Use cross products to test whether the typing rates are equal: 30 words in 6 minutes and 440 words in 8 minutes. _____

Name _____

Relating Proportions and Graphs

Is each table an equal ratio table? If so find the value of k.

1. _____   k = _____

x	3	4	5	10
y	24	32	40	80

2. _____   k = _____

x	9	12	15	20
y	6	8	10	15

3. _____   k = _____

x	4	6	8	10
y	9	12	15	18

4. _____   k = _____

x	4	12	20	28
y	1	3	5	7

5. If the value of k in $\frac{y}{x} = k$ is 18 and x = 5, what is the value of y? _____

6. If the value of k in $\frac{y}{x} = k$ is 11 and y = 33, what is the value of x? _____

7. Use a cm-ruler to measure the width and height of each rectangle. Graph the width on the x-axis and the height on the y-axis. Are the ratios of height to width equal? _____

Width (cm)				
Height (cm)				

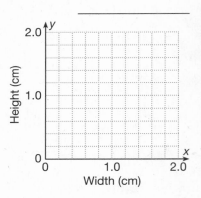

8. Science An object is suspended on a spring. The graph shows the relationship between the weight F of the object and the distance x that the spring is stretched by the weight.

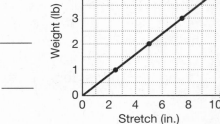

   a. Find the slope using any two points on the line. _____

   b. Make a table of values for the graph.
      Find the value of k.   k = _____

x				
F				

   c. Write a rate equation describing this relationship. _____

   d. What is the weight of an object that stretches the spring 18 in.? _____

Section 5A Review

Write a ratio comparing the number of vowels to the number of consonants in each word.

1. Washington _____   **2.** Roosevelt _____

Check each pair of ratios to see if a proportion is formed.
Use = or ≠ .

3. $\frac{9}{4} \bigcirc \frac{7}{3}$ **4.** $\frac{15}{25} \bigcirc \frac{6}{10}$ **5.** $\frac{17}{18} \bigcirc \frac{14}{15}$ **6.** $\frac{3.5}{4} \bigcirc \frac{1.4}{1.6}$

Complete each table to create ratios equal to the given ratio.

7.

7	14	21	28	35
3				

8.

		18		
10	20	30	40	50

9. The bar graph shows the number of thousands of miles of railroad tracks in each country.

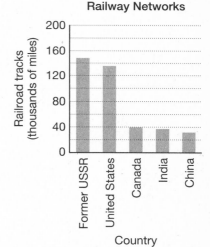

Railway Networks

   a. Estimate the ratio of the lengths of the railway networks in India and the former USSR.

   _____

   b. For what countries is the ratio about 5 to 4?

   _____

Is the table an equal ratio table? If so, find the value of k.

10. _____ $k =$ _____

x	3	6	9	11
y	15	25	35	45

11. _____ $k =$ _____

x	1	3	5	7
y	7	21	35	49

12. If the value of k in $\frac{y}{x} = k$ is 15 and $y = 45$, what is the value of x? _____

13. The Bitter Nut Company sells pecans for $4.50 per pound, plus $3.00 for shipping and handling. Use x for the number of pounds. Graph the relationship between the total cost and the number of pounds. *[Lesson 4-3]*

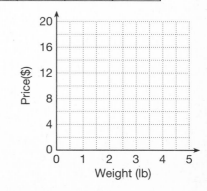

Name _____

Solving Proportions

Write a proportion for each situation. Do not solve.

1. How much should 5 pounds of potatoes cost
if 2 pounds cost $0.88?   _____

2. A recipe for 30 cookies uses 2 cups of flour.
How much flour would you use to make 54
cookies?   _____

Solve each proportion. Which method did you use? Why?

3. $\frac{18}{x} = \frac{9}{8}$ _____

_____

4. $\frac{16}{28} = \frac{x}{7}$ _____

_____

5. $\frac{32}{44} = \frac{48}{x}$ _____

_____

Which is the best estimate for *x* in each proportion? Explain your choice.

6. $\frac{6.2}{5.41} = \frac{51}{x}$ **(A)** 4.5 **(B)** 36 **(C)** 45 **(D)** 61

_____

7. $\frac{2134}{769} = \frac{x}{22}$ **(A)** 60 **(B)** 75 **(C)** 120 **(D)** 600

_____

Solve each proportion.

8. $\frac{12}{10} = \frac{42}{u}$ **9.** $\frac{10}{5} = \frac{14}{y}$ **10.** $\frac{n}{28} = \frac{21}{12}$ **11.** $\frac{18}{66} = \frac{t}{11}$

$u =$ _____ $y =$ _____ $n =$ _____ $t =$ _____

12. A typical paint roller uses 5 gallons of paint to cover 3250 square
feet. How much paint would be used to cover 5850 square feet? _____

Name _____

Using Unit Rates

For each of the following, find the
unit rate and create a rate formula.

1. $408 for 24 months _____

2. $38.50 for 7 hours of work _____

3. 160 students for 8 teachers _____

4. $18.00 for 12 pounds _____

5. 360 miles in 8 hours _____

6. $80 for 5 dictionaries _____

7. 42 meters in 7 seconds _____

8. Hong Kong has a population of about 5,550,000 and
an area of about 402 sq mi. Estimate the number of
people per square mile. _____

9. **Consumer** An insurance policy is advertised with the
phrase "only 75¢ per day!" What is the cost for one year? _____

Which is a better buy? (Underline the correct choice.)

10. A 24-exposure roll of film for $5.50, or a 36-exposure roll for $9.00

11. 8 binder clips for $0.88, or 10 binder clips for $1.00

12. 4 pounds of bananas for $1.00, or 1 pound for $0.22

13. A 3 hour equipment rental for $210, or 5 hours for $335

14. A 20-lb bag of dog food for $14, or a 25-lb bag for $18

15. 28 oz of honey for $6.30, or 16 oz for $3.76

16. A 2-lb watermelon for $0.37, or a 3-lb watermelon for $0.48

17. In 1992, the Disney Channel set a record by unveiling
a jar containing 2,910 lb of jelly beans. If there were
378,000 jelly beans in the jar, how many jelly beans
would be in a 1-lb jar? _____

Problem Solving Using Rates and Proportions

1. A 7-inch record turns 165 times to play a song lasting $3\frac{2}{3}$ minutes. How many times would a 7-inch record turn to play a song lasting $4\frac{1}{15}$ minutes? Explain how you solved this problem.

_____

2. For which two figures do the ratios of shaded area to unshaded area form a proportion?

_____

 (A)   (B)   (C)   (D)

3. The World Trade Center is about 240 m tall, and the Citicorp Center is about 280 m tall. If a scale model of New York includes a 33-cm tall replica of the World Trade Center, how tall is the replica of the Citicorp Center? Explain how you solved this problem.

_____

4. **Social Science** In San Francisco, about 27% of residents (that is, 27 out of every 100 residents) speak a foreign language at home. If there were about 195,500 foreign language speakers in 1990, what was the population? Explain how you solved this problem.

_____

5. Use the numbers 3, 6, 9, 12, and 18 to write as many true proportions as you can. (Use a number only once in each proportion.)

_____

_____

_____

6. **Social Science** The ratio of men to women in the United Arab Emirates is about 3 to 2. If there are about 1,680,000 men, how many women are there? Explain how you solved this problem?

_____

Name _____

Scale, Scale Drawings, and Models

Geography Use the map and a ruler.
What is the approximate distance from

1. Seattle to Miami _____

2. New York to Miami _____

3. Denver to Dallas _____

4. Seattle to New Orleans _____

5. Dallas to Milwaukee _____

Use the scale 3 cm = 10 km to find each missing measure.

	6.	7.	8.	9.	10.
Scaled dimension	2.7 cm		21 cm		13.5 cm
Actual dimension		50 km		243 km	

Geometry Find the missing measures in each pair of similar figures.

11. x = _____

x ◺ 24 ◺
33   44

12. y = _____

10 ▭ 5 ▭
  14   y

13. a = _____   b = _____

6 ◿ 12   9 ◿ b
   a   12

14. c = _____   d = _____   e = _____

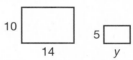

2.4 ⬡ 2.7
2.1
c

d ⬡ 4.5
e
7.5

15. Suppose you need to make a map of a 35 mi by 45 mi
region. The map needs to fit in an 8 in. by 10 in. frame.
What is the largest scale you could use?   _____

16. The Renaissance Tower in Dallas is 216 m tall. If a drawing
of the Renaissance Tower is made using a scale of
5 cm = 27 m, how tall will the drawing be?   _____

Name _____

Section 5B Review

Write and solve a proportion for each of the following situations.

1. How much should 22 notebooks cost if 4 cost $11? _____

2. Monte's Music Store has 7 jazz CDs for every 4 classical CDs.
If there are 1001 jazz CDs, how many classical CDs are there? _____

Solve each proportion. Which method did you use? Why?

3. $\dfrac{4}{12} = \dfrac{6}{u}$ _____

4. $\dfrac{s}{21} = \dfrac{24}{18}$ _____

For each of the following, find the unit rate and create a rate formula.

5. $180 for 4 tires _____

6. 45 children for 9 adults _____

Find the missing values for each pair of similar figures.

7. $u =$ _____ $v =$ _____

28 · 40 · u · v · 30 · 33

8. $w =$ _____ $x =$ _____ $y =$ _____

30 · w · 25 · 35 · 18 · 12 · x · y

9. A building is 56 ft wide and 378 ft tall. If a model of this
building is made with scale 3 in. = 28 ft, what are the width
and height of the model? _____

10. Consumer Henry can buy ink cartridges for his computer
printer for $7.50 each at a local store, or he can order them
by mail for $4.75 each. If he orders by mail, he will have to
pay $8.25 for shipping and handling. *[Lesson 4-6]*

a. Write a system of equations showing the total cost y
for each method of purchasing x cartridges.

_____

b. Graph the equations. For how many cartridges is
the price the same either way?

_____

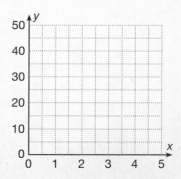

Name _____

Cumulative Review Chapters 1–5

Compute the following. *[Lessons 2-2, 2-3, and 2-4]*

1. $132 + (-18)$

2. $22 \times (-8)$

3. $-37 - 18$

4. $38 \div (-2)$

_____ _____ _____ _____

5. $47 - (-15)$

6. $-16 + 142$

7. $\dfrac{-275}{-11}$

8. $-12 \times (-4)$

_____ _____ _____ _____

Write an expression for each situation. *[Lesson 3-3]*

9. The number of feet in d miles

10. the number of eyes on c cats

_____ _____

11. the number of gallons in b quarts

12. the number of cans in t twelve-packs

_____ _____

For each line, find the slope, the x-intercept, and the y-intercept.
[Lesson 4-5]

13. Line through
   A and B

   slope: _____

   x-intercept: ____

   y-intercept: ____

14. Line through
   A and D

   slope: _____

   x-intercept: ____

   y-intercept: ____

15. Line through
   B and C

   slope: _____

   x-intercept: ____

   y-intercept: ____

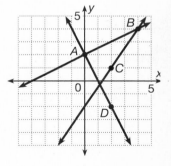

Complete each table to create ratios equal to the given ratio.
[Lesson 5-2]

16.

3	6	9	12	15
7				

17.

5				
2	4	6	8	10

Solve each proportion. *[Lesson 5-4]*

18. $\dfrac{7}{4} = \dfrac{x}{28}$

   $x = $ _____

19. $\dfrac{4}{z} = \dfrac{6}{18}$

   $z = $ _____

20. $\dfrac{h}{9} = \dfrac{7}{3}$

   $h = $ _____

21. $\dfrac{16}{22} = \dfrac{56}{u}$

   $u = $ _____

Percents, Decimals, and Fractions

1. Draw a diagram to show 60%.

2. Use the circle graph to answer the questions about music sales in 1994.

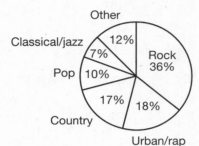

1994 Music Sales

a. What percent of music sold was classical or jazz? _____

b. What percent of music sold was rock? _____

c. What percent of music sold was *not* rock, country, or pop? _____

Write each fraction or decimal as a percent.

3. $\frac{2}{5}$ **4.** 0.53   **5.** $\frac{1}{4}$ **6.** 0.014

_____   _____   _____   _____

7. $\frac{3}{8}$ **8.** 0.0051   **9.** $\frac{5}{4}$ **10.** 1.39

_____   _____   _____   _____

Write each percent as a fraction in lowest terms and as a decimal.

11. 50%   **12.** 23%   **13.** 78%   **14.** 87.5%

_____   _____   _____   _____

15. 64%   **16.** 0.1%   **17.** 300%   **18.** 175%

_____   _____   _____   _____

19. A bag contains 8 green marbles, 7 blue marbles, and 5 clear marbles. What percent of the marbles are

a. green? _____   **b.** blue? _____   **c.** not green? _____

20. The House of Representatives has 435 members, of whom 52 are from California. What percent of the members are from California? _____

Name _____

Solving Problems with Percent

Solve.

1. What number is 85% of 560?

_____

2. What percent of 120 is 36?

_____

3. 75 out of 500 is what percent?

_____

4. 46 is $66\frac{2}{3}$% of what number?

_____

5. 150% of 84 is what number?

_____

6. What percent of 64 is 36?

_____

7. What number is 180% of 90?

_____

8. 250 is what percent of 400?

_____

9. About 15% of prime time television is devoted to commercials. How many minutes of commercials are broadcast each hour? _____

10. About 40% of the waste in American landfills is paper. This paper waste amounts to 420 lb per person, per year. How much garbage is generated by the average person each year? _____

11. 800 households were surveyed to determine how many children lived in each household.

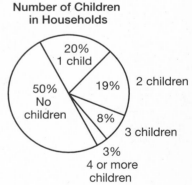

Number of Children in Households

   a. How many households had no children? _____

   b. How many households had 3 children? _____

   c. How many households had at least 2 children? _____

12. You can make a delicious peanut sauce by combining the ingredients shown in the order given, and then adding a dash of cayenne pepper. Complete the table to show how much of each ingredient you would use to make $1\frac{1}{2}$ cups (24 tablespoons) of sauce.

Ingredient	Peanut butter	Hot water	Cider vinegar	Soy sauce	Molasses
Percent	$33\frac{1}{3}$	$33\frac{1}{3}$	$16\frac{2}{3}$	$8\frac{1}{3}$	$8\frac{1}{3}$
Amount (tbls.)					

Name _____

Estimating Percents

Estimate each percent.

1. 83 out of 201

2. 43 out of 126

3. 73 out of 139

_____

_____

_____

4. 408 out of 991

5. 5 out of 485

6. 119 out of 121

_____

_____

_____

Estimate.

7. 91% of 385

8. 6% of 158

9. 32% of 1190

_____

_____

_____

Estimate the percent that each shaded region represents.

10. _____

11. _____

12. _____

Use mental math. Insert >, <, or =. Explain your answer.

13. 33% of 682 ◯ $\frac{1}{3}$ of 682

_____

14. 6% of 518 ◯ 0.006 · 518

_____

15. 14% of 82 ◯ 28% of 41

_____

_____

16. Health A serving of granola contains 38 g of carbohydrate, which is 13% of the daily requirement. What is the daily requirement for carbohydrate?

_____

17. The average per capita income in America was $20,800 in 1993. The city with the highest per capita income was New York, NY, where the per capita income was 251.3% of the national average. What was the average per capita income in New York?

_____

Name _____

Section 6A Review

For each figure, write the fraction, decimal, and percent that tells how much of the figure is shaded.

1. fraction: _____

   decimal: _____

   percent: _____

2. fraction: _____

   decimal: _____

   percent: _____

Write each fraction, mixed number, or decimal as a percent.

3. $1\frac{7}{20}$ _____

4. 0.025 _____

5. $\frac{11}{16}$ _____

6. 2.35 _____

Write each percent as a decimal and as a fraction or mixed number in lowest terms.

7. 4% _____

8. 21% _____

9. 270% _____

For Exercises 10–13, estimate each percent.

10. 17 out of 32

11. 154 out of 445

12. 63% of 144

13. 76% of 540

_____ _____ _____ _____

14. What number is 18% of 360? _____

15. 32 is 16% of what number? _____

16. 94.5 is what percent of 525? _____

17. 117 is 180% of what number? _____

18. Without evaluating, insert >, <, or =: 36% of 842 ◯ 35% of 842

19. In 1960, 56.1% of the U.S. civilian labor force was employed. If 65,778,000 civilians were employed, estimate the civilian labor force. _____

20. **Health** The recommended daily allowance for vitamin C is 60 mg. How much vitamin C is in a serving of fruit juice which provides 18% of the daily allowance? _____

21. **Science** The maximum depth of the Atlantic Ocean is 30,246 ft. This is 5,049 ft deeper than the maximum depth of the Caribbean Sea. What is the maximum depth of the Caribbean Sea? *[Lesson 3-4]* _____

22. Hal typed 385 words in 7 minutes. Val typed 495 words in 9 minutes. Use cross products to test whether the rates are equal. *[Lesson 5-2]* _____

Percent Increase

For Exercises 1–8, find the percent of increase.
Round to the nearest whole percent.

1. Old: 360
New: 392

2. Old: 35
New: 105

3. Old: 72
New: 100

4. Old: 365
New: 521

_____

_____

_____

_____

5. Old: $63.95
New: $75.60

6. Old: $18.00
New: $24.95

7. Old: $168
New: $195

8. Old: $3820
New: $5160

_____

_____

_____

_____

9. The average speed of a horse-drawn carriage was 8 mi/hr
in 1900. In New York City, the average speed for traffic
was 9.9 mi/hr in 1988. Find the percent increase.

_____

10. What is the wholesale price of a product if the percent
of increase is 35% and the amount of increase is $14.70?

_____

11. Consumer Find the total cost of a $22 toaster whose
price is increased 18%.

_____

12. The price of an average movie ticket increased 1880%
between 1940 and 1990. The average price was $0.24
in 1940. What was the average price in 1990?

_____

13. In 1993, the average cost for four people to go to a
major league baseball game was $90.81. This was an
increase of 4.7% over the average cost in 1992. What
was the average cost in 1992?

_____

14. The circulation of *YM* magazine increased 13.26%
from 1993 to 1994. If the 1993 circulation was
1,707,377, find the 1994 circulation.

_____

15. Social Science The fastest-growing major city in the
U.S. from 1980 to 1990 was Mesa, AZ, which grew
89% to a population of 288,091. What was the
1980 population?

_____

16. Consumer The wholesale cost of a computer is
$2250. Find the retail cost after an increase of 18%.

_____

Percent Decrease

For Exercises 1–8 find the percent decrease. Round to the nearest whole percent.

1. Old: 50
New: 47

_____

2. Old: 275
New: 230

_____

3. Old: 460
New: 240

_____

4. Old: 220
New: 98

_____

5. Old: $36.75
New: $32.50

_____

6. Old: $165
New: $94

_____

7. Old: $1.99
New: $1.25

_____

8. Old: $374
New: $197

_____

9. Consumer What is the sale price of a $200 removable computer disk drive that has been discounted 25%?

_____

10. There were 470 "top 40" radio stations in September, 1994. This is 43% fewer than there were in September, 1990. How many "top 40" stations were there in 1990?

_____

11. Consumer You want to buy a $128 tape player that is supposed to go on sale for 15% off next month. How much will you save if you wait until the sale to buy it?

_____

12. Social Science The population of Detroit, Michigan, declined 14.6% from 1980 to 1990. The 1980 population was 1,203,368. What was the 1990 population?

_____

13. Sarah invests in stocks. Unfortunately, she made some poor decisions last year, and the value of her stock portfolio fell from $24,638 to $13,874. What was the percent decrease?

_____

14. The number of American daily evening papers dropped 12.6% from 1990 to 1994. There were 1084 evening papers in 1990. How many were there in 1994?

_____

15. Consumer An advertisement for a bicycle reads "22% off, this week only! Your price $265.20." What is the regular price for the bicycle?

_____

16. The enrollment at Valley High School fell 18% from 1265 students last year. What is the enrollment now?

_____

Name _____

Applications of Percent Change

Start with 100. Find each result (+ means increase, − means decrease).

1. +40% followed by +40% _____   **2.** +40% followed by −40% _____

3. −40% followed by +40% _____   **4.** −40% followed by −40% _____

5. −40% followed by +60% _____   **6.** +75% followed by −60% _____

7. −37.5% followed by +60% _____   **8.** +600% followed by −100% _____

9. −50% followed by +300% _____   **10.** +400% followed by −75% _____

11. Consumer A $180 ring is discounted 20%, but you must pay 8% sales tax on the purchase. Find the total cost if

   a. you take off the discount first, then add the tax. _____

   b. you add the tax first, then calculate the discount. _____

12. In Houston, Texas, the median price for a pre-owned home was $78,600 in 1985. This amount fell 10.0% from 1985 to 1990, and increased 13.8% from 1990 to 1994. What was the median price in 1994? _____

Find the simple interest.

13. Savings Account
Principal: $1275
Rate: 7%
Time: 3 years

Interest: _____

14. Loan
Principal: $540
Rate: 13%
Time: 1.5 years

Interest: _____

15. Retirement Account
Principal: $8450
Rate: 8%
Time: 5 years

Interest: _____

16. Consumer Before traveling to France, Scott could have exchanged his 100 U.S. dollars for French francs, and the bank would have given him 4.60 francs for each dollar. But, when he arrived in France, he found that the franc had dropped 10%. Scott exchanged his francs there. How many francs did he receive? _____

17. History During the late 1970s and early 1980s, interest rates were very high by today's standards. Cecelia opened a savings account which paid 11.5% simple interest for 4 years. If her interest amounted to $386.40, what was her principal? _____

Section 6B Review

Find the percent of increase or decrease. Round to the nearest whole percent.

1. Old: 814
New: 675

2. Old: 381
New: 461

3. Old: 625
New: 419

_____

_____

_____

4. Old: $31.60
New: $35.95

5. Old: $142
New: $119

6. Old: $949
New: $325

_____

_____

_____

7. A sign in a music store reads, "15% off—You save $2.70!" What is the regular price?

_____

8. A stereo priced at $385.00 costs $406.18 after the sales tax is added. What is the tax rate?

_____

9. A suit is normally $364.95. Find its cost during a 25%-off sale.

_____

10. Connie took some friends out to dinner. The meal's regular price was $48. Connie had a 30%-off coupon, and she left a tip of 15% of the discounted amount. How much did she pay for the meal?

_____

11. Shares of stock in *XYZ* Corporation fell 42% from last year's price of $83.00 per share. What percent of increase would bring them back to last year's price?

_____

12. Find the simple interest earned in 3 years on a savings account that started at $1820.00 if the interest rate is 7.5%.

_____

13. The value of a home increased 10%, and then fell 5%. Find the total percent increase or decrease from the original price.

_____

14. Social Science The population of Rome, Italy, is about 3274 times the population of the Vatican City. If 2,688,000 people live in Rome, what is the population of the Vatican City? *[Lesson 3-5]*

_____

15. Tom is making miniature models of Chicago skyscrapers for a movie set. His model of the 700-ft Leo Burnett building is 63 in. tall. How tall is his model of the 900-ft building at Two Prudential Center? *[Lesson 5-6]*

_____

Practice

Cumulative Review Chapters 1–6

Plot each point on the coordinate grid. *[Lesson 2-6]*

1. $A(0, 2)$ **2.** $B(-1, -3)$

3. $C(0, 0)$ **4.** $D(2, 4)$

5. $E(-3, 0)$ **6.** $F(4, -2)$

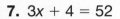

Solve each equation. *[Lesson 3-6]*

7. $3x + 4 = 52$ **8.** $7x - 5 = 51$ **9.** $6x - 10 = -76$ **10.** $11x + 18 = 62$

   $x =$ _____ $x =$ _____ $x =$ _____ $x =$ _____

11. $\frac{1}{2}y - 5 = 21$ **12.** $\frac{n}{12} + 6 = 8$ **13.** $2.5x - 5 = -10$ **14.** $16 = \frac{5}{7}x - 19$

   $y =$ _____ $n =$ _____ $x =$ _____ $x =$ _____

Determine whether each ordered pair is a solution of the equation.
[Lesson 4-2]

15. $y = x - 5$ **a.** $(7, 2)$ _____   **b.** $(2, -7)$ _____   **c.** $(2, 7)$ _____

16. $y = 7x$ **a.** $(6, 42)$ _____   **b.** $(6, 13)$ _____   **c.** $(42, 6)$ _____

17. $y = 3x - 7$ **a.** $(17, 8)$ _____   **b.** $(8, 17)$ _____   **c.** $(5, 8)$ _____

18. $2x - 5y = 7$ **a.** $(8, 3)$ _____   **b.** $(6, 1)$ _____   **c.** $(1, 6)$ _____

Write each fraction or decimal as a percent. *[Lesson 6-1]*

19. $\frac{3}{5}$ _____   **20.** 0.61 _____   **21.** $\frac{7}{8}$ _____   **22.** 0.84 _____

23. 0.162 _____   **24.** $\frac{5}{6}$ _____   **25.** 2.87 _____   **26.** $\frac{21}{4}$ _____

Find the percent of increase or decrease. Round to the nearest whole percent. *[Lessons 6-4 and 6-5]*

27. old: 614   **28.** old: 163   **29.** old: 217
     new: 321   new: 184   new: 365

_____   _____   _____

© Scott Foresman • Addison Wesley 8

Divisibility Patterns and Prime Factorization

Determine whether each given number is divisible by 2, 3, 4, 5, 6, 8, 9, or 10.

1. 290 _____

2. 420 _____

3. 156 _____

4. 4547 _____

5. 3576 _____

6. 8379 _____

List all of the factors for each number and identify the prime factors.

7. 110

Factors _____

Prime factors: _____

8. 72

Factors _____

Prime factors: _____

Use a factor tree to determine the prime factorization of
each number. Express your answer using exponents.

9. 182 _____

10. 735 _____

11. 198 _____

The equations below involve prime factorization. Solve for the variable
in each equation.

12. $y = 2^5$

13. $c = 11 \times 5^3$

14. $k = 2^2 \times 5$

15. $m = 2^4 \times 7$

$y =$ _____

$c =$ _____

$k =$ _____

$m =$ _____

16. A *perfect number* is a whole number that is equal to the sum
of its positive factors (excluding itself). For example, 6 is a
perfect number because 6 = 1 + 2 + 3. Find a perfect number
between 20 and 30.

_____

Name _____

Greatest Common Factors (GCF)

Find the GCF of each group of numbers.

1. 16, 40 _____   **2.** 9, 12 _____   **3.** 40, 112 _____

4. 42, 48 _____   **5.** 154, 147 _____   **6.** 35, 54 _____

7. 49, 91, 168 _____   **8.** 90, 50, 10 _____   **9.** 16, 72, 104 _____

Use prime factorization to find the GCF of each group of numbers.

10. 125 = _____   **11.** 24 = _____   **12.** 120 = _____

440 = _____   60 = _____   165 = _____

GCF = _____   GCF = _____   GCF = _____

13. 156 = _____   **14.** 100 = _____   **15.** 90 = _____

54 = _____   84 = _____   72 = _____

GCF = _____   GCF = _____   GCF = _____

16. 216 = _____   **17.** 132 = _____   **18.** 96 = _____

144 = _____   60 = _____   90 = _____

180 = _____   252 = _____   175 = _____

GCF = _____   GCF = _____   GCF = _____

Write each fraction in lowest terms.

19. $\frac{19}{38}$ _____   **20.** $\frac{58}{64}$ _____   **21.** $\frac{68}{114}$ _____   **22.** $\frac{10}{120}$ _____

23. $\frac{14}{18}$ _____   **24.** $\frac{85}{90}$ _____   **25.** $\frac{20}{196}$ _____   **26.** $\frac{112}{175}$ _____

27. $\frac{28}{62}$ _____   **28.** $\frac{42}{122}$ _____   **29.** $\frac{76}{236}$ _____   **30.** $\frac{56}{100}$ _____

31. The number of students in Mrs. Folsom's art classes are 28, 36, and 32. She wants to divide each class into groups for a class project. If all of the groups are to be the same size, what is the largest group size that will work? _____

Least Common Multiples (LCM)

Find the LCM for each pair of numbers.

1. 16, 12 _____   **2.** 12, 8 _____   **3.** 8, 3 _____   **4.** 20, 45 _____

5. 27, 15 _____   **6.** 34, 18 _____   **7.** 12, 15 _____   **8.** 6, 75 _____

9. 64, 20 _____   **10.** 12, 6 _____   **11.** 28, 8 _____   **12.** 36, 24 _____

Use prime factorization to find the LCM for each group of numbers.

13. 45 = _____   **14.** 22 = _____   **15.** 39 = _____

50 = _____   26 = _____   36 = _____

LCM = _____   LCM = _____   LCM = _____

16. 24 = _____   **17.** 30 = _____   **18.** 80 = _____

20 = _____   18 = _____   105 = _____

LCM = _____   LCM = _____   LCM = _____

19. 20 = _____   **20.** 33 = _____   **21.** 60 = _____

15 = _____   18 = _____   56 = _____

35 = _____   12 = _____   35 = _____

LCM = _____   LCM = _____   LCM = _____

Rewrite each group of fractions with the LCD.

22. $\frac{1}{3}$ and $\frac{7}{12}$ _____   **23.** $\frac{7}{10}$ and $\frac{2}{15}$ _____

24. $\frac{2}{3}, \frac{3}{5},$ and $\frac{5}{7}$ _____   **25.** $\frac{5}{12}, \frac{4}{9}, \frac{5}{16}$ _____

26. A carousel has two rows of plastic ponies going at different speeds. Ralph is riding a pony that goes around every 135 seconds, and Lucy is riding a pony that goes around every 150 seconds. If Ralph and Lucy start on the east side of the carousel at the same time, how soon will they again meet on the east side of the carousel?

_____

Name _____

Practice

Section 7A Review

Use divisibility rules. State whether the given number is divisible by
2, 3, 4, 5, 6, 8, 9, or 10. Indicate when the number is prime.

1. 1792 _____ **2.** 2748 _____ **3.** 1492 _____

4. 1947 _____ **5.** 331 _____ **6.** 4494 _____

Find the prime factorization of each number.

7. 150 _____ **8.** 360 _____ **9.** 96 _____

10. 168 _____ **11.** 555 _____ **12.** 378 _____

Find the GCF and the LCM of each group of numbers.

13. 20, 6 **14.** 15, 2 **15.** 28, 36 **16.** 15, 25, 40

GCF: _____ GCF: _____ GCF: _____ GCF: _____

LCM: _____ LCM: _____ LCM: _____ LCM: _____

Write each fraction in lowest terms.

17. $\frac{28}{140}$ _____ **18.** $\frac{25}{45}$ _____ **19.** $\frac{320}{380}$ _____ **20.** $\frac{54}{126}$ _____

Find the LCD for each group of fractions.

21. $\frac{5}{6}$ and $\frac{17}{18}$ _____ **22.** $\frac{9}{10}$ and $\frac{4}{25}$ _____ **23.** $\frac{3}{16}, \frac{7}{20},$ and $\frac{11}{24}$ _____

24. Do you think the LCM of an odd and even number is always even?
Explain your answer.

_____

_____

25. The Thrifty Copy Shop charges $0.10 per
copy, plus a service charge of $0.50 for the
entire order. Use *x* for the number of copies
made, and graph the price paid. *[Lesson 4-3]*

26. The population of Glendale, Arizona, increased
from about 97,000 in 1980 to 148,000 in 1990.
Find the percent increase. *[Lesson 6-4]*

_____

66 Use with page 342.

© Scott Foresman • Addison Wesley 8

Name _____

Defining Rational Numbers

Use >, <, or = to compare each pair of numbers.

1. $\frac{7}{8}$ ◯ 0.82   **2.** 1.03 ◯ 1.029   **3.** $\frac{-3}{6}$ ◯ 0.4   **4.** $\frac{3}{5}$ ◯ $\frac{4}{7}$

5. $\frac{8}{3}$ ◯ 2.6   **6.** 0.4 ◯ $\frac{2}{5}$ **7.** 2.34 ◯ 2.43   **8.** 0.4 ◯ $\frac{5}{12}$

9. −0.63 ◯ $\frac{-5}{8}$ **10.** $\frac{8}{25}$ ◯ 0.32   **11.** $\frac{-3}{16}$ ◯ −0.2   **12.** 1.333 ◯ $\frac{4}{3}$

Write each fraction as a decimal and state whether it is repeating or terminating.

13. $\frac{5}{8}$ _____   **14.** $-\frac{7}{10}$ _____

15. $\frac{16}{33}$ _____   **16.** $\frac{6}{7}$ _____

17. $\frac{21}{80}$ _____   **18.** $-\frac{5}{6}$ _____

Write each decimal as a fraction or mixed number in lowest terms.

19. 0.36 _____   **20.** 0.375 _____   **21.** 1.24 _____   **22.** $0.\overline{8}$ _____

23. $0.\overline{54}$ _____   **24.** 0.13 _____   **25.** $2.\overline{4}$ _____   **26.** $7.\overline{6}$ _____

Compare each group of numbers and order them on a number line.

27. 0.7, $0.\overline{7}$, $\frac{3}{4}$, $\frac{7}{8}$ **28.** $\frac{3}{5}$, 1.2, $\frac{5}{3}$, $0.\overline{3}$ **29.** $-0.\overline{5}$, $-\frac{2}{3}$, $-\frac{1}{2}$, $-\frac{3}{8}$

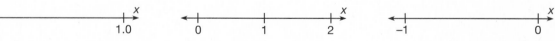

30. 8.2, $8.\overline{25}$, $8.\overline{3}$, $8\frac{1}{4}$ **31.** 0.6, −0.5, $\frac{1}{2}$, $-\frac{4}{5}$ **32.** $-2\frac{2}{3}$, $-2\frac{2}{5}$, −2.1, −2.25

33. During the 1992 Summer Olympic Games, the top three scorers for the women's long jump were Inessa Kravets ($23\frac{3}{8}$ ft), Jackie Joyner-Kersee ($23\frac{5}{24}$ ft), and Heike Drechsler ($23\frac{7}{16}$ ft). Write these women's names in order from the longest jump to the shortest.

_____

34. Social Science In 1990, 21.5% of the world's population lived in China. What fraction is this? _____

Add and Subtract Rational Numbers

Add or subtract each of the following. Write each answer in lowest terms.

1. $0.1465 + 0.28$

2. $2.73 - 1.2496$

3. $28.4167 + 7.9$

_____

_____

_____

4. $8.63 - (-4.721)$

5. $-3.6017 + 8.85$

6. $35.6408 - 8.59$

_____

_____

_____

7. $2.384 + (-12.9)$

8. $-3.8712 - 6.84$

9. $12.63821 + 7.38$

_____

_____

_____

10. $\frac{3}{5} + \frac{1}{5}$ _____

11. $\frac{15}{11} - \frac{7}{11}$ _____

12. $\frac{5}{4} + \frac{7}{4}$ _____

13. $9\frac{9}{16} - 2\frac{1}{24}$ _____

14. $2\frac{4}{5} + 20\frac{1}{4}$ _____

15. $5\frac{7}{8} - 2\frac{3}{8}$ _____

16. $18\frac{3}{4} - 16\frac{1}{5}$ _____

17. $6\frac{4}{11} + \left(-2\frac{1}{2}\right)$ _____

18. $5\frac{9}{20} + 1\frac{3}{5}$ _____

Find n.

19. $n - 1\frac{1}{3} = 9\frac{4}{5}$

20. $n + 7\frac{4}{11} = 21\frac{1}{33}$

21. $n - \frac{1}{3} = 5\frac{1}{6}$

$n =$ _____

$n =$ _____

$n =$ _____

22. $n + 6\frac{1}{6} = 7\frac{5}{21}$

23. $n + \left(-2\frac{1}{22}\right) = 5\frac{5}{11}$

24 $n + 3\frac{2}{3} = 5\frac{2}{5}$

$n =$ _____

$n =$ _____

$n =$ _____

25. $n - 7\frac{2}{5} = \frac{6}{35}$

26. $n + 8\frac{5}{7} = 13\frac{4}{35}$

27. $n - \left(-7\frac{1}{22}\right) = 20\frac{10}{11}$

$n =$ _____

$n =$ _____

$n =$ _____

28. In 1970, $\frac{13}{25}$ of the funding for U.S. public elementary and secondary schools came from local sources, and $\frac{2}{5}$ of the funding came from state governments. The remaining funds came from the federal government. What fraction of funding came from the federal government? _____

29. Miguel bought some stock that was priced at $14\frac{3}{8}$ per share. Find the value of the stock after it went up $2\frac{3}{4}$. _____

Name _____

Multiply and Divide Rational Numbers

Multiply or divide each of the following. Write each answer in lowest terms.

1. $97.98 \times (-0.2)$ **2.** 7.039×0.04 **3.** $-0.1 \times (-4.1)$ **4.** -0.05×0.014

_____   _____   _____   _____

5. $0.17\overline{)8.126}$ **6.** $-3.6\overline{)32.256}$ **7.** $-0.5\overline{)-423.55}$ **8.** $2.7\overline{)-19.899}$

9. -0.06×5.89 **10.** 4×0.478 **11.** $-5.8 \times (-7.2)$ **12.** $0.008 \times (-12.22)$

_____   _____   _____   _____

13. $-5.5\overline{)-34.1}$ **14.** $8.58\overline{)-0.1716}$ **15.** $0.091\overline{)8.6541}$ **16.** $-0.87\overline{)-4.524}$

17. $\frac{3}{8} \times \frac{5}{6}$ _____   **18.** $\frac{4}{9} \times \frac{6}{7}$ _____   **19.** $\frac{4}{5} \times \frac{11}{12}$ _____

20. $\frac{1}{2} \div \frac{7}{9}$ _____   **21.** $\frac{3}{5} \div \frac{7}{8}$ _____   **22.** $\frac{5}{7} \div \frac{15}{28}$ _____

23. $\frac{1}{5} \times 7\frac{1}{8}$ _____   **24.** $3 \times 6\frac{5}{9}$ _____   **25.** $2 \times 2\frac{1}{5}$ _____

26. $1\frac{2}{3} \div 3\frac{4}{5}$ _____   **27.** $1\frac{2}{5} \div 2\frac{6}{7}$ _____   **28.** $1 \div 14\frac{1}{2}$ _____

29. $4\frac{3}{7} \times 1\frac{1}{4}$ _____   **30.** $1\frac{6}{7} \times (-5)$ _____   **31.** $\frac{2}{5} \times 6\frac{3}{10}$ _____

32. $1\frac{1}{2} \div (-8)$ _____   **33.** $3\frac{1}{2} \div \frac{5}{7}$ _____   **34.** $-8\frac{1}{2} \div 9$ _____

35. $-3 \times 7\frac{2}{3}$ _____   **36.** $1\frac{1}{5} \times 5\frac{1}{6}$ _____   **37.** $6\frac{1}{4} \times 4\frac{1}{10}$ _____

38. $1\frac{11}{14} \div 2\frac{1}{7}$ _____   **39.** $16 \div 1\frac{2}{5}$ _____   **40.** $2\frac{5}{8} \div 7\frac{1}{2}$ _____

41. Social Science In 1994, about $\frac{27}{140}$ of the federal budget was spent on national defense. About $\frac{7}{25}$ of the money spent on defense was used for military personnel. What fraction of the federal budget was spent on military personnel?

_____

42. Geography The area of Colombia is about $1\frac{1}{4}$ times the area of Venezuela, which is about 352,000 square miles. What is the area of Colombia?

_____

Section 7B Review

Compare each group of numbers and order them on a number line.

1. $\frac{3}{4}, \frac{5}{6}, 0.\overline{8}, 0.8$

2. $5\frac{1}{3}, 5\frac{1}{5}, 5.25, 5.\overline{4}$

3. $-\frac{5}{8}, -\frac{3}{7}, -0.\overline{6}, -0.5$

Write each fraction as a decimal and determine whether it's terminating or repeating.

4. $\frac{5}{7}$ _____

5. $-\frac{7}{8}$ _____

Write each decimal as a fraction or mixed number.

6. 0.68 _____

7. $0.\overline{6}$ _____

8. $-8.\overline{36}$ _____

Calculate.

9. $5.63 + 2.073$

10. $9.6 - 3.176$

11. 8.36×7.4

_____

_____

_____

12. $7\frac{5}{8} + 3\frac{5}{6}$ _____

13. $1\frac{2}{3} \times 2\frac{1}{6}$ _____

14. $10\frac{2}{3} - 8\frac{1}{5}$ _____

Solve.

15. $\frac{8}{9} = \frac{1}{6} + x$

16. $x - \frac{3}{8} = \frac{9}{10}$

17. $3\frac{1}{2} = x - \left(-7\frac{3}{5}\right)$

$x =$ _____

$x =$ _____

$x =$ _____

18. For a party, a caterer needs to prepare twice as many chicken sandwiches as vegetarian sandwiches. There are to be 24 sandwiches altogether. Write a system of equations, using x for the number of vegetarian sandwiches and y for the number of chicken sandwiches. Then solve the system using a table or a graph to find the number of each kind of sandwich. *[Lesson 4-6]*

_____

19. Social Science The population of Chattanooga, Tennessee, was about 120,000 in 1970. The population increased 42% from 1970 to 1980, and decreased 11% from 1980 to 1990. What was the population in 1990? *[Lesson 6-6]* _____

Name _____

Perfect Squares and Square Roots

State whether or not each number is a perfect square.

1. 20 _____   **2.** 16 _____   **3.** 60 _____   **4.** 110 _____

5. 76 _____   **6.** 4 _____   **7.** 64 _____   **8.** 9 _____

9. 36 _____   **10.** 32 _____   **11.** 50 _____   **12.** 200 _____

13. 160 _____   **14.** 625 _____   **15.** 1 _____   **16.** 144 _____

17. 45 _____   **18.** 25 _____   **19.** 12 _____   **20.** 400 _____

Find the two consecutive integers that each is between.

21. $\sqrt{175}$ _____   **22.** $\sqrt{30}$ _____   **23.** $\sqrt{135}$ _____

24. $\sqrt{6}$ _____   **25.** $\sqrt{53}$ _____   **26.** $\sqrt{21}$ _____

27. $\sqrt{111}$ _____   **28.** $\sqrt{3}$ _____   **29.** $\sqrt{580}$ _____

30. $\sqrt{90}$ _____   **31.** $\sqrt{200}$ _____   **32.** $\sqrt{12}$ _____

33. $\sqrt{42}$ _____   **34.** $\sqrt{408}$ _____   **35.** $\sqrt{910}$ _____

Determine each square root and write in lowest terms.

36. $\sqrt{\frac{25}{36}}$ _____   **37.** $\sqrt{\frac{25}{400}}$ _____   **38.** $\sqrt{\frac{4}{36}}$ _____   **39.** $\sqrt{\frac{9}{64}}$ _____

40. $\sqrt{\frac{81}{144}}$ _____   **41.** $\sqrt{\frac{1}{4}}$ _____   **42.** $\sqrt{\frac{64}{25}}$ _____   **43.** $\sqrt{\frac{81}{36}}$ _____

44. $\sqrt{\frac{4}{100}}$ _____   **45.** $\sqrt{\frac{4}{9}}$ _____   **46.** $\sqrt{\frac{64}{400}}$ _____   **47.** $\sqrt{\frac{121}{400}}$ _____

48. $\sqrt{\frac{16}{49}}$ _____   **49.** $\sqrt{\frac{81}{225}}$ _____   **50.** $\sqrt{\frac{36}{121}}$ _____   **51.** $\sqrt{\frac{49}{144}}$ _____

52. A square cake pan has an area of 529 cm^2. How long is each side of the pan? _____

53. In the Japanese art of origami, square paper is folded to create animals and other objects. If a sheet of origami paper has area 324 cm^2, what is the length of each edge of the paper? _____

Name _____

Square Roots and Irrational Numbers

Identify each number as rational or irrational.

1 2.717711777 ...   **2.** 75   **3.** $\sqrt{36}$

_____   _____   _____

4. 6.18181818 ...   **5.** 18.7   **6.** $\frac{4}{7}$

_____   _____   _____

7. 13.61324   **8.** $\sqrt{21}$ **9.** $\sqrt{\frac{49}{64}}$

_____   _____   _____

Use a calculator to find each of the square roots and round to the nearest thousandth.

10. $\sqrt{35}$ _____   **11.** $\sqrt{23}$ _____   **12.** $\sqrt{50}$ _____   **13.** $\sqrt{44}$ _____

14. $\sqrt{27}$ _____   **15.** $\sqrt{18}$ _____   **16.** $\sqrt{69}$ _____   **17.** $\sqrt{56}$ _____

18. $\sqrt{79}$ _____   **19.** $\sqrt{39}$ _____   **20.** $\sqrt{314}$ _____   **21.** $\sqrt{73}$ _____

22. $\sqrt{62}$ _____   **23.** $\sqrt{108}$ _____   **24.** $\sqrt{48}$ _____   **25.** $\sqrt{1200}$ _____

Geometry Find the side length of each of the squares with the given area.

26. 150 in^2 _____   **27.** 144 m^2 _____   **28.** 14 cm^2 _____

29. 18.49 ft^2 _____   **30.** 2.89 km^2 _____   **31.** 94.09 yd^2 _____

32. 49 mm^2 _____   **33.** 0.2025 mi^2 _____   **34.** 85 cm^2 _____

35. 40.96 in^2 _____   **36.** 111 m^2 _____   **37.** 169 ft^2 _____

38. A square card table has a tabletop with area 1350 in^2.
Find the length of each side.   _____

39. Science The formula $t = \sqrt{\frac{d}{4.9}}$ gives the time (t), in seconds, for an object to free fall a distance (d), in meters. A rock is dropped from a 35-m-high cliff. How soon will it hit the beach below?   _____

Name _____

The Pythagorean Theorem

Find the length of the missing side for each right triangle.

1.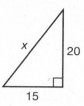

_____

2.

_____

3.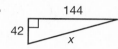

_____

4.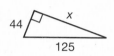

_____

5.

_____

6.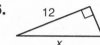

_____

7.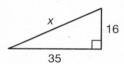

_____

8.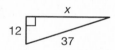

_____

9.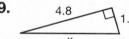

_____

10.

_____

11.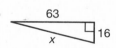

_____

12.

_____

13.

_____

14.

_____

15.

_____

16. An 8-ft ladder is leaning against a building. If the base of
the ladder is 3 ft from the base of the building, how far is
it up the building from the base of the ladder to the top of
the ladder?

_____

17. Geography Washington, DC, is 494 miles east of
Indianapolis, Indiana. Birmingham, Alabama, is 433 miles
south of Indianapolis. How far is Birmingham from
Washington, DC?

_____

Name _____

Section 7C Review

Use your calculator to determine whether each is a perfect square.

1. 3823 _____   **2.** 7245 _____   **3.** 1849 _____   **4.** 5916 _____

Determine each square root and write in lowest terms.

5. $\sqrt{\dfrac{25}{81}}$ _____   **6.** $\sqrt{49}$ _____   **7.** $\sqrt{441}$ _____   **8.** $\sqrt{\dfrac{100}{144}}$ _____

9. $-\sqrt{81}$ _____   **10.** $\sqrt{30.25}$ _____   **11.** $\pm\sqrt{169}$ _____   **12.** $\sqrt{68.89}$ _____

Identify each number as rational or irrational.

13. 2.141414 ... _____   **14.** $\dfrac{5}{11}$ _____   **15.** $5.8\overline{3}$ _____

Find the side length of a square with the given area.

16. 196 ft^2 _____   **17.** 75 m^2 _____   **18.** 116 yd^2 _____

19. 7.84 in^2 _____   **20.** 8.4 cm^2 _____   **21.** 12.8 km^2 _____

Find the missing side of each right triangle.

22. 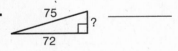 _____   **23.** 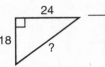 _____   **24.**  _____

25. This graph shows the price to item ratio for oranges. How many oranges could you buy for $9? Explain your reasoning. *[Lesson 5-3]*

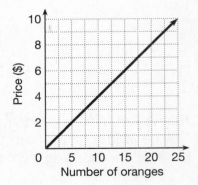

_____

_____

_____

26. In 1994, 36,521,700 Americans age 25 or older had completed at least 4 years of college. This was 22.2% of all Americans age 25 or older. How many Americans were at least 25 years old in 1994? *[Lesson 6-2]*

_____

Name _____

Cumulative Review Chapters 1–7

For each line, find the slope, the x-intercept, and the
y-intercept. *[Lesson 4-5]*

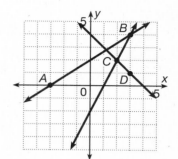

1. Line through *A* and *B* slope: _____

x-intercept: _____ y-intercept: _____

2. Line through *B* and *C* slope: _____

x-intercept: _____ y-intercept: _____

3. Line through *C* and *D* slope: _____

x-intercept: _____ y-intercept: _____

Complete each table to create ratios equal to the given ratio. *[Lesson 5-2]*

4.

3	6	9	42	66
7				

5.

8				
11	22	44	88	121

6.

9	18	27	54	81
5				

7.

6				
15	30	45	75	5

Estimate. *[Lesson 6-3]*

8. 63% of 12 _____ **9.** 80% of 365 _____ **10.** 35% of 67 _____

11. 12% of 582 _____ **12.** 28% of 737 _____ **13.** 125% of 89 _____

Calculate. *[Lessons 7-5 and 7-6]*

14. $6\frac{3}{4} + 7\frac{1}{3}$ _____ **15.** $12\frac{3}{7} - 4\frac{5}{8}$ _____ **16.** $3\frac{5}{6} \times 3$ _____ **17.** $\frac{3}{8} \div 1\frac{1}{5}$ _____

18. $3\frac{5}{6} + 8\frac{3}{8}$ _____ **19.** $23\frac{4}{5} - 8\frac{1}{4}$ _____ **20.** $4\frac{3}{8} \times 7\frac{2}{3}$ _____ **21.** $8\frac{3}{4} \div 2\frac{3}{8}$ _____

Determine the following square roots and write in lowest terms. *[Lesson 7-7]*

22. $\sqrt{361}$ _____ **23.** $\sqrt{1024}$ _____ **24.** $\sqrt{\frac{9}{16}}$ _____ **25.** $\sqrt{\frac{36}{49}}$ _____

26. $\sqrt{\frac{64}{121}}$ _____ **27.** $\sqrt{\frac{100}{36}}$ _____ **28.** $\sqrt{\frac{49}{144}}$ _____ **29.** $\sqrt{\frac{100}{169}}$ _____

Units of Measurement

What U.S. customary unit would you use for each measurement?

1. The weight of a whale

_____

2. The length of a freeway

_____

3. The capacity of a punch bowl

_____

4. The area of a window

_____

What metric unit would you use for each measurement?

5. The width of a computer monitor

_____

6. The amount of gasoline in a car

_____

7. The mass of a feather

_____

8. The volume of a closet

_____

Convert each measurement.

9. 38 min to sec

_____

10. 72 ft to in.

_____

11. 684 m to cm

_____

12. 25 lb to oz

_____

13. 46.3 kg to g

_____

14. 384 mL to L

_____

15. 64 qt to cups

_____

16. 84 mi to ft

_____

17. 1632 m to km

_____

18. 3000 lb to T

_____

19. 14.86 g to kg

_____

20. 2136 min to hr

_____

21. A group of students ran one lap around a track. Their times
were 132 sec, 1.83 min, 118 sec, 1.97 min, and 101 sec.
Give the average time in seconds. _____

22. The smallest street-legal car in the United States is 7 ft 4.75 in.
long. Convert this length to inches. _____

Significant Digits and Precision

Determine the number of significant digits in each measurement.

1. 1.063 in.   **2.** 12,000 g   **3.** 634 yd   **4.** 8300 qt

_____   _____   _____   _____

5. 0.0037 sec   **6.** 10.9 kg   **7.** 2.030 pt   **8.** 4.87 hr

_____   _____   _____   _____

Underline the more precise measurement.

9. 23 oz, 20.7 oz   **10.** 1830 g, 2.5 kg   **11.** 160 qt, 137 qt

12. 63.7 L, 63.70 L   **13.** 3.7 T, 5610 lb   **14.** 47 qt, 83 pt

15. 58.3 cm, 4.6 m   **16.** 12 L, 1735 mL   **17.** 61 lb, 63.7 lb

18. 3.008 pt, 0.95 pt   **19.** 7.3 min, 516 sec   **20.** 2.7 mL, 12 mL

Calculate each and give the answer with the correct number of significant digits.

21. 6.35 oz + 4.2 oz   **22.** 83 g − 1.8 g   **23.** 6.25 in. × 15.85 in.

_____   _____   _____

24. 4.20 yd × 8.64 yd   **25.** 21 cm × 5360 cm   **26.** 8137 hr − 500 hr

_____   _____   _____

27. 5.382 m × 8 m   **28.** 6.4 ft × 4300 ft   **29.** 30 mi × 165 mi

_____   _____   _____

30. 2.713 mL + 8.4 mL   **31.** 50 lb − 4.6 lb   **32.** 6.83 km × 10.3 km

_____   _____   _____

33. Geography Boundary Peak in Nevada is 13,000 ft high.
Guadalupe Peak in Texas is 8749 ft high. How much higher
than Guadalupe Peak is Boundary Peak? Use the correct
number of significant digits.   _____

34. A rectangular swimming pool has length 98 ft and width
33.5 ft. Use significant digits to express the area of the pool.   _____

Position

1. What city is located at 24°N and 104.5°W?

_____

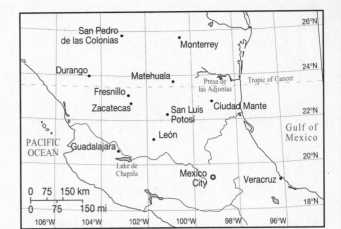

2. What is the position of Ciudad Mante relative to Mexico City?

_____

3. What is the position of Guadalajara relative to Veracruz?

_____

4. What is the absolute position of Monterrey using latitude and longitude?

_____

5. How many degrees of latitude are between Durango and Veracruz?

_____

6. How many degrees of longitude are between San Pedro and Mexico City?

_____

7. Locate the position 23°N, 95°W, on the map. Is this location in Mexico, in the Pacific Ocean, or in the Gulf of Mexico?

_____

Tell what state contains each location.

8. 40°N, 105°W _____

9. 32°N, 100°W _____

10. 47°N, 110°W _____

11. 45°N, 100°W _____

12. 35°N, 95°W _____

Name _____

Section 8A Review

What metric unit would you use for each measurement?

1. The mass of a television set

_____

2. The area of a football field

_____

Convert each measurement.

3. 75 in. to ft   **4.** 21 hr to min   **5.** 258 cm to m   **6.** 3.8 T to lb

_____   _____   _____   _____

Determine the number of significant digits in each measurement.

7. 5.360 mL ____   **8.** 748 lb _____   **9.** 21,000 ft ____   **10.** 0.0075 hr ____

Underline the more precise measurement.

11. 26.4 cm, 8.39 cm   **12.** 216 ft, 3106 in.   **13.** 4100 lb, 6123 lb

Calculate each and give the answer with the correct number of significant digits.

14. 2100 cm − 418 cm_____   **15.** 41.3 in. × 84 in._____

Geography Tell what country contains each location.

16. 30° N, 5° E _____

17. 15° N, 20° E _____

18. 20° N, 5° W _____

19. 10° N, 8° E _____

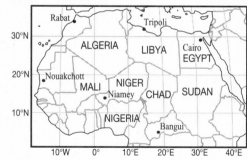

20. The American International Building is 950 ft tall, and the Statue of Liberty is 152 ft tall. If a scale model of New York City includes a 75 in. replica of the America International Building, how tall is the model Statue of Liberty? *[Lesson 5-6]*   _____

21. Explain the difference between the GCF and the LCM. *[Lessons 7-2 and 7-3]*

_____

_____

_____

Name _____

Lines and Angles

Classify each angle measurement as right, straight, obtuse, or acute.

1. 27° _____ **2.** 90.2° _____ **3.** 100° _____

4. 89° _____ **5.** 153° _____ **6.** 180° _____

7. 74° _____ **8.** 90° _____ **9.** 4° _____

Find the measure of the complement of each angle measure.

10. 82° _____ **11.** 31° _____ **12.** 7° _____ **13.** 64° _____

14. 35° _____ **15.** 0.7° _____ **16.** 50° _____ **17.** 12° _____

Find the measure of the supplement of each angle measure.

18. 34° _____ **19.** 100° _____ **20.** 67° _____ **21.** 125° _____

22. 2.3° _____ **23.** 53° _____ **24.** 176° _____ **25.** 84° _____

Use a protractor to measure each angle.

26. ∠ABC _____ **27.** ∠CDE _____

28. ∠BDE _____ **29.** ∠BCD _____

30. ∠EDF _____ **31.** ∠BDC _____

32. ∠CBD _____ **33.** ∠BDF _____

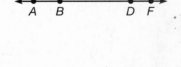

Identify each as a ray, line, or line segment and draw each.

34. $\overleftrightarrow{JK}$ _____ **35.** $\overrightarrow{ML}$ _____ **36.** $\overline{PQ}$ _____

37. a. Measure ∠WXY and ∠XYZ in the parallelogram
shown at the right.

   $m\angle WXY =$ _____ $m\angle XYZ =$ _____

b. Are these angles complementary, supplementary,
or neither?

_____

Parallel and Perpendicular Lines

In the figure shown at right, $\overleftrightarrow{PQ} \parallel \overleftrightarrow{RS}$. Use the figure for Exercises 1–7.

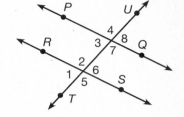

1. Name all interior angles. _____

2. Name all exterior angles. _____

3. Name the transversal. _____

4. Name two pairs of alternate interior angles. _____

5. Name two pairs of alternate exterior angles. _____

6. Name four pairs of corresponding angles.

_____

7. If $m\angle 6 = 75°$, find each angle measure.

$m\angle 1 =$ _____ $m\angle 2 =$ _____ $m\angle 3 =$ _____ $m\angle 4 =$ _____

$m\angle 5 =$ _____ $m\angle 7 =$ _____ $m\angle 8 =$ _____

In the figure on the right, $\overleftrightarrow{VW} \parallel \overleftrightarrow{XY}$. Use the figure to find the measure of each angle.

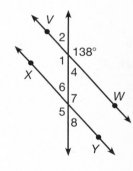

8. $m\angle 1 =$ _____   9. $m\angle 2 =$ _____

10. $m\angle 4 =$ _____   11. $m\angle 5 =$ _____

12. $m\angle 7 =$ _____   13. $m\angle 8 =$ _____

Complete each statement to make it true.

14. When a transversal crosses _____ lines, the alternate exterior angles are congruent.

15. Two pairs of congruent angles called _____ angles are formed whenever two lines intersect.

The map shows some streets in downtown San Francisco. Use it for Exercises 16–17.

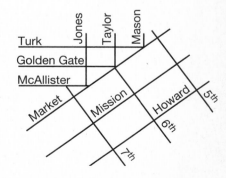

16. Name the streets that are parallel to Market. _____

17. Name the streets that are perpendicular to Market. _____

Name _____

Polygons

Identify each polygon. Be as specific as possible.

1. _____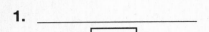

2. _____

3. _____

4. _____

5. _____

6. _____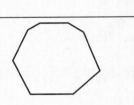

Decide whether each statement is true or false.

7. All squares are parallelograms.

_____

8. All quadrilaterals are parallelograms.

_____

9. Some rhombuses are rectangles.

_____

10. Some scalene triangles are isosceles.

_____

Find the measure of the missing angle.

11. _____

12. _____

13. _____

14. _____

Determine the sum of all angles in each polygon.

15. nonagon
(9-sided polygon)

_____

16. decagon
(10-sided polygon)

_____

17. dodecagon
(12-sided polygon)

_____

18. Name the polygon that describes the shape
of a stop sign.

_____

3-D Views

1. Draw the right, front, and top views for the 3-D object shown.

Draw a base plan for the cube towers shown.

2.

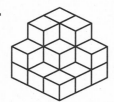

3.

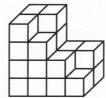

Draw a net for the following objects:

4. a rectangular prism

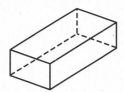

5. a regular triangular prism

6. Draw a net for the number cube shown. Show the dots in the correct position.

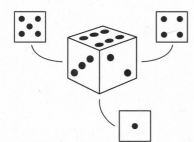

Name _____

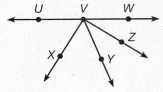

Section 8B Review

Use a protractor to measure each angle. Classify each angle as right, straight, obtuse, or acute.

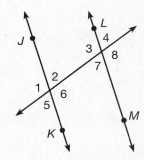

1. ∠UVX _____   **2.** ∠XVZ _____

3. ∠WVY _____   **4.** ∠UVW _____

5. ∠UVY _____   **6.** ∠XVW _____

7. Find the angle measure complementary to 23.8°. _____

8. Find the angle measure supplementary to 81°. _____

Use figure at right to answer Exercises 9–16.
$\overrightarrow{JK} \parallel \overleftrightarrow{LM}$. If $m\angle 2 = 70°$, find each angle measure.

9. $m\angle 4$ _____   **10.** $m\angle 7$ _____

11. $m\angle 5$ _____   **12.** $m\angle 3$ _____

Match each pair of angles with the angle classification.

13. ∠6 and ∠8 _____   **A.** alternate interior angles

14. ∠3 and ∠6 _____   **B.** alternate exterior angles

15. ∠4 and ∠7 _____   **C.** corresponding angles

16. ∠1 and ∠8 _____   **D.** vertical angles

Identify each polygon. Be as specific as possible.

17. _____   **18.** _____   **19.** _____

20. The largest hotel lobby is the 160 ft by 350 ft lobby at the Hyatt Regency in San Francisco. What is the largest scale that could be used to make a scale drawing of this lobby on an 8-in. by 10-in. sheet of paper? *[Lesson 5-7]*

_____

21. Geography Tucson, Arizona, is about 75 miles south and 70 miles east of Phoenix. What is the distance from Phoenix to Tucson? *[Lesson 7-9]*

_____

Cumulative Review Chapters 1–8

Solve each proportion. *[Lesson 5-4]*

1. $\dfrac{15}{21} = \dfrac{x}{35}$

2. $\dfrac{33}{t} = \dfrac{48}{64}$

3. $\dfrac{45}{33} = \dfrac{105}{p}$

4. $\dfrac{k}{54} = \dfrac{36}{81}$

$x =$ _____

$t =$ _____

$p =$ _____

$k =$ _____

5. $\dfrac{n}{26} = \dfrac{40}{65}$

6. $\dfrac{85}{51} = \dfrac{15}{r}$

7. $\dfrac{30}{48} = \dfrac{u}{104}$

8. $\dfrac{45}{c} = \dfrac{27}{66}$

$n =$ _____

$r =$ _____

$u =$ _____

$c =$ _____

Find the percent of increase or decrease. Round to the nearest whole percent. *[Lessons 6-4 and 6-5]*

9. old: 7.3
new: 11.4

10. old: 27.6
new: 21.8

11. old: 384
new: 400

12. old: $129.95
new: $113.60

_____

_____

_____

_____

13. old: 16.4
new: 12.8

14. old: $84.30
new: $89.90

15. old: 57
new: 42

16. old: 38
new: 157

_____

_____

_____

_____

Determine whether the given number is divisible by
2, 3, 4, 5, 6, 8, 9, or 10. *[Lesson 7-1]*

17. 532 _____

18. 817 _____

19. 486 _____

20. 860 _____

21. 178 _____

22. 135 _____

Use a protractor to measure each angle. Classify each angle as right, straight, obtuse, or acute. *[Lesson 8-4]*

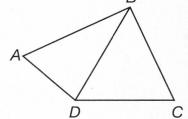

23. $\angle BAD$ _____

24. $\angle BCD$ _____

25. $\angle ABC$ _____

26. $\angle ABD$ _____

27. $\angle ADC$ _____

28. $\angle BDC$ _____

Identify each polygon. Be as specific as possible. *[Lesson 8-6]*

29. _____

30. _____

31. _____

Name _____

Perimeter and Area of Polygons

Find the perimeter and area of each polygon.

1. P = _____

A = _____

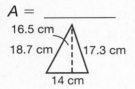
39 in. 89 in.
80 in.

2. P = _____

A = _____

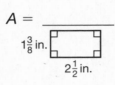
36 cm / 39 cm
40 cm

3. P = _____

A = _____

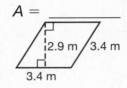
18 mi
18 mi

4. P = _____

A = _____

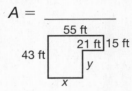
23 m
29 m / 20 m / 25 m
59 m

5. P = _____

A = _____

16.5 cm
18.7 cm / 17.3 cm
14 cm
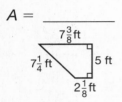

6. P = _____

A = _____

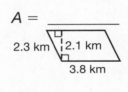
$1\frac{3}{8}$ in.
$2\frac{1}{2}$ in.

7. P = _____

A = _____

2.9 m / 3.4 m
3.4 m
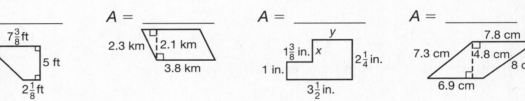

8. P = _____

A = _____

55 ft
21 ft / 15 ft
43 ft
y
x
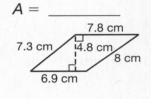

9. P = _____

A = _____

$7\frac{3}{8}$ ft
$7\frac{1}{4}$ ft / 5 ft
$2\frac{1}{8}$ ft

10. P = _____

A = _____

2.3 km / 2.1 km
3.8 km

11. P = _____

A = _____

y
$1\frac{3}{8}$ in. / x / $2\frac{1}{4}$ in.
1 in.
$3\frac{1}{2}$ in.

12. P = _____

A = _____

7.8 cm
7.3 cm / 4.8 cm / 8 cm
6.9 cm

Use the figure to the right for Exercises 13–15.

13. Give the value of x and the value of y.

x = _____   y = _____

14. Find each area.

Square: _____   Rectangle: _____

Triangle: _____   Total: _____

15. Find the perimeter of the figure. _____

y
x   x
80 cm
36 cm
48 cm   36 cm
108 cm

16. Fine Arts In 1871, James Abbott McNeill Whistler painted
his mother's portrait. The painting measures 144 cm × 162 cm.
Find the perimeter and area of this portrait.

Perimeter: _____   Area: _____

Name _____

Scale and Area

Find the perimeter and area of each polygon after the given dilation.

1. Scale factor = $\frac{1}{3}$

P = _____

A = _____

15 cm
15 cm

2. Scale factor = 2

P = _____

A = _____

45 ft 53 ft
28 ft

3. Scale factor = 0.8

P = _____

A = _____

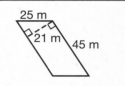
25 m
21 m 45 m

4. Scale factor = 3.6

P = _____

A = _____

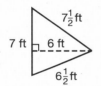
$7\frac{1}{2}$ ft
7 ft 6 ft
$6\frac{1}{2}$ ft

5. Scale factor = 0.4

P = _____

A = _____

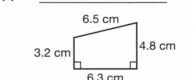
6.5 cm
3.2 cm 4.8 cm
6.3 cm

6. Scale factor = 1.8

P = _____

A = _____

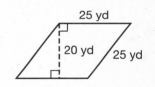
25 yd
20 yd 25 yd

7. Scale factor = 4

P = _____

A = _____

$1\frac{3}{8}$ in.
$\frac{7}{8}$ in.

8. Scale factor = 7.5

P = _____

A = _____

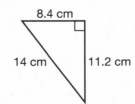
8.4 cm
14 cm 11.2 cm

9. Scale factor = $\frac{1}{2}$

P = _____

A = _____

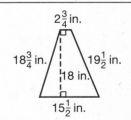
$2\frac{3}{4}$ in.
$18\frac{3}{4}$ in. $19\frac{1}{2}$ in.
18 in.
$15\frac{1}{2}$ in.

10. Carolyn's construction business has been hired to provide new carpet and baseboard for a rectangular hotel lobby. A floor plan, drawn at a scale factor of $\frac{1}{20}$, measures 3 ft × $1\frac{3}{4}$ ft.

   a. What is the area of the carpet for the lobby? _____

   b. The length of baseboard required is equal to the perimeter of the lobby. How much baseboard is needed? _____

Name _____

Circles

Sketch each figure.

1. Octagon inscribed in a circle

2. Hexagon circumscribed about a circle

Find the circumference of each circle. Use π = 3.14.

3. _____

4. _____

5. _____

6. _____

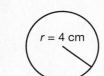

Find the area of each circle. Use π = 3.14.

7. _____

8. _____

9. _____

10. _____

11. _____

12. _____

13. _____

14. _____

15. Science Saturn is surrounded by hundreds of rings of tiny particles in orbit about the planet. The innermost rings have a circumference of about 260,000 mi. Find the radius.

_____

16. A round clock face has a diameter of 15 in. Find the area.

_____

Surface Area of Prisms and Cylinders

Sketch a net for each, then find the surface area.

1. SA = _____

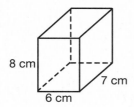

2. SA ≈ _____

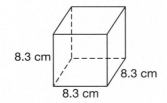

3. SA = _____

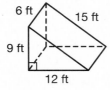

4. SA = _____

5. A birthday present is packaged in a tube that has
length 8 in. and diameter 3 in. How much paper is
needed to wrap the present? (Ignore any overlap.)   _____

6. A shoebox is 4 in. tall with a 6-in. × 10-in. base.
If there is no lid, how much cardboard is needed
to make this box?   _____

Name _____

Surface Area of Pyramids and Cones

For each figure, find **a.** the slant height; **b.** the surface area.

1. a. _____

   b. _____

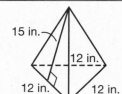

2. a. _____**Given**_____

   b. _____

   15 in.

   12 in.

   12 in.   12 in.

3. a. _____

   b. _____

   $h = 16.8$ m

   $r = 9.5$ m

4. a. _____**Given**_____

   b. _____

   5 cm

   4 cm   4 cm

   4 cm

5. a. _____

   b. _____

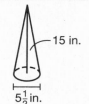

   15 in.

   $5\frac{1}{2}$ in.

6. a. _____

   b. _____

   $h = 13.2$ m

   17 m

   17 m

7. a. _____

   b. _____

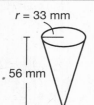

   $r = 33$ mm

   56 mm

8. a. _____

   b. _____

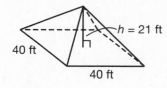

   $h = 21$ ft

   40 ft

   40 ft

9. a. _____**Given**_____

   b. _____

   8.6 cm   11.3 cm

   8.6 cm   8.6 cm

10. **History** The largest of the Egyptian pyramids was built almost 5000 years ago. Its square base has sides of length 755 ft, and it was originally about 482 ft tall. Find the slant height and the surface area (do not include the base).

    Slant height: _____   Surface area: _____

11. A circular cone has a surface area of 282.6 cm². The base of the cone has radius 5 cm. Find the slant height. Then use the Pythagorean Theorem to find the height of the cone.

    Slant height: _____   Height: _____

Section 9A Review

Fill in the appropriate vocabulary term for each sentence.

1. A _____ is a 3-D figure with a single vertex and a circular base.

2. The circumference of a circle is 2π times the _____.

3. The _____ of a polyhedron can be found by adding the areas of all the faces.

Find the perimeter/circumference and area for each figure.

4. $P =$ _____

$A =$ _____

12.7 cm
12.7 cm

5. $P =$ _____

$A =$ _____

$2\frac{3}{4}$ in. $3\frac{1}{8}$ in.
$3\frac{3}{4}$ in.

6. $P =$ _____

$A =$ _____

6.5 m   5.2 m
3.9 m

7. $P =$ _____

$A =$ _____

7.3 m
13.7 m   10.5 m
16.1 m

8. $P =$ _____

$A =$ _____

14.3 km
11.2 km   6.6 km
x y
4.5 km

9. $C =$ _____

$A =$ _____

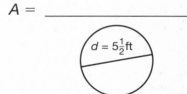
$d = 5\frac{1}{2}$ ft

Find the surface area of each figure.

10. _____

40 cm
9 cm

11. _____

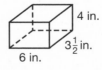
4 in.
$3\frac{1}{2}$ in.
6 in.

12. _____

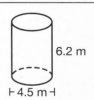
6.2 m
4.5 m

13. The population of Cleveland, Ohio, decreased 11.9% from 1980 to 1990. If the 1990 population was 505,600, what was the 1980 population? *[Lesson 6-5]*

_____

14. Tell what metric unit you would use to measure the height of a cathedral. *[Lesson 8-1]*

_____

Name _____

Volume of Rectangular Prisms

Find the volume of each figure.

1. _____
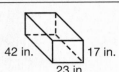
42 in.   17 in.
23 in.

2. _____
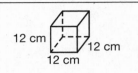
12 cm   12 cm
12 cm

3. _____
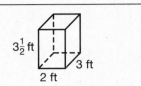
$3\frac{1}{2}$ ft   3 ft
2 ft

4. _____
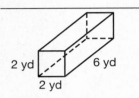
2 yd   6 yd
2 yd

5. _____
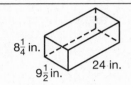
$8\frac{1}{4}$ in.   24 in.
$9\frac{1}{2}$ in.

6. _____
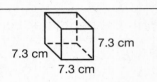
7.3 cm   7.3 cm
7.3 cm

7. _____
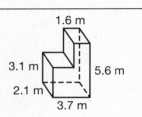
1.6 m
3.1 m   5.6 m
2.1 m
3.7 m

8. _____
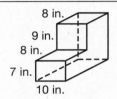
8 in.
9 in.
8 in.
7 in.
10 in.

9. _____
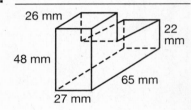
26 mm   22 mm
48 mm
27 mm   65 mm

Sketch the figure, then find its volume.

10. A cassette box that measures
1.7 cm by 7 cm by 10.9 cm

$V =$ _____

11. A recycling bin that is 15 in.
wide, $20\frac{1}{2}$ in. long and 13 in. tall

$V =$ _____

12. The lobby of the Hyatt Regency Hotel in San Francisco,
California measures 350 ft by 160 ft. Its ceiling is 170 ft tall.
Find the volume of a rectangular prism with these dimensions.

_____

Scale and Volume

Find the volume of each prism after scaling one dimension by the indicated scale factor.

1. Scale factor = 3

$V =$ _____

14 cm 6 cm
8 cm

2. Scale factor = $\frac{1}{16}$

$V =$ _____

8 in. 8 in.
8 in.

3. Scale factor = $\frac{3}{7}$

$V =$ _____

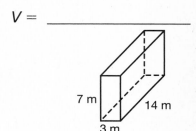

7 m 14 m
3 m

Find the volume of each figure after the dilation.

4. Scale factor = $\frac{1}{2}$

$V =$ _____

9.3 cm
18 cm 12.4 cm

5. Scale factor = $\frac{2}{3}$

$V =$ _____

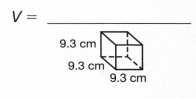

$7\frac{1}{2}$ in. 20 in.
$7\frac{1}{2}$ in.

6. Scale factor = 10

$V =$ _____

9.3 cm
9.3 cm
9.3 cm

7. Scale factor = $\frac{1}{10}$

$V =$ _____

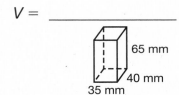

65 mm
40 mm
35 mm

8. Scale factor = 3

$V =$ _____

2 ft
$2\frac{1}{2}$ ft
$7\frac{1}{2}$ ft

9. Scale factor = $\frac{1}{7}$

$V =$ _____

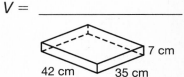

7 cm
42 cm 35 cm

10. Some sponges expand when they become wet. A dry sponge measures $\frac{3}{8}$ in. by $1\frac{3}{4}$ in. by $2\frac{3}{4}$ in. If water dilates this sponge by a scale factor of 2, find the volume of the wet sponge.

_____

11. Science Every cubic foot of air weighs about 0.26 lb. Find the weight of the air in a 11-ft by 13-ft room with an 8-ft ceiling.

_____

Name _____

Practice
9-8

Volume of Prisms and Cylinders

Find the volume of each solid. Use 3.14 for π.

1. _____

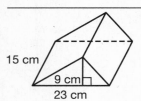

15 cm
9 cm
23 cm

2. _____

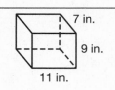

7 in.
9 in.
11 in.

3. _____

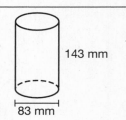

143 mm
83 mm

4. _____

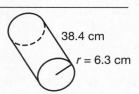

38.4 cm
$r = 6.3$ cm

5. _____

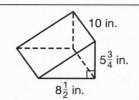

10 in.
$5\frac{3}{4}$ in.
$8\frac{1}{2}$ in.

6. _____

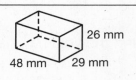

26 mm
48 mm   29 mm

7. _____

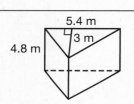

5.4 m
3 m
4.8 m

8. _____

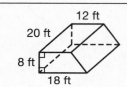

12 ft
20 ft
8 ft
18 ft

9. _____

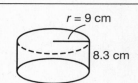

$r = 9$ cm
8.3 cm

10. _____

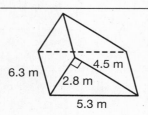

6.3 m
4.5 m
2.8 m
5.3 m

11. _____

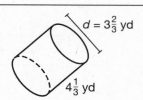

$d = 3\frac{2}{3}$ yd
$4\frac{1}{3}$ yd

12. _____

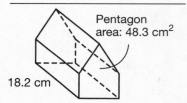

Pentagon area: 48.3 cm^2
18.2 cm

13. The attic of Karen's house has the shape of the triangular prism shown at the right. Find the volume of the attic.

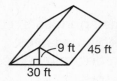

9 ft   45 ft
30 ft

_____

14. A cylindrical cookie tin has a diameter of 10 in. and a height of $3\frac{1}{2}$ in. How many cubic inches of cookies can it hold? Round your answer to the nearest cubic inch.

_____

94 Use with pages 487–491.

© Scott Foresman • Addison Wesley 8

Name _____

Practice
9-9

Volume of Pyramids and Cones

Find the volume of each solid. Use 3.14 for π.

1. _____

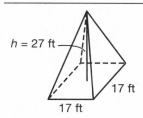

h = 27 ft
17 ft
17 ft

2. _____

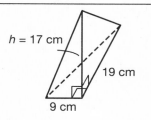

h = 17 cm
19 cm
9 cm

3. _____

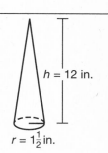

h = 12 in.
r = 1½ in.

4. _____

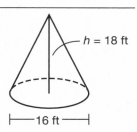

h = 18 ft
16 ft

5. _____

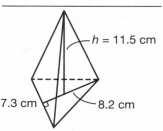

h = 11.5 cm
7.3 cm
8.2 cm

6. _____

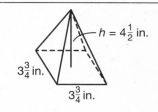

h = 4½ in.
3¾ in.
3¾ in.

7. _____

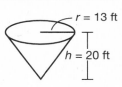

r = 13 ft
h = 20 ft

8. _____

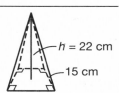

h = 22 cm
15 cm

9. _____

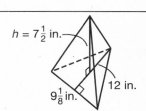

h = 7½ in.
12 in.
9⅛ in.

10. _____

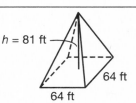

h = 81 ft
64 ft
64 ft

11. _____

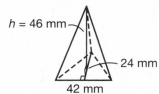

h = 46 mm
24 mm
42 mm

12. _____

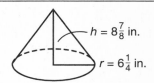

h = 8⅞ in.
r = 6¼ in.

13. The base of a square pyramid has sides of length 15 in. If the pyramid has volume 1050 in³, what is the height? _____

14. A special cushion designed to go in a corner is shaped like a triangular pyramid. The base is a right triangle with sides of length 42 cm, 56 cm, and 70 cm. If the height of the pillow is 64 cm, what is the volume? _____

© Scott Foresman • Addison Wesley 8

Use with pages 492–496. **95**

Name _____

Section 9B Review

Find the volume of each solid. Use 3.14 for π.

1. _____

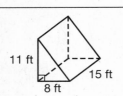

2. _____

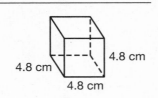

3. _____

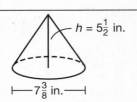

4. _____

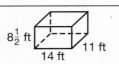

5. _____

6. _____

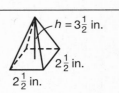

Find the volume for each after the given dilation.

7. Scale factor = 4

V = _____

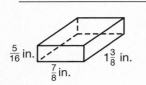

8. Scale factor = $\frac{2}{3}$

V = _____

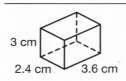

9. Scale factor = 0.75

V = _____

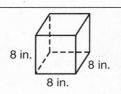

10. Which has the greater volume: a cone with radius 8 in. and height 12 in. or a cylinder with diameter 9 in. and height 12 in.?

_____

11. A decorative pedestal has the shape of a prism with a square pyramid on top, as shown. What is the volume of the pedestal?

_____

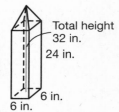

12. **Geography** Springfield, Illinois, is 193 mi due west of Indianapolis, Indiana. Jeanette drove due north from Indianapolis until she was 215 mi from Springfield. How far did she drive? *[Lesson 7-9]*

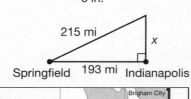

_____

13. **Geography** A portion of Utah is shown. Name all cities in 2B. If none, write "None." *[Lesson 8-3]*

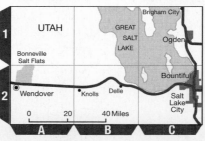

_____

Cumulative Review Chapters 1–9

Write each percent as a fraction in lowest terms and as a decimal. *[Lesson 6-1]*

1. 82% _____

2. 60% _____

3. 13% _____

4. 25% _____

5. 8% _____

6. 35% _____

Identify each number as rational or irrational. *[Lesson 7-8]*

7. $\sqrt{36}$ _____

8. $\sqrt{0.64}$ _____

9. $\sqrt{28}$ _____

10. $\sqrt{\dfrac{49}{81}}$ _____

11. $\sqrt{12}$ _____

12. $\sqrt{\dfrac{144}{25}}$ _____

In the figure shown at right, $\overleftrightarrow{VW} \parallel \overleftrightarrow{XY}$. *[Lesson 8-5]*

13. Name a pair of alternate interior angles. _____

14. Name a pair of corresponding angles. _____

15. Name a pair of vertical angles. _____

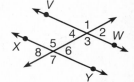

16. Name the angles that are congruent to ∠3. _____

Find the perimeter and area of each polygon after the given dilation. *[Lesson 9-2]*

17. Scale factor = 4

18. Scale factor = 2

19. Scale factor = $\dfrac{1}{5}$

P = _____

A = _____

P = _____

A = _____

P = _____

A = _____

Find the volume of each solid. Use 3.14 for π. *[Lesson 9-9]*

20. _____

21. _____

22. _____

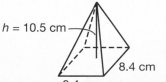

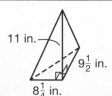

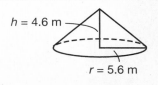

Name _____

Functions

For the function machine shown, find the output value for each
input value.

1. Input of 20 _____   **2.** Input of 5 _____

3. Input of −35 _____   **4.** Input of 13 _____

Input → | Divide by 5 and subtract 3 | → Output

For the function machine shown, find the input value for each
output value.

5. Output of 6 _____   **6.** Output of 12 _____

7. Output of −28 _____   **8.** Output of −13 _____

Input → | Add 7 | → Output

What is a possible rule for the input and output shown in each table?

9.

Input	1	3	5	9
Output	16	18	20	24

10.

Input	−1	0	1	2
Output	−5	−2	1	4

_____   _____

11.

Input	−8	−3	2	7
Output	7	7	7	7

12.

Input	64	4	−4	−8
Output	16	1	−1	−2

_____   _____

13. At Roy's Donut Shop, if you buy 1 to 4 donuts, you pay $0.50
per donut. If you buy 5 to 8 donuts, the price is $0.40 each.
Roy limits each customer to 8 donuts.

a. Complete the table by finding the *total* purchase price for
each number of donuts.

Number of donuts	0	1	2	3	4	5	6	7	8
Total price ($)									

b. Is the price a function of the number of donuts? Explain. _____

_____

c. Is the number of donuts a function of the price? Explain. _____

_____

Name _____

Linear Functions

Given the following function rules, complete the table of values.

1. $y = 4x - 8$

Input (x)	Output (y)
−1	
0	
1	
2	
3	

2. $y = -2x + 3$

Input (x)	Output (y)
−1	
0	
1	
2	
3	

3. $y = -5x - 2$

Input (x)	Output (y)
−1	
0	
1	
2	
3	

Graph each linear equation. Does the equation describe a function?

4. $y = -2$ _____

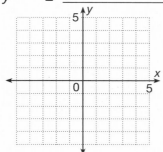

5. $y = x - 3$ _____

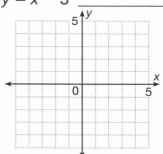

6. $x = 1$ _____

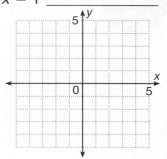

Does each table of values represent a function? Explain your answer.

7.

Input (x)	−1	3	1	5	3
Output (y)	3	4	7	2	8

_____

_____

8.

Input (x)	−4	2	6	7	8
Output (y)	3	5	1	5	7

_____

_____

9. Science The speed of sound in air is about 1088 ft/sec.

a. Write an equation to show the relationship
between distance d and time t.   _____

b. Use your equation to find how far a sound travels
in 2 seconds, 5 seconds, and 10 seconds.

2 seconds _____   5 seconds _____   10 seconds _____

Name _____

**Practice
10-3**

Quadratic Functions

Graph each set of functions.

1. $y = x^2 - 2$, $y = x^2$,
and $y = x^2 + 2$

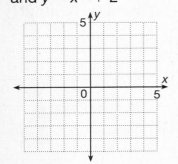

2. $y = x^2$, $y = -2x^2$
and $y = 3x^2$

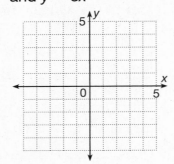

3. $y = -x^2$, $y = -x^2 + 2$
and $y = -x^2 + 5$

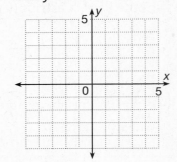

Match each graph with the function that describes it.

4. _____

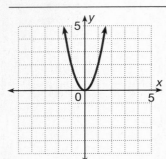

5. _____

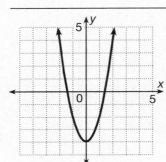

6. _____

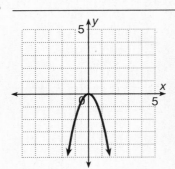

7. _____

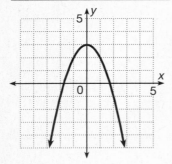

8. _____

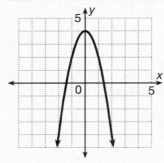

9. _____

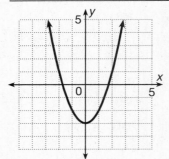

A. $y = -2x^2$
D. $y = -2x^2 + 4$

B. $y = 2x^2$
E. $y = -x^2 + 3$

C. $y = 2x^2 - 4$
F. $y = x^2 - 3$

10. For a group of n people, the formula $h = \frac{1}{2}(n^2 - n)$ gives the number of
handshakes that would occur if each person shook hands once with each
other person. Find the number of handshakes for each number of people.

a. $n = 1$ _____   **b.** $n = 4$ _____   **c.** $n = 9$ _____   **d.** $n = 25$ _____

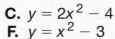

© Scott Foresman • Addison Wesley 8

Name _____

Other Functions

Graph each function.

1. $y = 3x$

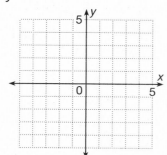

2. $y = 3^x$

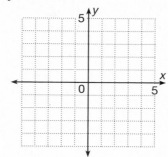

3. $y = 0.4x$

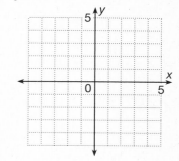

4. $y = 0.4^x$

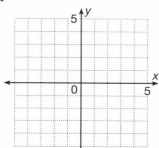

5. $y = \left(\dfrac{4}{3}\right)^x$

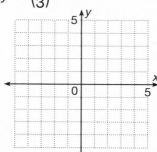

6. $y = \left(\dfrac{3}{4}\right)^x$

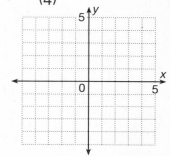

Identify each function as linear, quadratic, exponential, or step.

7. $y = 2x + 5$ _____

8. $y = 5^x$ _____

9. $y =$ round up to the next hundred _____

10. $y = 0.3^x$ _____

11. $y = 4x^2$ _____

12. $y =$ multiply by 7 _____

13. $y = x + 8$ _____

14. $y = -x^2 + 3$ _____

15. $y =$ round to the nearest 0.1 _____

16. Consumer A mail-order catalog lists the following
charges for shipping and handling:

Price of Order ($)	Under 10	10 to 25	Over 25
Shipping Charge ($)	2.50	4.00	7.00

a. Graph the function.

b. What kind of function is this? _____

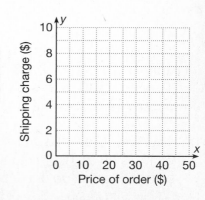

Name _____

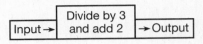
Section 10A Review

For the function machine shown, find each missing value.

1. Input 3, output _____

2. Input _____, output 5

3. Input −9, output ____

4. Input ____, output −3

```
              ┌─────────────┐
              │  Divide by 3│
Input →       │  and add 2  │ → Output
              └─────────────┘
```

Sketch an example of a graph for each kind of function.

5. Exponential

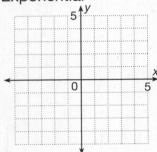

6. Step

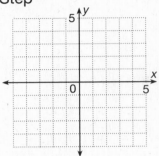

7. Quadratic

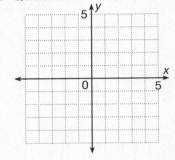

8. Is y a function of x? Explain.

x	1	0	1	2	3
y	−2	−1	0	1	2

_____

_____

9. Graph $y = 2$, $y = 2x$, $y = x^2$, and $y = 2^x$. Describe the similarities and differences.

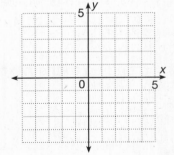

_____

_____

10. Science An elephant can run about 25 mi/hr at maximum speed. If distance is a function of time, write an equation to show the relationship between distance and time. Use your equation to show how far the elephant could travel in 3 hours at this speed. _____

11. The population of San Francisco, California, was about 716,000 in 1970. It decreased 5.2% from 1970 to 1980, and increased 6.6% from 1980 to 1990. What was the population in 1990? *[Lesson 6-6]* _____

12. The floor plan of a home shows a kitchen that is $6\frac{2}{3}$ in. by 8 in. If the scale factor is 18, what is the area of the actual kitchen? *[Lesson 9-2]* _____

Name _____

Polynomials

Identify each expression as a monomial, binomial, or trinomial.

1. $2x^3$ _____   **2.** $5y - 7$ _____   **3.** $x^5 - 3x^2 + 2$ _____

4. $c^3 - 5$ _____   **5.** $8d + 2 - d^5$ _____   **6.** $215k$ _____

Write each polynomial expression in descending order. Then find the degree of each polynomial.

7. $7 - 5x + 2x^3$ Deg.: ___   **8.** $12 + 3x$ Deg.: _____   **9.** $3x + 2 + x^2$ Deg.: _____

_____   _____   _____

10. $-x^3 + 2x^7$ Deg.: _____   **11.** $7x^4 - 2x^3$ Deg.: _____   **12.** $4x - 3 + x^5$ Deg.: _____

_____   _____   _____

Evaluate each polynomial for $x = -5$.

13. $4x + 7$ _____   **14.** $-7x + 3$ _____   **15.** $4x^2 + 18x$ _____

16. $x^2 - 3x + 8$ _____   **17.** x^3 _____   **18.** $x^2 - 5x + 7$ _____

Evaluate each polynomial for $t = 3$ and for $t = 8$.

19. $t^3 - 5$ **20.** $-3t^2 + 12t$ **21.** $56 - 9t$

    $t = 3$: _____ $t = 3$: _____ $t = 3$: _____

    $t = 8$: _____ $t = 8$: _____ $t = 8$: _____

22. $5 + 8t^2 - t$ **23.** $8t - 4 + t^2$ **24.** $t^3 - 2t - 12$

    $t = 3$: _____ $t = 3$: _____ $t = 3$: _____

    $t = 8$: _____ $t = 8$: _____ $t = 8$: _____

25. Science A ball is thrown upward at a speed of 48 ft/sec.
Its height h, in feet, after t seconds, is given by
$h = 48t - 16t^2$. Find the height after 2 seconds. _____

26. Geometry The formulas $S = 4\pi r^2$ and $V = \frac{4}{3}\pi r^3$ give the
surface area S and volume V of a sphere with radius r. The
moon has radius 1080 mi. Find the surface area and volume.
Use 3.14 for π.

Surface area: _____   Volume _____

Adding Polynomials

Simplify each if possible. If the expression cannot be simplified, write "simplified." Write answers in descending order.

1. $5p^2 + 7p^2$ _____

2. $3x^4 - 3x + 4x^2 + 8x$ _____

3. $9t^3 - 5t^2 - 4t^3$ _____

4. $6w^3 - 4w^2 + 6w - 4$ _____

5. $7x + 9x^2 - 12x + 3$ _____

6. $4u^3 + 7u - 21u^3$ _____

7. $8g^5 + 3g^3 - 2g + 3$ _____

8. $3k - 9 - 2k + 35$ _____

Find each polynomial sum. Write the answers in simplest form.

9. $(3x^2 + 4x) + (x^2 + 7x - 3)$

10. $(2j - 5) + (3j^2 - 7j + 14)$

_____

_____

11. $(-z^3 + 8z - 2) + (2z^2 - 3z + 2)$

12. $(5s^2 - 4s + 7) + (3s^2 + 4s + 11)$

_____

_____

13. $\begin{array}{r} (7g^2 - 5g + 4) \\ + (4g^2 + 7g - 6) \\ \hline \end{array}$

14. $\begin{array}{r} (-4y^2 + 2y - 3) \\ + \quad\quad (-6y - 7) \\ \hline \end{array}$

15. $\begin{array}{r} (m^2 + 4m + 3) \\ + (2m^2 - m + 4) \\ \hline \end{array}$

Find the total floor area of each birdhouse.

16. _____

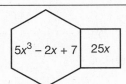

$x^2 + 5$

$2x^2 - 3x + 2$

17. _____

$5x^3 - 2x + 7$ $25x$

18. _____

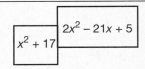

$2x^2 - 21x + 5$

$x^2 + 17$

19. A tabletop is $4x^2 - 2x + 7$ in. above the floor. A computer monitor with height $7x - 3$ in. is on the table. Write a polynomial in simplest form to represent the distance from the top of the monitor to the floor. What is the distance if $x = 3$?

_____

20. If you know x^2, the square of an even number x, you can find the square of the next even number by adding $4x + 4$ to x^2. The square of 46 is 2116. Show how you can add polynomials and evaluate to find 48^2.

_____

Name _____

Subtracting Polynomials

Find the additive inverse of each polynomial.

1. $3x + 7$ _____

2. $4x^2 - (-2x) - 7$ _____

3. $x^2 + 2x + (-9)$ _____

4. $3x^3 - 7x + 5$ _____

Subtract. Write your answers in simplest form.

5. $(4x - 3) - (9x + 4)$

6. $(3x^2 - 2x + 7) - (x^2 + 2x + 5)$

_____

_____

7. $(4p + 7) - (p^2 + 8p - 3)$

8. $(7t^2) - (3t^2 + 5t + 8)$

_____

_____

9. $\begin{array}{r} (8k^2 + 2k + 3) \\ -(3k^2 - 6k + 4) \end{array}$

10. $\begin{array}{r} (5u^2 + 7u + 9) \\ -(2u^2 + 3u + 9) \end{array}$

11. $\begin{array}{r} (c^3 - 2c^2 + 4) \\ -(c^3 + 3c^2 + 8) \end{array}$

Find an expression for the area of each shaded region, given the total area A of each figure.

12. _____

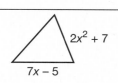

$4x - 9$

$A = x^2 - 3x + 6$

13. _____

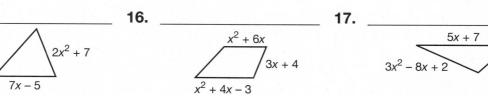

$2x^2 - 3x + 11$

$A = 3x^2 - 7x - 2$

14. _____

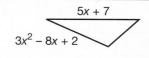

$3x^2 - 5$

$A = 4x^2 - 8x + 2$

Find the missing side length, based on the perimeter of each figure.

15. _____

$2x^2 + 7$

$7x - 5$

$p = 5x^2 + 3x - 2$

16. _____

$x^2 + 6x$

$3x + 4$

$x^2 + 4x - 3$

$p = 3x^2 + 10x - 6$

17. _____

$5x + 7$

$3x^2 - 8x + 2$

$p = 4x^2$

18. Physics A ball is dropped from the top of a 128-foot building at the same time that Sam begins riding up on the elevator. The ball's height, in feet, is given by $-16t^2 + 128$, and Sam's height, in feet, is given by $4t$, where t is the number of seconds. Find a polynomial that tells how far above Sam that ball is after t seconds.

_____

Multiplying Polynomials and Monomials

Multiply.

1. $3^7 \cdot 3^4$ _____

2. $x^3 \cdot x^5$ _____

3. $3t^6 \cdot t^8$ _____

4. $(5c^8)(7c^{12})$ _____

5. $(11u^2)(3u^0)$ _____

6. $(7p)(5p^3)$ _____

7. $(12y^2)(3y^9)$ _____

8. $(-5g^3)(2g)$ _____

9. $(6k^2)(-8k^4)$ _____

10. $4x(x^2 + 5x - 3)$

11. $-7r(4r^7 - 8r^3 + 9)$

_____

_____

12. $\frac{1}{3}h^2(6h^3 - 12h^2 + 15)$

13. $8v^3(-2v^2 + 7v - 3)$

_____

_____

14. $-2n^6(5n^4 + 3n^2 + 4)$

15. $b^2(5b^2 - 8b + 3)$

_____

_____

16. $-\frac{3}{4}q^3(-8q^2 + 64)$

17. $20w^6(6w^8 - 3w^6 + w^4)$

_____

_____

Multiply each of the following. Write your answers in scientific notation.

18. $(2.3 \times 10^3)(1.7 \times 10^4)$ _____

19. $(4.6 \times 10^{11})(3.9 \times 10^9)$ _____

20. $(3.2 \times 10^3)(1.4 \times 10^3)$ _____

21. $(1.6 \times 10^6)(4.1 \times 10^5)$ _____

22. $(6.8 \times 10^7)(1.1 \times 10^1)$ _____

23. $(8.3 \times 10^{10})(7.9 \times 10^8)$ _____

24. $(3.0 \times 10^2)(1.9 \times 10^7)$ _____

25. $(2.4 \times 10^4)(3.1 \times 10^9)$ _____

26. $(6.3 \times 10^9)(1.4 \times 10^6)$ _____

27. $(8.4 \times 10^8)(1.0 \times 10^5)$ _____

28. Social Science Japan has about 3.35×10^2 people per square kilometer of land. The area of Japan is about 3.78×10^5 km^2. Find the population of Japan. Give your answer in scientific notation.

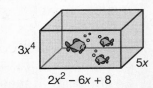

$3x^4$

$5x$

$2x^2 - 6x + 8$

_____

29. Multiply to find an expression for the volume of the aquarium. Simplify if possible.

_____

Section 10B Review

Identify each polynomial expression as a monomial, binomial, trinomial, or polynomial. Explain your choice.

1. $3x^5 + 2x - 4$

_____

2. $7x^3$

_____

3. $x^7 - 2$

_____

4. $-4x^3 + 2x - x + 3$

_____

Find the degree of each polynomial expression. Write the polynomial expression in descending order.

5. $4x + 3x^5 - 6$ Deg.: __

_____

6. $-7 + 3x^2 - 5x$ Deg.: __

_____

7. $8x^3 - 5x^2 + x^4$ Deg.: __

_____

Simplify each if possible. If the expression cannot be simplified, write "simplified." Write your answer in descending order.

8. $5x + x^2 - 8x + x^2$ _____

9. $-7k^3 - 6k^2 + 2k - 3$ _____

10. $\begin{aligned} &(\ c^2\ -\ 7c\ +\ 11\,)\\ +\,&(\,4c^2\ +\ 4c\ \ +\ 5\,)\end{aligned}$

11. $\begin{aligned} &(\,15x^2\ +\ 4x\ +\ 12\,)\\ -\,&(\ \ 7x^2\ +\ 5x\ -\ \ 3\,)\end{aligned}$

12. A rectangle has length $3x$ and width $2x + 1$. After a dilation of scale factor x, the area of the new rectangle is $x^2(3x)(2x + 1)$. Simplify this expression.

_____

13. Multiply to find an expression for each area. Simplify if possible.

a. _____

b. _____

c. _____

d. _____

$3x$	a.	b.	c.	d.
	$8x - 4$	$2x + 1$	$3x$	$7x - 5$

14. Four students were asked their heights. The answers were 4 ft, 51 in., 55 in., and $4\frac{1}{2}$ ft. What was the average height? *[Lesson 8-1]*

_____

15. A 1.44-megabyte computer disk uses a circular piece of magnetic media with radius $1\frac{11}{16}$ in. Find the circumference and the area. *[Lesson 9-3]*

Circumference: _____   Area: _____

Cumulative Review Chapters 1–10

Add, subtract, multiply or divide each of the following. Write each answer in simplest form. *[Lessons 7-5, 7-6]*

1. $3\frac{1}{5} + 2\frac{1}{4}$ _____ **2.** $5\frac{1}{3} - 2\frac{1}{2}$ _____ **3.** $4\frac{3}{7} + 8\frac{1}{2}$ _____ **4.** $6\frac{1}{5} - \frac{5}{8}$ _____

5. $\frac{3}{4} \times \frac{5}{7}$ _____ **6.** $2\frac{1}{2} \div 3\frac{1}{3}$ _____ **7.** $2\frac{5}{8} \times 3\frac{3}{7}$ _____ **8.** $8\frac{2}{3} \div 2\frac{3}{5}$ _____

Identify each polygon. Be as specific as possible. *[Lesson 8-6]*

9.  _____ **10.** _____

11. _____ **12.** _____

Find the surface area of each figure. *[Lesson 9-4]*

13. _____ **14.** _____ **15.** _____ **16.** _____

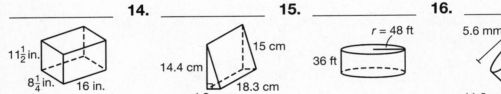

$11\frac{1}{2}$ in. $8\frac{1}{4}$ in. 16 in.

14.4 cm 15 cm 18.3 cm 4.2 cm

$r = 48$ ft 36 ft

5.6 mm 11.6 mm

Graph each linear equation. Does the equation describe a function? *[Lesson 10-2]*

17. $x = -4$ _____ **18.** $y = 3x$ _____ **19.** $y = -2x + 1$ _____

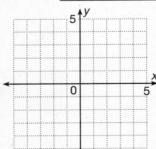 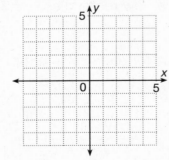 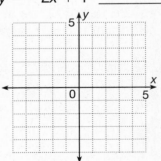

Add or subtract. Write the answers in simplest form. *[Lesson 10-6]*

20.
$$(x^2 - 5x - 6)$$
$$-(3x^2 + 2x - 4)$$

21.
$$(2x^2 \qquad + 7)$$
$$+(-x^2 - 2x + 3)$$

22.
$$(5x - 3)$$
$$-(4x^2 + x - 7)$$

Similar Figures

Decide whether each pair of figures is similar.

1. _____

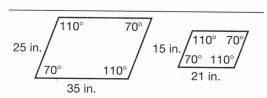

2. _____

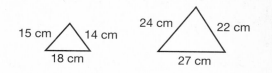

3. _____

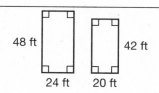

4. _____

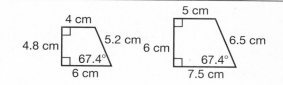

5. The two triangles are similar.

   a. Find x. _____

   b. Find the measure of ∠1. _____

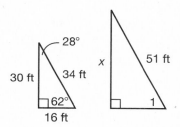

6. The two parallelograms are similar.

   a. Find y. _____

   b. Find the measure of ∠2. _____

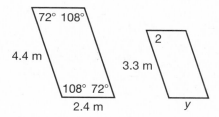

7. The two trapezoids are similar.

   a. Find z. _____

   b. Find the measure of ∠3. _____

8. The two car drawings are similar.
Find x, the length of the larger car.

_____

9. The Society Tower in Cleveland, Ohio, is 271 m tall. A scale
drawing shows the tower at 10.84 cm. What is the scale
factor of the drawing?

_____

Congruent Figures

The two quadrilaterals are congruent.

1. Find $m\angle JKH$. _____

2. Find $m\overline{HI}$. _____

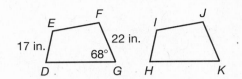

The two hexagons are congruent.

3. Find $m\angle STU$. _____

4. Find $m\overline{MN}$. _____

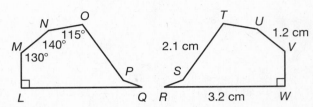

Determine whether each pair of figures is congruent.

5. _____

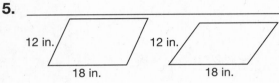

6. _____

7. _____

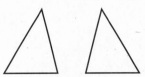

8. _____

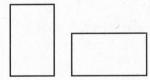

9. Algebra In the figure, the polygons are congruent. Find the values of x and y.

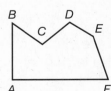

$x =$ _____ $y =$ _____

10. Construct a polygon congruent to the one shown. Label the vertices and complete the statements.

$\overline{AB}$ corresponds to _____

$\overline{AF}$ corresponds to _____

$\overline{DE}$ corresponds to _____

Triangle Congruence

For each pair, what rule tells you that the two triangles are congruent?

1. _____

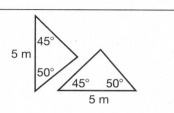

2. _____

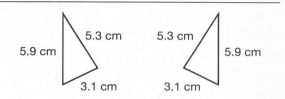

3. _____

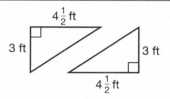

4. _____

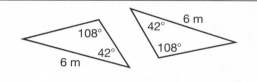

State whether each pair of triangles has congruence; if it does, give the rule that justifies your answer.

5. _____

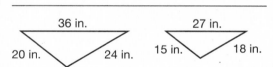

6. _____

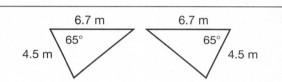

7. _____

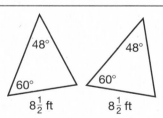

8. _____

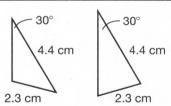

9. A craftsman building a stained glass window determines that $\overline{BC}$ and $\overline{CD}$ are the same length. State the rule used to determine this.

_____

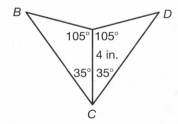

Name _____

Trigonometry

Use the lengths of the sides to evaluate the sine, cosine, and tangent ratios for each of the labeled angles.

1. sin ∠A = _____

cos ∠A = _____

tan ∠A = _____

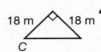

2. sin ∠B = _____

cos ∠B = _____

tan ∠B = _____

3. sin ∠C = _____

cos ∠C = _____

tan ∠C = _____

4. sin ∠D = _____

cos ∠D = _____

tan ∠D = _____

5. sin ∠E = _____

cos ∠E = _____

tan ∠E = _____

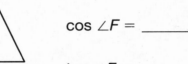

6. sin ∠F = _____

cos ∠F = _____

tan ∠F = _____

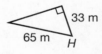

7. sin ∠G = _____

cos ∠G = _____

tan ∠G = _____

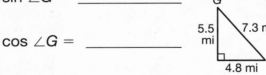

8. sin ∠H = _____

cos ∠H = _____

tan ∠H = _____

Find the length represented by x.

9. _____

10. _____

11. The top of the Landmark Tower in Yokohama, Japan, forms a 72° angle with a point $315\frac{1}{2}$ ft away from the tower's base, as shown. How tall is the Landmark Tower?

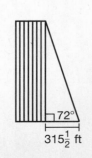

_____

Indirect Measurement

1. Find the length of side $\overline{YZ}$.

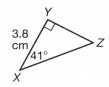

2. The two triangles are similar. If $\overline{UW}$ measures 6.3 m, find $m\overline{UV}$.

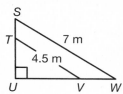

_____

_____

3. Fine Arts Giorgione's 1508 painting, *The Tempest*, is about 82 cm tall. A 16-cm-tall reproduction of this painting in a book features a bridge that is about 5.3 cm long. How long is the bridge on the actual painting?

_____

4. Eve is 55 in. tall. Find the length of her shadow if the sun makes an angle of 38° as shown.

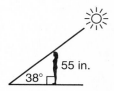

_____

5. Larry wants to know the distance between two trees, *A* and *B*, on the opposite side of a river. He knows the river is 25 m wide. He marks off and measures a right triangle as shown. The two triangles are similar. How far apart are the trees?

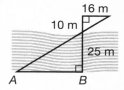

_____

6. Geography Santa Fe, New Mexico, is about 480 mi from Fort Worth, Texas. Find the distance from Fort Worth to Oklahoma City, Oklahoma, if the three cities form a right triangle as shown.

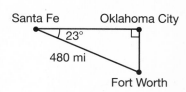

_____

7. Harold is 4 ft tall. When he stands 9 ft away from the base of a streetlight, his shadow is 3 ft long. How tall is the streetlight? (Start by finding the length of the base of the larger triangle.)

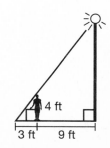

_____

Name _____

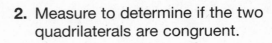

Section 11A Review

1. The pentagons are similar. Find the length represented by *x*.

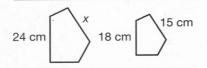

2. Measure to determine if the two quadrilaterals are congruent.

State whether each pair of triangles has congruence; if it does, give the rule that justifies your answer.

3. _____

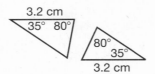

4. _____

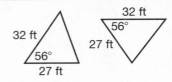

5. A small table is supported by diagonal legs as shown. If △*ABC* ~ △*EDC*, find the width *m*$\overline{AB}$ of the table.

_____

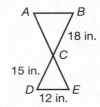

6. Kelly is flying a kite. If the kite string is 24 m long and makes an angle of 55° with the ground, how high is the kite? _____

7. A cone-shaped container for a crushed ice drink is 5 in. tall and has a $3\frac{1}{2}$-in. diameter. How many cubic inches of crushed ice can the container hold? *[Lesson 9-5]* _____

8. A ball is thrown upwards at a speed of 96 ft/sec. Its height, in feet, after *t* seconds is given by $h = 96t - 16t^2$. *[Lesson 10-3]*

a. Graph the function $h = 96t - 16t^2$.

b. Estimate when the ball has height 108 ft.

_____

c. When does the ball hit the ground?

_____

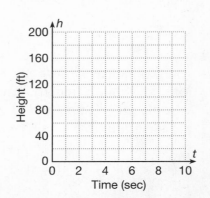

Transformations and Congruence

Tell what transformation of the lightly shaded figure produced the dark one.

1. _____
2. _____
3. _____

Across which axis was each figure reflected?

4. _____
5. _____

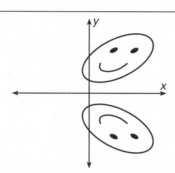
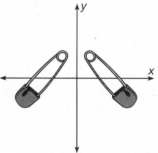

6. Find the coordinates of points *P* and *Q* on the triangle that has been translated 4 units to the right and 2.5 units up.

P _____   Q _____

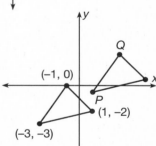

(−1, 0)   Q
P
(1, −2)
(−3, −3)

7. Find the coordinates of points *R* and *S* on the trapezoid that has been rotated 90° clockwise about the origin.

R _____   S _____

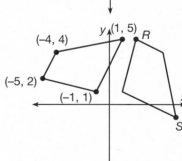

(−4, 4)   (1, 5) R
(−5, 2)
(−1, 1)
S

8. a. Name each polygon, if any, that is a translation of 1.

_____

b. Name each polygon, if any, that is a reflection of 4.

_____

c. Name each polygon, if any, that is a rotation of 6.

_____

Name _____

Transformations and Similarity

1. Hexagon 2 is a dilation of hexagon 1. Classify the dilation as a reduction or enlargement, and find the scale factor.

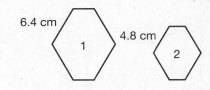

   _____

2. The larger dinosaur is a dilation of the smaller one. Classify the dilation as a reduction or enlargement, and find the scale factor.

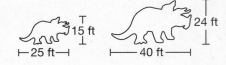

   _____

3. **a.** Use a scale factor of 1.5 to dilate trapezoid *ABCD.* Find the coordinates of the vertices of the dilation.

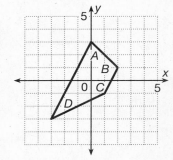

   A' _____   *B'* _____

   C' _____   *D'* _____

   b. Graph trapezoid *A'B'C'D'.*

4. Complete the sentence: The scale factor of a(n) _____ is less than 1.

5. Draw a reduction of this envelope. Use a scale factor of $\frac{1}{3}$.

6. Draw an enlargement of this paper clip. Use a scale factor of 1.75.

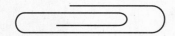

7. An APS camera uses a 1.6-cm by 2.8-cm negative to produce a photograph measuring 10.16 cm by 17.78 cm. Think of the photograph as a dilation of the negative. What is the scale factor? _____

Name _____

Symmetry

1. a. What kinds of symmetry does this figure have?

_____

b. Identify any lines of symmetry and rotation points.

2. a. What kinds of symmetry does this figure have?

_____

b. Identify any lines of symmetry and rotation points.

3. a. How many degrees can this figure be
turned and end up unchanged?   _____

b. Does the figure have rotational symmetry?   _____

4. a. How many degrees can this figure be
turned and end up unchanged?   _____

b. Does the figure have rotational symmetry?   _____

5. How many lines of symmetry does the flower
pattern have?   _____

For each letter shown, draw any and all lines of symmetry.

6.   U   7.   H   8.   L   9.   D

10. Language Arts The word BED has a horizontal line of symmetry. Find
at least three other words that have a horizontal lines of symmetry.

_____

11. An adapter like the one shown can be used to make a
45-rpm record ("single") play on a standard record player.

a. Draw all lines of symmetry, if any.

b. How many degrees can this figure be turned and end
up unchanged?   _____

Name _____

Covering the Plane

1. Use 8 translations of the figure to produce a tessellation.

2. What transformation would have to be used for the tessellation of triangles shown?

_____

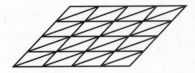

3. How many square tiles with 8-in. sides would it take to cover a wall with area 108 ft^2?

_____

4. Is this pattern a tessellation of octagons? Explain.

_____

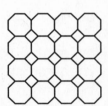

5. Sketch a tessellation of a figure that is not a polygon.

6. How many square tiles with 3-in. sides would it take to cover a floor with area 45 ft^2?

_____

7. What polygon is used for the tessellation shown?

_____

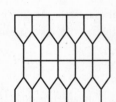

8. Could the pattern in Exercise **7** be created using

a. Only translations? _____   **b.** Only rotations? _____

c. Only reflections? _____   **d.** A combination? _____

Section 11B Review

1. What transformation is used in each of the two pairs of figures?

a. _____   b. _____

2. The shape is reflected across the *x*-axis. What are the corresponding vertex coordinates of the reflected figure?

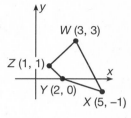

W' _____   *X'* _____

Y' _____   *Z'* _____

3. What is the general rule for reflecting point (*x*, *y*) across the *x*-axis?

_____

4. A parallelogram with vertices *P*(3, 3), *Q*(0, −3), *R*(−4, −2), and *S*(−1, 4) is dilated with respect to the origin, by a factor of $\frac{4}{5}$. What are the new coordinates of the vertices?

P' _____   *Q'* _____   *R'* _____   *S'* _____

5. a. How many degrees can this figure be turned and look just as it did before?   _____

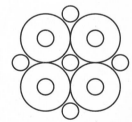

b. What kind or kinds of symmetry does it have?

_____

6. Geography What is the absolute position of Mexico City using latitude and longitude? *[Lesson 8-3]*

_____

7. Science The heaviest door in the world is designed to protect people from radiation at the Natural Institute for Fusion Science in Japan. It is 11.7 m high, 11.4 m wide, and 2.0 m thick. Find the volume of the door. *[Lesson 9-6]*

_____

Name _____

Cumulative Review Chapters 1–11

Use a protractor to measure each angle. *[Lesson 8-4]*

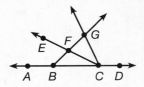

1. ∠FBC _____   **2.** ∠BFE _____   **3.** ∠BGC _____

4. ∠BCF _____   **5.** ∠DCG _____   **6.** ∠ECD _____

Find the volume of each figure after the dilation. *[Lesson 9-7]*

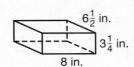

7. Scale factor = $\frac{2}{3}$ Volume = _____

8. Scale factor = 6   Volume = _____

Graph each function. *[Lesson 10-4]*

9. $y = \left(\frac{2}{3}\right)^x$

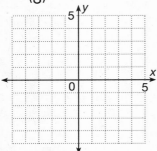

10. y = round to the nearest even number

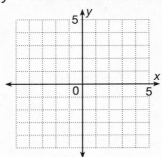

State whether each pair of triangles has congruence; if it does, give
the rule that justifies your answer. *[Lesson 11-3]*

11. _____

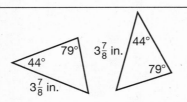

12. _____

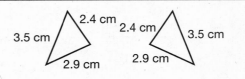

13. a. What polygon is used to produce the
tessellation shown? *[Lesson 11-9]*

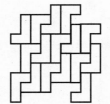

_____

b. Can the pattern be produced using:

Only translations? _____   Only rotations? _____

Only reflections? _____   A combination? _____

Tree Diagrams and the Counting Principle

1. A restaurant offers a choice of apple pie or pecan pie. Each slice of pie can be ordered with whipped cream, ice cream, or fresh fruit.

   a. How many choices of pie are there? _____

   How many choices of garnish or topping are there? _____

   b. Use the Counting Principle to find the number of different ways to order a slice of pie with topping or garnish. You may want to check it by drawing a tree diagram. _____

2. Make a tree diagram to show the possible results of spinning both spinners.

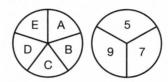

3. How many choices do you have in each situation?

   a. 4 types of muffin, 3 types of spread _____

   b. 5 t-shirt color choices, 4 sizes _____

   c. 12 ice cream flavors, cone or cup, with or without sprinkles _____

The early bird special from the Mighty Cafe is shown. Use it to answer Exercises 4 and 5.

> **Early Bird Special $6.49**
> • Soup or Salad
> • Quiche, Casserole, or Pasta
> • Potatoes, Peas, Broccoli, or Carrots
> • Milk, Juice, or Soda

4. How many different early bird specials can be ordered?

   _____

5. If the Mighty Café runs out of soup and pasta, how many different early bird specials can be ordered? _____

6. **Geography** Rich is trying to get from San Francisco to San Jose, California. He needs to stop in San Bruno on the way. There are 3 major roads or freeways from San Francisco to San Bruno, and 3 major roads or freeways from San Bruno to San Jose. How many routes can Rich take? _____

Permutations and Arrangements

1. Show all arrangements of the letters R, E, A, and D.

_____

_____

_____

Evaluate.

2. 4! _____

3. (5!)(3!) _____

4. (8 − 5)! _____

5. $\frac{6!}{3!}$ _____

6. 7(6!) _____

7. 7! _____

8. $\frac{12!}{9!}$ _____

9. (11 − 6)! _____

10. (6 − 2)! _____

11. $\frac{7!}{2!}$ _____

12. (4!)(6!) _____

13. $\frac{8!}{(8 − 2)!}$ _____

How many ways can the letters of each of these words be arranged? (No letter is used twice.) The letters do not have to form a word.

14. WORDS

15. THE

16. EQUATION

_____

_____

_____

17. SALE

18. SWITZERLAND

19. NATURE

_____

_____

_____

20. A librarian has 7 books to arrange on a shelf. How many ways can he order them? _____

21. Five runners are competing in the 100-yard dash. In how many orders can the runners finish? Assume there are no ties. _____

22. Jill bought 4 new CD singles. In how many orders can she play them? _____

23. An 18-member club is choosing its president, vice president, secretary, and treasurer. In how many ways can these four officers be chosen? _____

24. Geography On vacation in Hawaii, Kevin wants to visit the islands of Maui, Kauai, Hawaii, Molokai, and Oahu. He only has time to visit 3 islands. In how many ways can he select and order the islands he will visit? _____

Combinations and Groups

Evaluate.

1. $\dfrac{8!}{3! \times 5!}$ _____

2. $\dfrac{5!}{4! \times 1!}$ _____

3. $\dfrac{7!}{5! \times 2!}$ _____

4. $\dfrac{11!}{8! \times 3!}$ _____

5. $\dfrac{6!}{5!(6-5)!}$ _____

6. $\dfrac{4!}{2!(4-2)!}$ _____

7. $\dfrac{9!}{6!(9-6)!}$ _____

8. $\dfrac{5!}{3!(5-3)!}$ _____

9. In how many ways can 9 Senators be selected from among 100 Senators to serve on a committee? Write in factorial notation.

_____

10. In how many ways can a used car lot manager choose 12 of his 45 cars to feature in a newspaper advertisement? Write in factorial notation.

_____

11. Becky wants to buy 12 of the posters at a poster shop, but she only has enough money for 3 posters. How many ways can she select 3 out of 12 posters?

_____

12. A test instructs you to "answer 2 of the next 5 questions." How many ways can you choose 2 questions to answer?

_____

13. A teacher wants 5 of her 25 students to write solutions on the board. How many ways can she select a group of 5 students?

_____

14. **Social Science** In 1995, President Clinton had 20 men and women on his cabinet. How many ways could he select 4 cabinet members to consult regarding a particular issue?

_____

15. Patrick read 10 short stories for his English class. He needs to write an essay describing 3 of the stories. How many ways can he choose 3 stories to write about?

_____

16. A pancake restaurant has 8 different syrups, jams, and honeys. Tammy wants to put a different topping on each of her 4 pancakes. How many ways can she choose 4 toppings?

_____

17. Chih is joining a music club. He needs to choose 4 out of 65 compact discs for his first shipment. How many ways can he choose? Write in factorial notation.

_____

18. A computer drawing program has 256 colors available, but you can only use 16 colors at a time. How many ways can you choose 16 out of 256 colors? Write in factorial notation.

_____

Name _____

Section 12A Review

Evaluate.

1. 9! _____ **2.** 11! _____ **3.** $(15 - 8)!$ _____

4. 8(7!) _____ **5.** $\dfrac{12!}{7!}$ _____ **6.** $\dfrac{14!}{4!(14 - 4)!}$ _____

7. A bag contains many blue, green, and red marbles. Make an organized list showing the possible outcomes of removing two marbles, one after the other.

_____

_____

_____

_____

8. Suppose you remove one marble from the bag in Exercise 7, then flip a coin twice. Make a tree diagram to show the possible outcomes.

How many ways can the letters of each of these words be arranged if no letter is used twice? The letters do not have to form a word.

9. SQUARE _____ **10.** IOWA _____ **11.** SURVEY _____

12. At an amusement park, Faye and Gary have chosen 5 rides they want to go on. In how many different orders can they go on the rides? _____

13. A group of friends plan to share 6 of the 36 dishes on the menu at a Chinese restaurant. How many ways can they choose what dishes to order? Write in factorial notation. _____

14. **Science** A ball is thrown upward at a speed of 48 ft/sec from a height of 12 ft. After t seconds, the height (in feet) is given by the sum of $-16t^2$ and $48t + 12$. What is the height of the ball after 2.5 sec? *[Lesson 10-6]* _____

15. The Renaissance Tower in Dallas, Texas, is 216 m tall. A scale model of it is 54 cm tall. What is the scale factor of the model? *[Lesson 11-1]* _____

Probability

List all outcomes in each sample space.

1. Tossing a coin   _____

2. Choosing one of 7 cards labeled with the days of the week

_____

3. Asking a student at your school what grade he or she is in

_____

Express the probability as a fraction, decimal, and percent.

4. Tossing a coin that lands heads   _____

5. Having 60 minutes in the next hour   _____

6. Having a birthday that is *not* in January
   (assuming that all months are equally likely)   _____

7. Drawing a white marble out of a bag that contains
   3 white and 7 black marbles   _____

The blue, gold, and white sectors of the spinner are each $\frac{1}{5}$ of the spinner area.

8. Which color or colors have the same
   probability as gold?   _____

9. What is the probability of spinning black?   _____

10. What is the probability of spinning blue?   _____

11. What is the probability of *not* spinning black? _____

12. Suppose you choose someone at random from your
   school. What is the probability that he or she was
   born on the same day of the week as you?   _____

13. In the game of Monopoly™, the probability of going to
   jail in any one turn is about 4.5%. What is the probability
   of *not* going to jail?   _____

Experimental and Geometric Probability

1. Toss 4 coins 40 times and complete the table to record your results. Use the data to find the experimental probability of each event. Give each probability as a percent.

Outcome	4 heads	3 heads 1 tails	2 heads 2 tails	1 heads 3 tails	4 tails
Frequency					
Experimental Probability					

2. Compare the experimental probability of tossing 4 tails and no heads with the theoretical probability.

_____

3. Helen works in an ice cream shop. For the last three hours, she has recorded what flavor each customer purchased. Her data is shown.

   a. What is the probability that a customer purchased chocolate? _____

   b. What is the probability that a customer purchased vanilla or strawberry? _____

   c. What is the probability that the next customer will *not* purchase strawberry?

   _____

Outcome	Customers
Vanilla	27
Chocolate	14
Strawberry	16
Other	13

4. A player tosses a coin onto the game board.

   a. What is the probability that the coin lands in the circle? _____

   b. What is the probability that the coin lands outside the circle? _____

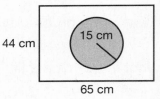

44 cm

15 cm

65 cm

5. **Social Science** The stem-and-leaf diagram shows the ages of U.S. Presidents at inauguration.

```
stem | leaf
  4  | 2 3 6 6 8 9 9
  5  | 0 0 1 1 1 1 2 2 4 4 4 4 5 5 5 5 6 6 6 7 7 7 7 8
  6  | 0 1 1 1 2 4 4 5 8 9
```

   a. What is the probability that a President was 57? _____

   b. What is the probability that a President was over 59? _____

Conditional Probability

Suppose that a fly lands on the 7 by 7 game board shown.
What is the probability that it lands:

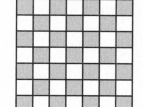

1. On a white square? _____

2. In the fifth row? _____

3. On a white square in the fifth row? _____

4. On a shaded square in the first row? _____

5. If you know that the fly landed on a shaded square, what is
the probability that it landed on the top right corner square? _____

6. You roll a pair of number cubes. If the first one comes up 3,
find the probability that the sum of the 2 number cubes is:

a. 6 _____   **b.** less than 7 _____   **c.** 5 or 8 _____

The graph shows the percent of people in Gambia who
belong to various ethnic groups.

Ethnic Groups in Gambia

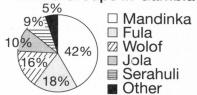

7. Two Gambians are chosen at random. What is
the probability that both are Fulas?

_____

8. The 1994 population of Gambia was about
960,000. Estimate the number of Jolas.   _____

9. If you know that a Gambian is not Mandinka,
what is the probability that he or she is Fula?   _____

10. The table shows how many people live in each
area of Smalltown, U.S.A. What is the probability
that a randomly chosen small town resident:

a. Lives north of Main St.? _____

b. Lives east of Broadway, if you already know
that the resident lives south of Main Street?

_____

	West of Broadway	East of Broadway
North of Main St.	106	243
South of Main St.	158	174

Dependent and Independent Events

State whether each pair of events is independent or dependent.

1. You roll a 6 on a number cube and then flip a coin that comes up heads. _____

2. A person was born in winter and born in February. _____

3. You get an A in science and an A in math. _____

4. A man is 42 years old and his phone number begins with the digits 4 and 2. _____

5. You draw a red marble from a bag, and then another red marble (without replacing the first marble). _____

Suppose that two tiles are drawn from the collection shown at the right. The first tile is replaced before the second is drawn. Find each probability.

6. P(A, A) _____

7. P(R, C) _____

8. P(E, not E) _____

9. P(vowel, vowel) _____

10. P(vowel, not R) _____

11. P(consonant, vowel) ___

Suppose that two tiles are drawn from the collection shown above. The first tile is *not* replaced before the second is drawn. Find each probability.

12. P(A, A) _____

13. P(R, C) _____

14. P(E, not E) _____

15. P(vowel, vowel) _____

16. P(vowel, not R) _____

17. P(consonant, vowel) _____

Suppose you're new in town and you do not know your way around, so you choose your path randomly. Assume that you always travel in a northbound direction.

18. If you take path 1, what is the probability that you end up at Karl's house? _____

19. If you take path 2, what is the probability that you end up at Leo's house? _____

20. Find the probability that you end up at:

Jane's house _____ Karl's house _____ Leo's house _____ Mary's house _____

Section 12B Review

1. Identify the sample space for the experiment of randomly choosing a letter from the word C O M P U T E R. Find the number of outcomes in each event, and find the probability of each event.

   Sample space: _____

   Events: **a.** Choosing *R*   **b.** Choosing a vowel   **c.** Not choosing *P*

   Number of outcomes: _____   _____   _____

   Probability: _____   _____   _____

2. If you toss two number cubes, what are the following probabilities?

   a. *P*(sum of 10) _____   **b.** *P*(sum < 7) _____   **c.** *P*(sum of 8, 9, or 12) ____

3. You draw two chips from a bag containing 2 white, 3 red, and 5 blue chips. Find each probability if the first chip is replaced. Then find each probability if it is not replaced.

   a. *P*(blue then blue)   **b.** *P*(white then red)   **c.** *P*(red then *not* red)

   If replaced: _____   _____   _____

   If not replaced: _____   _____   _____

4. What is the probability of spinning orange?   _____

5. If you don't spin pink, what is the probability of spinning brown?   _____

6. If you spin the spinner twice, what is the probability of spinning orange then brown?   _____

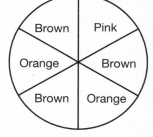

7. If the first spin lands on brown, what is the probability that both spins land on brown?   _____

8. A living room on a floor plan is 4 in. by $5\frac{1}{2}$ in. If the scale factor is 36, what are the perimeter and area of the living room? *[Lesson 9-2]*

   Perimeter: _____   Area: _____

9. The top of the Commerzbank Tower in Frankfurt, Germany, forms a 71° angle with a point 89.2 m from the tower's base. How tall is the Commerzbank Tower? *[Lesson 11-4]*   _____

Name _____

Cumulative Review Chapters 1–12

Find the surface area of each figure. *[Lesson 9-4]*

1. _____

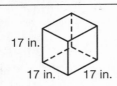

17 in.
17 in.   17 in.

2. _____

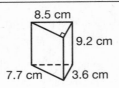

8.5 cm
9.2 cm
7.7 cm   3.6 cm

3. _____

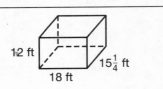

12 ft
18 ft
$15\frac{1}{4}$ ft

Multiply. *[Lesson 10-8]*

4. $(3x^2)(4x^5)$

5. $2p(p^2 - 3p + 5)$

6. $-t^3(t^3 - 8t)$

_____   _____   _____

7. $3u^2(u^4 - 5u^2 + 7)$

8. $\frac{2}{3}c(12c^2 - 18)$

9. $8d(3d^2 - 4d - 11)$

_____   _____   _____

Tell what transformation of the left figure in each pair produces the
right one. *[Lesson 11-6]*

10. _____

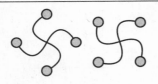

11. _____

12. _____

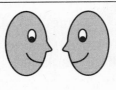

How many ways can the letters of each of these words be arranged?
(No letter is used twice.) The letters do not have to form a word. *[Lesson 12-2]*

13. MYOPIA _____

14. BARN _____

15. MONKEYS _____

16. FORMALITY _____

17. DINOSAUR _____

18. POWER _____

Express the probability as a fraction, decimal, and percent. *[Lesson 12-4]*

19. Rolling a 3 or 5 on a single roll of a number cube _____

20. Drawing a rectangle that is also a pentagon _____

21. Selecting a purple marble from a bag that
contains 8 purple and 22 red marbles _____

22. A randomly chosen person being born on a
Saturday or Sunday _____

Name _____

Practice 1-1

Line Plots and Stem-and-Leaf Diagrams

State the range and draw a line plot for each data set.

1. Some students were asked "How many magazines do you subscribe to?" Their answers were 3, 0, 2, 3, 0, 0, 5, 1, 3, and 2.

range __0 to 5, or 5__

2. Jorge wrote down the number of songs on each of his ten favorite CDs. The numbers he wrote were 8, 10, 14, 11, 7, 10, 9, 10, 12, and 9.

range __7 to 14, or 7__

3. Career A real estate agent wrote the number of bedrooms in each of the homes on Cedar Avenue. They were 2, 3, 3, 2, 4, 3, 2, 2, 5, 3, 2, 2, and 1.

range __1 to 5, or 4__

State the range and draw a stem-and-leaf diagram for each data set.

4. The number of pages in the books on Syd's bookshelf are 84, 96, 132, 115, 100, 97, 89, 126, 98, 115, 86, 135, and 92.

range __84 to 135, or 51__

stem	leaf
8	469
9	2678
10	0
11	55
12	6
13	25

5. Ms. Trejo's history class took a test last week. The scores were 89, 92, 74, 87, 98, 86, 79, 83, 94, 100, 68, 80, 93, 70, 84, 73, 62, 83, 91, 86, 77, and 87.

range __62 to 100, or 38__

stem	leaf
6	28
7	03479
8	033466779
9	12348
10	0

Use with pages 6–10. **1**

Name _____

Practice 1-2

Measures of Central Tendency

Find the mean, median, and mode(s) of each data set.

1. The number of students in classes at Johnson School are 30, 27, 31, 26, 33, 29, 21, 31, 30, 28, and 26.

mean __About 28.36__   median __29__   mode(s) __26, 30, and 31__

2. The number of children in families on Memory Lane are 3, 0, 2, 1, 2, 1, 1, 0, 3, and 4.

mean __1.7__   median __1.5__   mode(s) __1__

3. The daily wages for employees at Burrito Hut are $62, $47, $75, $59, and $49.

mean __$58.40__   median __$59__   mode(s) __None__

Health The table shows the calcium and potassium content of several vegetable foods. Use the table for Exercises 4–7.

Food	1 raw carrot	1 ear corn	1/2 cup lentils	1/2 cup raw mushrooms	1 baked potato	1/2 cup tofu	1 raw tomato
Calcium (mg)	19	2	19	2	20	130	9
Potassium (mg)	233	192	366	130	844	150	255

4. Find the mean, median, and mode(s) for the amount of calcium.

mean __About 28.71 mg__   median __19 mg__   mode(s) __2 mg and 19 mg__

5. Identify the outlier in the calcium data. __130 mg__

Recalculate the mean and median as if the outlier were not in the data set.

mean __About 11.83 mg__   median __14 mg__

6. Find the mean, median, and mode(s) for the amount of potassium.

mean __310 mg__   median __233 mg__   mode(s) __None__

7. Is there an outlier in the potassium data? Explain.

__No. The data is spread out over a large range.__

2 Use with pages 11–16.

Name _____

Practice 1-3

Box-and-Whisker Plots

Sketch a box-and-whisker plot for each set of data. Between what range does the middle half of the data fall?

1. Howard counted the number of convenience stores he saw the last six times he went for a drive with his parents. The numbers were 7, 4, 12, 3, 6, and 8.

__4 to 8__

Number of Convenience Stores

2. The last fifteen people to leave the library checked out 1, 5, 3, 0, 4, 1, 2, 0, 3, 6, 12, 6, 4, 8, and 2 books.

__1 to 6__

Number of Books

3. From 1980 to 1994, the winning scores in the British Open men's golf championship were 271, 276, 284, 275, 276, 282, 280, 279, 273, 275, 270, 272, 272, 267, and 268.

__271 to 279__

British Open - Winning Scores

4. The number of faces of regular polyhedra are 6, 4, 8, 20, and 12.

__5 to 16__

Number of Faces of Regular Polyhedra

The box-and-whisker plot shows the 1990 populations of the 20 largest U.S. metropolitan areas. Use it for Exercises 5–7.

Population of Major U.S. Metropolitan Areas (millions)

5. Give the range, median, and quartiles of the data (in millions).

range __2.1 to 18.0, or 15.9__   median __3.45__

lower quartile __2.5__   upper quartile __5.3__

6. What fraction of the 20 areas have a population between 3.45 million and 5.3 million? __$\frac{1}{4}$__

7. What is shown by the whisker right of the median?

__One-fourth, or 5, of the 20 areas have a population between 5.3 million and 18.0 million.__

Use with pages 17–21. **3**

Name _____

Practice 1-4

Bar Graphs and Line Graphs

1. Create a bar graph to represent the data, showing the five rhythm and blues performers with the most number-one singles since 1965.

Performer	James Brown	Aretha Franklin	Marvin Gaye	The Temptations	Stevie Wonder
#1 singles	16	20	13	14	18

Rhythm & Blues Performers

2. Career The data shows the approximate number of civilians (in thousands) working for the military in a given year. Create a line graph to represent the data. Draw a conclusion about the civilian staff in the military from 1985 to 1993.

Year	'85	'86	'87	'88	'89	'90	'91	'92	'93
Civilians	980	960	970	950	960	930	900	890	850

__The number of civilian staff decreased from 1985 to 1993.__

Civilian Staff in the Military

3. The table shows the median age of American men and women at the time of their first marriage. Create a double line graph to represent this data. What conclusions can you draw?

Year	1940	1950	1960	1970	1980	1990
Men	24.3	22.8	22.8	23.2	24.7	26.1
Women	21.5	20.3	20.3	20.8	22.0	23.9

__On the average, men get married at an older age than women. The median marriage age for both men and women has been increasing since 1960.__

Median Age at First Marriage

4 Use with pages 22–27.

131

Section 1A Review

1. Edwin counted the number of cars that passed him as he walked to school each day for two weeks. The numbers were 8, 7, 5, 9, 7, 6, 9, 6, 7, and 10. Find the mean, median, and mode(s) of these numbers. Draw a line plot to show the mode(s).

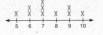

   mean __7.4__   median __7__   mode(s) __7__

The table shows the number of outlets (in thousands) and the sales (in billions of dollars) of the ten largest American fast-food chains in 1991.

Chain	Arby's	Burger King	Dairy Queen	Domino's Pizza	Hardee's	KFC	McDonald's	Pizza Hut	Taco Bell	Wendy's
Outlets	2.2	6.1	5.2	5.2	3.2	7.9	11.2	7.4	3.1	3.8
Sales	1.3	5.7	2.2	2.5	2.9	5.3	17.3	4.1	2.1	3.0

2. Create a stem-and-leaf diagram for the sales data. (Use the digit after the decimal point for each leaf.)

stem	leaf
1	3
2	1 2 5 9
3	0
4	1
5	3 7
17	3

3. Find the mean number of outlets and sales of these fast-food chains.

   mean number of outlets __5530__

   mean sales __$4.64 billion__

4. Create a box-and-whisker plot for the amount of sales, in billions of dollars.

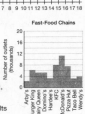

5. Create a box-and-whisker plot and a bar graph for the number of outlets of these fast-food chains.

6. Describe a possible relationship between the number of outlets and the amount of sales. Use your results from Exercises 2–5.

   __The sales increase as the outlets increase.__

7. On April 30, 1986, Ashrita Furman performed 8341 somersaults in 630 minutes. About how many somersaults did he perform each minute? [Previous Course]

   __13.24 somersaults__

Understanding Surveys

For Exercises 1–4, state whether or not the sample is random.

1. For the population of popular music fans: a top-40 radio station asks listeners to call in and name their three favorite songs.   __Not random__

2. For the population of students in Ellen's history class: Ellen chooses the seven students she feels most comfortable talking to.   __Not random__

3. For the population of students at Horton Junior High School: Each student's name is written on a separate card. The cards are mixed in a barrel, and a blindfolded student removes 15 cards from the drum.   __Random__

4. For the population of all residents in a particular area code: A computer is used to select 7-digit numbers at random, and the telephone numbers are dialed until the surveyor is able to contact 25 people who are willing to answer some questions.   __Not random__

5. A publisher wants to know whether their new book about rocket science will appeal to high school students. The publisher sends free copies of the book to science clubs at 100 high schools nationwide. The students like the book very much. Can the publisher be reasonably certain that the book will sell well to high school students? Explain.

   __No. Their sample included only students with a keen interest in science.__

6. A software manufacturer offers a World Wide Web site where users can ask questions about the software. Most of the users who write in report that they are having trouble using the software. Should the manufacturer conclude that most people who buy the software are having problems? Explain.

   __No. The people who are having trouble are more likely to write than those who are not having trouble.__

7. A pharmaceutical company distributed 31,600 trial samples of acne soap to high school students. Each sample was packaged with a questionnaire, and 8,350 of the questionnaires were returned.

   a. What is the population of this survey?   __High school students__

   b. What is the sample size of this survey?   __8,350__

Recording and Organizing Data

1. Mr. Ishii made a histogram showing his students' performance on a recent English test.

   a. What is the interval width in this histogram?   __10__

   b. How many students scored between 80 and 89 points?   __4__

English Test Scores

   c. Make a frequency table for the histogram.

Score	50-59	60-69	70-79	80-89	90-99
Students	1	5	11	4	7

   d. Can you tell how many students scored 73 points? Explain.

   __No. It could be any number from 0 to 11.__

2. The frequency table shows the ages of U.S. Senators in the 103rd Congress in 1994. Create a histogram to represent the data.

Age	under 40	40–49	50–59	60–69	70 or over
Number	1	16	48	22	12

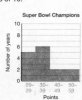

1994 Ages of Senators

3. The data shows the number of points scored by the winning team of each Super Bowl for the years 1980 to 1994. Create a frequency table and a histogram to represent the data. Use intervals of 10.

Year	'80	'81	'82	'83	'84	'85	'86	'87
Points	31	27	26	27	38	38	46	39

Year	'88	'89	'90	'91	'92	'93	'94
Points	42	20	55	20	37	52	30

Points	20-29	30-39	40-49	50-59
Number of Years	5	6	2	2

Super Bowl Champions

Scatterplots and Trends

1. The data shows the results of the 1994 NBA Eastern Conference Semi-finals. Create a scatterplot for the data. Determine a trend and draw a trend line if possible.

Away	86	91	102	83	86	79	77	96	69	81	86	76	79
Home	90	96	104	95	87	93	87	85	92	101	102	88	98

   __No trend line possible__

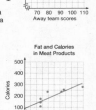

1994 NBA Eastern Conference Semi-finals

2. Health The table gives the fat and calorie content of a 3-oz serving of some common meat products. Create a scatterplot for the data. Determine a trend and draw a trend line if possible.

Food	Fat (g)	Calories
Raw clams	1	63
Fish sticks	10	231
Canned tuna	7	169
Lean ground beef	16	231
Lamb chop	17	252
Ham, canned, roasted	7	140
Fried chicken wings	7	103
Frankfurters, beef and pork	25	274

Fat and Calories in Meat Products

   __The number of calories rises as the amount of fat increases.__

3. Health An *outpatient* is someone who receives treatment at a hospital without being confined to the hospital. The table shows the approximate number of every 100 hospital surgeries performed on outpatients from 1982 to 1992. Create a scatterplot for the data. Determine a trend and draw a trend line.

Outpatient Surgeries per 100 Hospital Surgeries

Year	'82	'83	'84	'85	'86	'87	'88	'89	'90	'91	'92
Outpatients	21	28	31	37	40	45	48	50	52	57	60

   __The number of outpatient surgeries has been increasing.__

Designing a Survey

1. Provide a possible question that would appear on a survey card that comes with a new book.

_____ Answers will vary. _____

2. Provide a possible question that would appear on a survey card that comes with a frozen dinner.

_____ Answers will vary. _____

3. Provide a possible question that would appear on a survey card that comes with a new calculator.

_____ Answers will vary. _____

4. The organizers of a youth troop in downtown Dallas, Texas, plan to print some brochures to target young people in their community. To find out what images and activities appeal to these young people, they plan to take a survey.

   a. Who is the population of the survey?

   _____ Young people in downtown Dallas, Texas _____

   b. Why do the organizers want to know what images and activities appeal to the target population?

   The brochure will be more successful if the target

   population finds it interesting.

   c. The organizers discover that a similar survey has already been taken in a rural Pennsylvania community. Should they use the results of that survey instead of taking a new survey? Explain.

   No. The young people in a rural Pennsylvania community

   probably have interests that differ from those of the target

   population.

5. The bar graph shows the results of a survey that asked, "On the average, how many minutes do you exercise every day?"

   a. What was the most frequent answer? __15–29 min__

   b. How many people exercise an hour or more? __1__

   c. How many people were surveyed? __21__

Section 1B Review

1. Josh is surveying the students in his class. He does not want to bias his results, so he talks only to students he does not know. Is the following survey random or not random? If the sample is not random, state the part of the population that is not represented.

   _____ Not random; Josh's friends _____

2. The scatterplot shows the price and fuel efficiency of several automobile models. What trend is evident in the data? Why might this be true?

   More expensive cars tend to get fewer

   miles per gallon; expensive cars tend

   to be larger and heavier.

3. The table shows the land area of midwestern states (in thousands of square miles). Make a frequency chart of the data, using intervals of 10,000 square miles. Then make a histogram.

   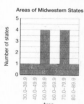

State	IA	IL	IN	KS	MI	MN	MO
Area	56.0	55.6	35.9	81.8	57.0	79.5	68.9

State	ND	NE	OH	SD	WI
Area	70.7	76.6	41.0	76.0	54.0

Area	30.0–39.9	40.0–49.9	50.0–59.9	60.0–69.9	70.0–79.9	80.0–89.9
States	1	1	4	1	4	1

4. The data gives the number of points scored by each player of the Vancouver Canucks hockey team during the 1993–1994 season. Make a box-and-whisker plot to represent the data. *[Lesson 1-3]*

   107, 70, 68, 66, 61, 55, 55, 38, 37, 32, 29, 28, 28, 27, 20, 15, 14, 12, 11, 10, 9, 7, 7, 6, 6, 5

Cumulative Review Chapter 1

Add, subtract, multiply, or divide. *[Previous Course]*

1. 32 + 67 __99__
2. 91 − 27 __64__
3. 6 × 7 __42__
4. 296 ÷ 8 __37__

5. 365 + 83 __448__
6. 38 − 29 __9__
7. 9 × 28 __252__
8. 952 ÷ 17 __56__

9. 127 + 98 __225__
10. 183 − 76 __107__
11. 37 × 24 __888__
12. 1932 ÷ 23 __84__

State the range and draw a stem-and-leaf diagram for each data set. *[Lesson 1-1]*

13. 84, 59, 63, 72, 87, 63, 61, 62, 70, 65, 74, 62, 77, 75, 71

   range __59 to 87, or 28__

stem	leaf
5	9
6	122335
7	012457
8	47

14. 94, 87, 103, 76, 100, 83, 79, 87, 85, 82, 98, 92, 79, 84, 89, 96

   range __76 to 103, or 27__

stem	leaf
7	699
8	2345779
9	2468
10	03

Find the mean, median, and mode(s) of each data set. *[Lesson 1-2]*

15. 6.8, 9.3, 15.8, 12.7, 13.7, 22.8

   mean __13.52__ median __13.2__

   mode(s) __None__

16. 3, 8, 7, 6, 8, 11, 8, 2, 9, 6

   mean __6.8__ median __7.5__

   mode(s) __8__

17. Create a scatterplot of the data below. Draw a trend line. *[Lesson 1-7]*

Price ($)	3.75	8.25	2.50	7.00	4.50	9.00	6.25
Size (oz)	9	23	8	17	12	22	16

Integers and Absolute Value

Name the opposite of each number.

1. 7 __−7__
2. −8 __8__
3. 11 __−11__
4. −47 __47__

5. −15 __15__
6. 28 __−28__
7. −98 __98__
8. 638 __−638__

Describe a situation that could be represented by each integer.

9. 4 __Answers will vary.__
10. −16 __Answers will vary.__

11. −2 hours __Answers will vary.__
12. −$3 __Answers will vary.__

Use >, <, or = to compare each set of numbers.

13. −$4 ◯ −$8
14. −7 ◯ |−7|
15. 6 ◯ −6
16. 0 ◯ −8

17. −9 ◯ 3
18. −2 ◯ −1
19. 15 ◯ |15|
20. 17 ◯ −35

Find each absolute value.

21. |−3| __3__
22. |8| __8__
23. |635| __635__
24. |−56| __56__

25. |−845| __845__
26. |12 − 3| __9__
27. |35 − 7| __28__
28. |−3487| __3487__

29. What integer is described by the following? The absolute value is 21 and the number is to the right of 0 on a number line. __21__

30. Henrietta's business lost $3200 last month. She told her cousin that her profit for the month was −$3200. Name a profit amount lower than −$3200.

   __Possible answer: −$3400__

31. In 1979, Jon Brower Minnoch set a world record for weight loss by losing 920 pounds in 16 months. Use an integer to represent the change in his weight. __−920 pounds__

32. What integer is described by the following? The absolute value is 10 and the number is to the left of 0 on a number line. __−10__

Addition of Integers

Write the addition problem for each model.

1. $7 + (-4)$

2. $-3 + 5$

3. $-2 + 6$

Add.

4. $17 + 12$
29

5. $-17 + 12$
-5

6. $17 + (-12)$
5

7. $-17 + (-12)$
-29

8. $81 + (-53)$
28

9. $-21 + 32$
11

10. $-18 + (-14)$
-32

11. $56 + (-16)$
40

12. $3 + (-7) + 12$
8

13. $-4 + (-11) + (-5)$
-20

14. $18 + 5 + (-24)$
-1

15. $-14 + 3 + 11$
0

16. $29 + (-8) + (-7)$
14

17. $-13 + 41 + (-8)$
20

Decide whether the sum is always, sometimes, or never positive.

18. three positive numbers   Always positive

19. zero and a negative number   Never positive

20. five negative numbers   Never positive

21. a positive number and a negative number   Sometimes positive

22. One night the temperature in Fairbanks, Alaska, was $-22°F$. By the next afternoon, the temperature had increased 13°. What was the new temperature? $-9°F$

23. **Career** A real estate appraiser determined that a home was worth $127,000 plus adjustments of $-2,000$ (no fireplace) and $+4,500$ (extra bedroom). How much was the home worth? $129,500

Subtraction of Integers

Write each problem as an addition problem. Compute the answer.

1. $16 - 5$ $16 + (-5) = 11$

2. $-6 - 11$ $-6 + (-11) = -17$

3. $31 - (-8)$ $31 + 8 = 39$

4. $47 - 83$ $47 + (-83) = -36$

5. $-12 - (-15)$ $-12 + 15 = 3$

6. $-38 - (-12)$ $-38 + 12 = -26$

Add or subtract.

7. $9 - 15$
-6

8. $16 - 7$
9

9. $-32 - (-18)$
-14

10. $-38 - 41$
-79

11. $-23 + 57$
34

12. $-41 - 85$
-126

13. $-17 - (-4)$
-13

14. $-23 - (-47)$
24

15. $8 - (-63)$
71

16. $12 - (-5)$
17

17. $83 - 184$
-101

18. $63 + (-28)$
35

19. A roller coaster, beginning 24 feet above ground level, goes up 15 feet, down 8 feet, up 23 feet, down 14 feet, up 35 feet, and finally down 75 feet. How far above or below ground level is it at the end of the ride?   At ground level

20. **Consumer** A checking account is overdrawn if it has a negative balance. Marc's account is overdrawn by $52. What will his balance be after he deposits $200 and writes a check for $18? $130

21. The average temperature in Caribou, Maine, is 18°C in July, and $-12°C$ in January. What is the difference between these temperatures? $30°C$

22. Polyus Nedostupnosti, Antarctica, is the coldest place in the world. Its annual mean temperature is 166° colder than that of Dallol, Ethiopia, the world's hottest place where the annual mean temperature is 94°F. What is the annual mean temperature of Polyus Nedostupnosti? $-72°F$

Multiplication and Division of Integers

Multiply or divide.

1. $4 \cdot (-7)$
-28

2. $-2 \cdot 10$
-20

3. $4 \cdot (-18)$
-72

4. $-21 \div 3$
-7

5. $18 \div (-6)$
-3

6. $86 \div 43$
2

7. $-52 \div (-13)$
4

8. $(15)(-11)$
-165

9. $-6(7)$
-42

10. -5×18
-90

11. $3 \times (-8)$
-24

12. $-18 \times (-16)$
288

13. $38 \div -2$
-19

14. $-45 \div (-3)$
15

15. $-164 \div (-4)$
41

16. $3 \cdot (-2) \cdot (-5)$
30

17. $-8 \cdot (-9) \cdot 10$
720

18. $-3 \cdot (-12) \cdot 2$
72

19. $\frac{21}{-7}$
-3

20. $\frac{35}{5}$
7

21. $\frac{-90}{-15}$
6

22. $\frac{64}{-16}$
-4

23. $\frac{-88}{11}$
-8

24. $\frac{-221}{-13}$
17

Evaluate.

25. $|-4 \times (-3)|$
12

26. $|-81| \div |9|$
9

27. $|12 \cdot (-9)|$
108

28. $|100 \div (-5)|$
20

29. The value of Jim's telephone calling card decreases 15 cents for every minute he uses it. Yesterday he used the card to make a 6-minute call. How much did the value of the card change? -90 cents

30. One day the temperature in Lone Grove, Oklahoma fell 3 degrees per hour for 5 consecutive hours. Give the total change in temperature. -15 degrees

31. The population of New Orleans, Louisiana, decreased from about 558,000 in 1980 to 497,000 in 1990. About how much did the population change each year? -6100

Evaluating Expressions Using Integers

Evaluate each pair of expressions.

1. $3 \cdot 4 + 5$ 17
$3 \cdot (4 + 5)$ 27

2. $(10 - 3) \times 5$ 35
$10 - 3 \times 5$ -5

3. $30 \div 2 \times 3$ 45
$30 \div (2 \times 3)$ 5

Evaluate each expression two different ways.

4. $8(3 + 7)$
$8 \cdot 10 = 80$
$24 + 56 = 80$

5. $-6(12 - 15)$
$-6(-3) = 18$
$-72 - (-90) = 18$

6. $7(3 - 5)$
$7(-2) = -14$
$21 - 35 = -14$

7. $6(7 + 5)$
$6(12) = 72$
$42 + 30 = 72$

8. $-5(8 + 1)$
$-5(9) = -45$
$-40 + (-5) = -45$

9. $2(-3 - 4)$
$2(-7) = -14$
$-6 + (-8) = -14$

Evaluate each expression.

10. $8 \cdot 9 + 10 \cdot 11$
182

11. $-24 \div 6 \times 2 - (-4)$
-4

12. $7(11 - 5) + 2$
44

13. $-18 + 3 \cdot (-9) + 15$
-30

14. $12 - \frac{7 + 8}{5 - 2}$
7

15. $\frac{30}{2(-6 + 9)} - 1$
4

Insert parentheses to make each sentence true.

16. $12 \div (3 - 6) + 5 = 1$

17. $(8 + 16) \div 2 + 2 = 14$

18. $63 - (9 - 15) - 4 = 65$

19. $3 - (12 + 4) \times 6 = -93$

20. $12 - (3 \times 5) - 7 = -10$

21. $5 \times (7 \times 2 - 8) = 30$

22. Stan bought donuts for the Drama Club meeting. He bought 6 regular donuts for 45 cents each and 9 premium donuts for 55 cents each.

  a. How much did he spend? $7.65

  b. What was the mean price per donut?   51 cents

Section 2A Review

Name _____

1. Refer to the number line.   —•—•—•—•—•—•—•—•—•—
   $-8\ -6\ -4\ -2\ 0\ 2\ 4$

   a. Which of the labeled numbers are positive? ___ 2, 4 ___

   b. Which of the labeled numbers are negative? ___ $-8, -6, -4, -2$ ___

   c. Name the pairs of opposites shown. ___ -2 and 2; -4 and 4 ___

   d. Which labeled number is the greatest? ___ 4 ___

   e. Which labeled number has the greatest absolute value? ___ -8 ___

Use the distributive property to evaluate.

2. $8(-12 + 4)$ ___ -64 ___   3. $-5(5 - 9)$ ___ 20 ___   4. $7(7 + 13)$ ___ 140 ___

Evaluate the following.

5. $|-8|$ ___ 8 ___   6. $|10|$ ___ 10 ___   7. $|20 - 6|$ ___ 14 ___

Compute the following.

8. $8 - (-4)$ ___ 12 ___   9. $42 \div (-3)$ ___ -14 ___   10. $8 + \dfrac{50}{14 - 9}$ ___ 18 ___

11. The data gives the number of runs scored by New York Mets players in 1994. Make a histogram using this data. *[Lesson 1-6]*

   16, 53, 60, 11, 18, 39, 47, 23, 20, 20, 46, 26, 45, 39, 5, 1

12. A fast-food restaurant chain plans to make a new sandwich intended to appeal to teenagers throughout Ohio, where the restaurants are located. To find out what foods appeal to this age group, the restaurant will take a survey. *[Lesson 1-8]*

   a. Who is the population of the survey? ___ Teenagers in Ohio ___

   b. Would a sample of teenagers in downtown Cleveland be a representative sample? Explain.
   ___ No. The sample should include teenagers throughout the state. ___

Integers in the Coordinate System

Name _____

Plot and label each point on the coordinate grid at the right.

1. $A(2, 0)$ 2. $B(1, 4)$

3. $C(0, -4)$ 4. $D(-4, -1)$

5. $E(-3, 2)$ 6. $F(3, -1)$

Find the coordinates of each point.

7. G ___ $(2, -2)$ ___   8. I ___ $(2, 4)$ ___

9. L ___ $(-3, 4)$ ___   10. M ___ $(-3, 0)$ ___

11. P ___ $(-2, -4)$ ___   12. Q ___ $(1, -4)$ ___

Name the point for each ordered pair.

13. $(4, -2)$ ___ R ___   14. $(0, 1)$ ___ J ___

15. $(-2, 2)$ ___ K ___   16. $(1, 3)$ ___ S ___

17. $(-2, -1)$ ___ N ___   18. $(3, 1)$ ___ H ___

19. **Geometry** Name the ordered pairs for the vertices of the figures.
   ___ $(4, 1), (1, 4), (-2, 4), (-3, 3), (-3, -2),$ ___
   ___ $(-1, -4), (2, -4), (4, -2)$ ___

Geography Using the map, estimate the approximate coordinates of the following capitol cities.

20. Daker, Senegal

   latitude ___ About 15° N ___

   longitude ___ About 17° W ___

21. Abidjan, Ivory Coast

   latitude ___ About 3° N ___

   longitude ___ About 4° W ___

Powers and Exponents

Name _____

Geometry A shortcut to finding the area of a square is to square the length of a side. Find each area.

1. ___ $25\ cm^2$ ___ (5 cm × 5 cm)
2. ___ $100\ in^2$ ___ (10 in. × 10 in.)
3. ___ $49\ m^2$ ___ (7 m × 7 m)
4. ___ $144\ ft^2$ ___ (12 ft × 12 ft)

Geometry A shortcut to finding the volume of a cube is to cube the length of a side. Find each volume.

5. ___ $512\ ft^3$ ___ (8 ft)
6. ___ $64\ mm^3$ ___ (4 mm)
7. ___ $1000\ in^3$ ___ (10 in.)
8. ___ $8000\ m^3$ ___ (20 m)

Evaluate.

9. 3^5 ___ 243 ___   10. -2^4 ___ -16 ___   11. $(-2)^4$ ___ 16 ___   12. $(-2)^5$ ___ -32 ___

13. -2^5 ___ -32 ___   14. 7^3 ___ 343 ___   15. 15^2 ___ 225 ___   16. $(-8)^2$ ___ 64 ___

17. $(-7)^0$ ___ 1 ___   18. 4^5 ___ 1024 ___   19. $(-17)^1$ ___ -17 ___   20. -25^2 ___ -625 ___

21. $3^4 + 5^6$ ___ 15,706 ___   22. $8^2 - 3^3$ ___ 37 ___   23. $15 + 3^7$ ___ 2202 ___   24. $1^5 - 2^4$ ___ -15 ___

25. $(3^3 + 4^4 + 5^5) \div 4^2$ ___ 213 ___   26. $3(5 - 7)^5 + 8^0$ ___ -95 ___   27. $(8 + 4)^2 \times (8 - 3)^3$ ___ 18,000 ___

28. A gray whale can weigh more than 3^{10} pounds. Write 3^{10} in standard form. ___ 59,049 ___

Scientific Notation Using Positive Exponents

Name _____

Social Science Exercises 1–6 give approximate 1993 populations.

Write each population in scientific notation.

1. California: 31 million   2. N. Dakota: 635 thousand   3. Rhode Island: 1.0 million

   ___ 3.1×10^7 ___   ___ 6.35×10^5 ___   ___ 1.0×10^6 ___

Write each population in standard notation.

4. Utah: 1.9×10^6 5. Alaska: 5.99×10^5 6. Pennsylvania: 1.2×10^7

   ___ 1,900,000 ___   ___ 599,000 ___   ___ 12,000,000 ___

Write each calculator display in standard notation.

7. `8.375   E 14`   8. `-3.4   E 8`

   ___ 837,500,000,000,000 ___   ___ $-340,000,000$ ___

9. `9.0207   12`   10. `-7.23   11`

   ___ 9,020,700,000,000 ___   ___ $-723,000,000,000$ ___

Without actually calculating, tell which number in each pair is greater. Explain.

11. 3.87×10^{12} or 3.9×10^{12}
   ___ 3.9×10^{12}, since $3.9 > 3.87$ and the exponents are the same ___

12. 2.1×10^{11} or 8.9×10^{10}
   ___ 2.1×10^{11}, since $2.1 \times 10^{11} > 10^{11} > 8.9 \times 10^{10}$ ___

13. Two of the wealthiest American families are the DuPont family, with assets estimated at $\$1.5 \times 10^{11}$, and the Walton retailing family, with assets estimated at $\$2.35 \times 10^{10}$. Find the combined net worth of the two families. Show how you found this.
   ___ $1.5 \times 10^{11} + 2.35 \times 10^{10} = 1.5 \times 10^{11} + 0.235 \times 10^{11} =$ ___
   ___ $(1.5 + 0.235) \times 10^{11} = 1.735 \times 10^{11}$, or about \$174 billion ___

Practice 2-9

Scientific Notation Using Negative Exponents

Write each number in scientific notation.

1. five billionths
5×10^{-9}

2. forty-seven thousandths
4.7×10^{-2}

3. eighteen hundredths
1.8×10^{-1}

4. two hundred thirty-seven millionths
2.37×10^{-4}

5. eighty-two billionths
8.2×10^{-8}

6. five hundred three thousandths
5.03×10^{-1}

Science These are the approximate masses or weights of atoms. Write each in scientific notation.

7. bismuth: 0.000000000000000000347 mg
3.47×10^{-19} mg

8. hydrogen: 0.00000000000000000000000000394 lb
3.94×10^{-27} lb

9. oxygen: 0.00000000000000000000000266 g
2.66×10^{-23} g

Measurement Write these very small amounts in standard notation.

10. second: 3.17×10^{-8} year
0.0000000317 year

11. angstrom: 10^{-10} meter
0.0000000001 meter

12. centimeter: 6.214×10^{-6} mile
0.000006214 mile

13. mile: 1.701×10^{-13} light-year
0.0000000000001701 light-year

Write each of these calculator displays in standard notation.

14. `3.47    -9`
0.00000000347

15. `-8.62    -11`
−0.0000000000862

16. `1.003  E -5`
0.00001003

17. In 1926, Alfred McEwen set a world record for small writing. He wrote 56 words in a space of area 0.00000128 square inches. Write 0.00000128 in scientific notation.
1.28×10^{-6}

Practice

Section 2B Review

Plot and label the following points. What quadrant is each point in?

1. $A(0, -2)$; quadrant None
2. $B(-3, 4)$; quadrant II
3. $C(2, -3)$; quadrant IV
4. $D(1, 3)$; quadrant I

Geography Using the map, locate the approximate latitude and longitude of these cities.

5. Pittsburgh, PA
latitude 40.5° N
longitude 80.0° W

6. Baltimore, MD
latitude 39.3° N
longitude 76.6° W

Find the area or volume of the following.

7. area 36 units^2

8. volume 729 units^3

Write each number in scientific notation.

9. In 1990, about 64,000 Native Americans lived in Texas.
6.4×10^4

10. One ounce is equal to 0.00003125 ton.
3.125×10^{-5}

Write each of these calculator displays in standard notation.

11. `4.25    E -8`
0.0000000425

12. `-3.8      14`
−380,000,000,000,000

13. `6.25    -10`
0.000000000625

14. Put these numbers in order from smallest to largest.
b., c., a., d.

a. 4.23×10^4 **b.** 9.37×10^{-4} **c.** 38,000 **d.** 4.23×10^5

15. The Carson family has three dogs and two cats. Each dog weighs 46 pounds and each cat weighs 16 pounds. Write an expression for the mean weight of the five animals. Evaluate the expression to find the mean weight. *[Lesson 2-5]*
$\dfrac{3 \times 46 + 2 \times 16}{5} = 34$ pounds

Practice

Cumulative Review Chapters 1–2

1. State the range and draw a line plot for the data set. *[Lesson 1-1]*

Jose asked passengers on his bus how many hours they worked that day. Their answers were 8, 9, 8, 6, 8, 4, 8, 7, 2, 0, 8, and 6

0 to 9, or 9

Hours of work

Find the mean, median, and mode(s) for each data set. *[Lesson 1-2]*

2. 12, 18, 16, 14, 13, 20, 15, 16, 19
mean About 15.89
median 16
mode(s) 16

3. 83, 77, 128, 63, 92, 77, 101, 118
mean About 92.38
median 87.5
mode(s) 77

Add or subtract. *[Lessons 2-2, 2-3]*

4. $7 + (-8)$ −1
5. $8 - (-3)$ 11
6. $7 + (-18)$ −11
7. $-15 - 3$ −18
8. $24 + (-8)$ 16
9. $35 - (-21)$ 56
10. $-21 - (-5)$ −16
11. $16 + (-18)$ −2
12. $38 + (-18)$ 20

Evaluate each expression two different ways. *[Lesson 2-5]*

13. $5(3 + 7)$
$5 \cdot 10 = 50$
$15 + 35 = 50$

14. $6(-8 - 4)$
$6(-12) = -72$
$-48 - 24 = -72$

15. $-3(5 + 3)$
$-3(8) = -24$
$-15 + (-9) = -24$

Plot and label each point.

16. $A(-3, -1)$
17. $B(0, -2)$
18. $C(1, 4)$
19. $D(4, 2)$
20. $E(-4, 1)$
21. $F(3, -3)$

Practice 3-1

Formulas and Variables

Solve each formula for the values given. The purpose of the formula is given.

1. $d = rt$, for $r = 25$ and $t = 3$ (*Distance*, given *rate* and *time*)
$d =$ 75

2. $P = 4s$, for $s = 11$ (*Perimeter* of a square, given *side length*)
$P =$ 44

3. $K = C + 273$, for $C = 37$
(*Kelvin* temperature, given *Celsius* temperature)
$K =$ 310

4. $S = 180(n - 2)$, for $n = 7$
(*Sum* of the angles, given *number* of sides)
$S =$ 900

5. $m = \frac{a + b + c}{3}$, for $a = 11.2$, $b = 12.3$, and $c = 11.9$
(*Mean*, given *three values*)
$m =$ 11.8

6. $A = \pi r^2$, for $r = 8.5$; use 3.14 for π
(*Area* of a circle, given *radius*)
$A =$ 226.865

7. $P = 2b + 2h$, for $b = 3\frac{1}{8}$ and $h = 4\frac{1}{2}$
(*Perimeter* of a rectangle, given *base* and *height*)
$P =$ 15.25

8. $V = \frac{1}{3}Bh$, for $B = 17$ and $h = 12$
(*Volume* of a pyramid, given *base area* and *height*)
$V =$ 68

9. $A = 2(\ell w + wh + \ell h)$, for $\ell = 8$, $w = 5$, and $h = 3$ (*Surface area* of a rectangular prism, given *length*, *width*, and *height*)
$A =$ 158

10. $C = \frac{5}{9}(F - 32)$, for $F = 77$
(*Celsius* temperature, given *Fahrenheit* temperature)
$C =$ 25

11. $T = 0.0825p$, for $p = \$160.00$ (*Tax*, given *price*)
$T =$ \$13.20

12. $F = ma$, for $m = 12$ and $a = 9.8$
(*Force*, given *mass* and *acceleration*)
$F =$ 117.6

13. In 1989, Dutch ice skater Dries van Wijhe skated 200 km at an average speed of 35.27 km/hr. How long was he skating?
About 5.67 hr

14. **Career** A roofer calculates his bid price using the formula $P = 1.85s + 4.2f$, where s is the area of the roof in square feet and f is the length of the fascia in feet. Find the price for a roof with area 1800 square feet and 190 feet of fascia.
\$4128

Algebraic Expressions and Equations

Evaluate each expression. Remember that operations within parentheses should be done first.

1. $5y + 3x$, for $x = 7$ and $y = 6$
____51____

2. $10(x - 5)$, for $x = 3$
____−20____

3. $2y - 17$, for $y = 21$
____25____

4. $20 - \frac{3}{4}x$, for $x = 16$
____8____

5. $(3x - 2)y$, for $x = -8$ and $y = -5$
____130____

6. $(3x + 4y) \cdot 8$, for $x = 10$ and $y = -2$
____176____

Solve each equation.

7. $3 + z = 18$
$z =$ __15__

8. $k - 7 = 10$
$k =$ __17__

9. $3d = 12$
$d =$ __4__

10. $j = 9(-8 + 3)$
$j =$ __−45__

11. $p = \frac{2 + 7}{-3}$
$p =$ __−3__

12. $y + 8 = 30$
$y =$ __22__

13. $-2g = 6$
$g =$ __−3__

14. $u = 4(-15)$
$u =$ __−60__

15. $5t = 35$
$t =$ __7__

16. $h = 3(8 + 3)$
$h =$ __33__

17. $w - 5 = -10$
$w =$ __−5__

18. $s = \frac{8 + (-4)}{2}$
$s =$ __2__

19. Geometry Each angle of a regular polygon can be found using the expression $\frac{180(n - 2)}{n}$, where n is the number of sides. A nonagon has 9 sides. Find the measure of each angle in a regular nonagon. __140°__

20. Technology Complete the table showing the rents collected in an apartment complex. Entries in column D are obtained by multiplying columns B and C.

	A	B	C	D
1	Unit Type	Number of Units	Unit Rent	Total Rent
2	Efficiency	14	$520	$7,280
3	1-bedroom	28	$595	$16,660
4	2-bedroom	18	$695	$12,510

Use with pages 127–131. **25**

Writing Algebraic Expressions

Write an expression for each situation.

1. the number of corners on c cubes _____$8c$_____

2. the number of gallons in h half-gallon containers _____$\frac{h}{2}$_____

3. the number of cans in s six-packs of soda _____$6s$_____

4. the number of fingers on p people _____$10p$_____

5. To square a number ending with 5, multiply 5 less than the number by 5 more than the number, and then add 25. Write an expression or equation for this situation.

Answers will vary. Possible formula: $x^2 = (x - 5)(x + 5) + 25$

Write a formula for each situation. Then solve for two values and explain the solution in terms of the problem situation.

6. Science To find the force on a certain spring, multiply the displacement by 12.

Answers will vary. Possible formula: $F = 12x$

7. Consumer To find the cost of ordering shirts by mail, multiply the number of shirts by $22.50 and then add $6.75 for shipping and handling.

Answers will vary. Possible formula: $P = \$22.50x + \$6.75$

8. Geometry To find the approximate surface area of a sphere, find the square of the radius and multiply by 12.57.

Answers will vary. Possible formula: $SA = 12.57r^2$

9. Accounting To find the 1995 federal income tax of a single person earning between $23,350 and $56,550, multiply 0.28 times the amount of income over $23,350, and then add $3502.50.

Answers will vary. Possible formula:
$T = 0.28(x - \$23,350) + \$3502.50$

26 Use with pages 132–136.

Section 3A Review

Evaluate each formula for the values given.

1. $V = \ell wh$, for $\ell = 11$, $w = 8$, and $h = 9$ $V =$ ____792____

2. $F = 1.8C + 32$, for $C = 27$ $F =$ ____80.6____

3. The speed limit on many freeways is 55 mi/hr. How far can you travel in 4 hours at this speed? ____220 mi____

Evaluate each expression.

4. $15x - 4y$ for $x = 8$ and $y = 12$
____72____

5. $10y(x + 7)$ for $x = 4$ and $y = 2$
____220____

Solve each equation. Use number sense or "guess and check."

6. $x + 2 = 20$
$x =$ __18__

7. $y - 5 = 10$
$y =$ __15__

8. $u = 4(3 + 2)$
$u =$ __20__

9. $c = -5 \cdot 11$
$c =$ __−55__

10. $3a = 21$
$a =$ __7__

11. $n = \frac{42}{-7}$
$n =$ __−6__

12. $\frac{t}{5} = 8$
$t =$ __40__

13. $p = \frac{100}{18 + 2}$
$p =$ __5__

Write an expression for each situation.

14. the number of wings on b birds ____$2b$____

15. the number of centimeters in m meters ____$100m$____

16. A mountain climber started one morning at an altitude of 6380 ft and began to climb to higher altitudes at a rate of 1500 ft per hour.

a. Write an expression to find her height after t hours. ____$6380 + 1500t$____

b. What was her height after $3\frac{1}{2}$ hours? ____11,630 ft____

17. Suppose you wanted to draw a graph showing the ages of all people living on your street. Which would be better, a line plot or a histogram? Explain. *[Lesson 1-6]*

Possible answer: A histogram would be more practical due to the large range of the data.

Use with page 138. **27**

Solving Equations by Adding or Subtracting

What is the next step in solving each equation?

1. $x + 7 = 39$
__Subtract 7 from each side.__

2. $x - 4 = 13$
__Add 4 to each side.__

3. $-4 = x + 17$
__Subtract 17 from each side.__

4. $3 = x - 12$
__Add 12 to each side.__

Solve each equation. Check your solution.

5. $t - 4 = 17$
$t =$ __21__

6. $-14 = r - 5$
$r =$ __−9__

7. $s + 9 = -13$
$s =$ __−22__

8. $7 = w - 15$
$w =$ __22__

9. $11 = k + 25$
$k =$ __−14__

10. $e - 5 = -13$
$e =$ __−8__

11. $b + 17 = 31$
$b =$ __14__

12. $y - 21 = -4$
$y =$ __17__

13. $8.3 = j + 2.7$
$j =$ __5.6__

14. $a - 8.1 = 3.6$
$a =$ __11.7__

15. $8 = n - 4.9$
$n =$ __12.9__

16. $3.8 = m + 9.7$
$m =$ __−5.9__

17. $v - 18.4 = 3.9$
$v =$ __22.3__

18. $f + 8.7 = 9.3$
$f =$ __0.6__

19. $z - 4.6 = 12.7$
$z =$ __17.3__

20. $c + 21.9 = 8.4$
$c =$ __−13.5__

21. $10 = q - 4\frac{1}{2}$
$q =$ __$14\frac{1}{2}$__

22. $u - \frac{2}{3} = 21$
$u =$ __$21\frac{2}{3}$__

23. $h + \frac{1}{2} = 5\frac{1}{4}$
$h =$ __$4\frac{3}{4}$__

24. $x - 3\frac{1}{8} = 21$
$x =$ __$24\frac{1}{8}$__

25. $d + 17 = 4$
$d =$ __−13__

26. $g - 2\frac{1}{2} = 7$
$g =$ __$9\frac{1}{2}$__

27. $8 = p + \frac{1}{3}$
$p =$ __$7\frac{2}{3}$__

28. $w - 8\frac{1}{2} = 23$
$w =$ __$31\frac{1}{2}$__

29. Consumer In 1996, Pacific Gas and Electric offered customers a $150 rebate on the purchase of an efficient washing machine. If the machine cost $849 with the rebate, how much would it cost without the rebate? ____$999____

30. The formula $K = C + 273$ relates Kelvin temperature, K, to Celsius temperature, C. What Celsius temperature is equivalent to 287° Kelvin? ____14°C____

28 Use with pages 140–144.

Practice 3-5

Name _____

Solving Equations by Multiplying or Dividing

Solve each equation.

1. $5n = 40$

$n = \underline{8}$

2. $10c = 120$

$c = \underline{12}$

3. $7g = 28$

$g = \underline{4}$

4. $15x = 180$

$x = \underline{12}$

5. $6f = 84$

$f = \underline{14}$

6. $\frac{1}{2}s = 21$

$s = \underline{42}$

7. $4r = 12$

$r = \underline{3}$

8. $9k = 63$

$k = \underline{7}$

9. $\frac{1}{5}u = 17$

$u = \underline{85}$

10. $\frac{h}{3} = 17$

$h = \underline{51}$

11. $\frac{b}{17} = 7$

$b = \underline{119}$

12. $\frac{s}{20} = 11$

$s = \underline{220}$

13. $\frac{3}{4}t = 81$

$t = \underline{108}$

14. $3a = 33$

$a = \underline{11}$

15. $13q = 78$

$q = \underline{6}$

16. $\frac{2}{3}m = 42$

$m = \underline{63}$

17. $\frac{x}{4} = 35$

$x = \underline{140}$

18. $\frac{d}{7} = 15$

$d = \underline{105}$

19. $\frac{1}{4}z = 21$

$z = \underline{84}$

20. $\frac{u}{8} = 13$

$u = \underline{104}$

21. $7r = 91$

$r = \underline{13}$

22. $11e = 99$

$e = \underline{9}$

23. $8w = 40$

$w = \underline{5}$

24. $16d = 144$

$d = \underline{9}$

25. $12d = 180$

$d = \underline{15}$

26. $\frac{1}{3}n = 24$

$n = \underline{72}$

27. $\frac{3}{5}h = 45$

$h = \underline{75}$

28. $20k = 150$

$k = \underline{7.5}$

29. $\frac{1}{6}x = 7$

$x = \underline{42}$

30. $\frac{a}{5} = 24$

$a = \underline{120}$

31. $\frac{u}{7} = 12$

$u = \underline{84}$

32. $\frac{m}{10} = 6.1$

$m = \underline{61}$

33. Accounting In 1995, the federal income tax for married couples earning less than $39,000 was 0.15 times the taxable income. If the Jacksons paid $4054 in federal income tax, what was their taxable income?

About $27,027

34. A box of oatmeal has instructions to use $\frac{1}{3}$ cup of oats for each serving. Han used 4 cups of oats. How many servings did he make?

12

Practice 3-6

Name _____

Solving Two-Step Equations

Solve each equation.

1. $6x + 5 = -19$

$x = \underline{-4}$

2. $2x + 12 = 24$

$x = \underline{6}$

3. $15x - 9 = 21$

$x = \underline{2}$

4. $5x - 11 = -36$

$x = \underline{-5}$

5. $18x - 6 = 84$

$x = \underline{5}$

6. $9x + 2.3 = -10.3$

$x = \underline{-1.4}$

7. $11x + 4 = -29$

$x = \underline{-3}$

8. $8x + 15 = 71$

$x = \underline{7}$

9. $\frac{1}{2}x + 3 = 5$

$x = \underline{4}$

10. $\frac{x}{6} - 7 = 3$

$x = \underline{60}$

11. $\frac{1}{4}x + 10 = -7$

$x = \underline{-68}$

12. $\frac{x}{9} - 15 = 5$

$x = \underline{180}$

13. $12x + 7 = 139$

$x = \underline{11}$

14. $3x - 8 = 55$

$x = \underline{21}$

15. $7x - 5.8 = 13.1$

$x = \underline{2.7}$

16. $4x + 13 = 61$

$x = \underline{12}$

17. $\frac{x}{8} - 7 = -12$

$x = \underline{-40}$

18. $\frac{1}{5}x + 8 = -2$

$x = \underline{-50}$

19. $\frac{n}{11} + 2 = 6$

$n = \underline{44}$

20. $\frac{x}{7} - 9 = -4$

$x = \underline{35}$

21. $20n - 2 = 138$

$n = \underline{7}$

22. $10x - 3 = -83$

$x = \underline{-8}$

23. $8x - 3.2 = 37.6$

$x = \underline{5.1}$

24. $12x - 10 = -130$

$x = \underline{-10}$

25. $\frac{w}{10} - 11 = 6$

$w = \underline{170}$

26. $\frac{1}{3}x + 3 = -9$

$x = \underline{-36}$

27. $\frac{u}{12} + 4 = 8$

$u = \underline{48}$

28. $\frac{x}{25} - 8 = -3$

$x = \underline{125}$

29. The Drama Club's production of "Oklahoma!" is going to cost $1250 to produce. How many tickets will they need to sell for $8 each in order to make a profit of $830?

260

30. Consumer In 1995, the monthly cost to use America Online was $9.95 (including the first 5 hours of usage), plus $2.95 for each additional hour. Phil paid $30.60 in March.

a. Let x be the number of "additional" hours that Phil used. Write and solve an equation to find x.

$9.95 + 2.95x = 30.6; \; x = 7$

b. How many hours did Phil use America Online in March?

12 hours

Practice 3-7

Name _____

Solving Inequalities

Write an inequality for each graph.

1. $u > 0$

$-4\ -3\ -2\ -1\ 0\ 1\ 2\ 3\ 4$

2. $x < -2$

$-4\ -3\ -2\ -1\ 0\ 1\ 2\ 3\ 4$

3. $r \geq 1$

$-4\ -3\ -2\ -1\ 0\ 1\ 2\ 3\ 4$

4. $t \geq -3$

$-4\ -3\ -2\ -1\ 0\ 1\ 2\ 3\ 4$

5. $y \leq 2$

$-4\ -3\ -2\ -1\ 0\ 1\ 2\ 3\ 4$

6. $k < -1$

$-4\ -3\ -2\ -1\ 0\ 1\ 2\ 3\ 4$

Determine whether -3 is a solution for each inequality.

7. $x + 3 \geq 0$

Yes

8. $2x < -4$

Yes

9. $-3x < 9$

No

10. $x - 5 \geq 8$

No

Solve each inequality. Graph the solution.

11. $x + 8 \leq 10$ $\quad x \leq 2$

$-4\ -3\ -2\ -1\ 0\ 1\ 2\ 3\ 4$

12. $y - 5 > -6$ $\quad y > -1$

$-4\ -3\ -2\ -1\ 0\ 1\ 2\ 3\ 4$

13. $8h < 16$ $\quad h < 2$

$-4\ -3\ -2\ -1\ 0\ 1\ 2\ 3\ 4$

14. $7f \geq 21$ $\quad f \geq 3$

$-4\ -3\ -2\ -1\ 0\ 1\ 2\ 3\ 4$

15. $6n > 6$ $\quad n > 1$

$-4\ -3\ -2\ -1\ 0\ 1\ 2\ 3\ 4$

16. $3r + 5 > 5$ $\quad r > 0$

$-4\ -3\ -2\ -1\ 0\ 1\ 2\ 3\ 4$

17. $2t - 3 \leq 5$ $\quad t \leq 4$

$-4\ -3\ -2\ -1\ 0\ 1\ 2\ 3\ 4$

18. $3k + 5 < 10$ $\quad k < \frac{5}{3}$

$-4\ -3\ -2\ -1\ 0\ 1\ 2\ 3\ 4$

19. $4c + 20 \geq 9$ $\quad c \geq -\frac{11}{4}$

$-4\ -3\ -2\ -1\ 0\ 1\ 2\ 3\ 4$

20. A rental car costs $25.00 per day, plus $0.30 per mile. Dan wants to know how far he can drive each day and still keep his cost under $85.00 per day. Help him by solving $0.3x + 25 < 85$.

$x < 200$ mi

21. The volume of a pyramid is given by $\frac{1}{3}Bh$, where B is the area of the base and h is the height. Zelda is making a solid pyramid out of modeling clay. The base is to be a 5 in. by 5 in. square, and she has 50 in³ of clay available. Solve $\frac{1}{3} \cdot 5^2 \cdot h < 50$ to find the possible heights of her pyramid.

$h < 6$ in.

Practice

Name _____

Section 3B Review

Solve each equation.

1. $y + 7 = 24$

$y = \underline{17}$

2. $g - 10 = -3$

$g = \underline{7}$

3. $x + 5.7 = 8.3$

$x = \underline{2.6}$

4. $t - 7\frac{3}{8} = 2\frac{1}{4}$

$t = \underline{9\frac{5}{8}}$

5. $18c = 90$

$c = \underline{5}$

6. $\frac{u}{12} = 7$

$u = \underline{84}$

7. $1.3k = 7.93$

$k = \underline{6.1}$

8. $\frac{s}{7.81} = 11$

$s = \underline{85.91}$

9. $5n - 8 = -18$

$n = \underline{-2}$

10. $3p + 15 = 36$

$p = \underline{7}$

11. $\frac{3}{5}z - 14 = 25$

$z = \underline{65}$

12. $20r - 5 = 9$

$r = \underline{\frac{7}{10}}$

13. Blazin' Bakery has a jar of cookie samples on the counter. Each cookie sample weighs 0.75 oz, and the jar weighs 27 oz. If the total weight is 45.75 oz, how many cookie samples are in the jar?

25

Solve and graph each inequality.

14. $m - 5 < -4$

$m < 1$

$-4\ -3\ -2\ -1\ 0\ 1\ 2\ 3\ 4$

15. $g + 7 \geq 10$

$g \geq 3$

$-4\ -3\ -2\ -1\ 0\ 1\ 2\ 3\ 4$

16. $8d > -24$

$d > -3$

$-4\ -3\ -2\ -1\ 0\ 1\ 2\ 3\ 4$

17. $5t \leq 12$

$t \leq \frac{12}{5}$

$-4\ -3\ -2\ -1\ 0\ 1\ 2\ 3\ 4$

18. $3a + 4 > 13$

$a > 3$

$-4\ -3\ -2\ -1\ 0\ 1\ 2\ 3\ 4$

19. $4u - 7 < 3$

$u < \frac{5}{2}$

$-4\ -3\ -2\ -1\ 0\ 1\ 2\ 3\ 4$

20. Tien's library allows her to check out a maximum of 10 books at a time. She has selected 3 history books and 4 science fiction novels she wants to read. Solve $3 + 4 + x \leq 10$ to find how many additional books she might check out.

$x \leq 3$

21. Ardeshir bought 4 pints of ice cream for $1.65 each and 2 cans of baked beans for $0.83 each. He also redeemed 3 coupons for $0.20 each. How much did he spend? *[Lesson 2-5]*

$7.66

22. The area of a typical postage stamp is about 0.00000000022 mi². Write this number in scientific notation. *[Lesson 2-9]*

2.2×10^{-10}

Cumulative Review Chapters 1–3

1. The data gives the number of dogs and cats in animal shelters in Roverton. Create a scatterplot and draw a trend line. *[Lesson 1-7]*

Dogs	13	27	41	35	21
Cats	7	10	28	23	16

Multiply or divide. *[Lesson 2-4]*

2. $-3 \cdot 4$ **3.** $52 \div (-4)$ **4.** $-8(-5)$ **5.** $126 \div (-18)$

$\underline{-12}$ $\underline{-13}$ $\underline{40}$ $\underline{-7}$

6. $-135 \div 9$ **7.** $11 \cdot (-4)$ **8.** $-96 \div 8$ **9.** $-7 \cdot 8$

$\underline{-15}$ $\underline{-44}$ $\underline{-12}$ $\underline{-56}$

Write each number using an exponent. *[Lesson 2-7]*

10. $8 \cdot 8 \cdot 8 \cdot 8$ **11.** $-2 \cdot (-2)$ **12.** $7 \cdot 7 \cdot 7$ **13.** $-13 \cdot (-13)$

$\underline{8^4}$ $\underline{(-2)^2}$ $\underline{7^3}$ $\underline{(-13)^2}$

Write an expression for each situation. *[Lesson 3-3]*

14. the number of sides in k rectangles $\underline{4k}$

15. the number of legs on d dogs $\underline{4d}$

16. the number of weeks in x days $\underline{\frac{x}{7}}$

Solve each inequality. Graph the solution. *[Lesson 3-7]*

17. $3x > -6$ **18.** $2p - 4 \le 3$ **19.** $8w - 5 < -13$

$\underline{x > -2}$ $\underline{p \le \frac{7}{2}}$ $\underline{w < -1}$

Understanding Two-Variable Relationships

Find the value of y when $x = 7$ in each of the following equations.

1. $y = 10x$ **2.** $y = x - 4$ **3.** $y = 14x$ **4.** $y = x + 23$

$\underline{70}$ $\underline{3}$ $\underline{98}$ $\underline{30}$

Complete each table of values.

5.
x	0	1	2	3	4	5
y = x + 5	5	6	7	8	9	10

6.
x	0	1	2	3	4	5
y = 4x	0	4	8	12	16	20

7.
x	0	1	2	3	4	5
y = x - 7	-7	-6	-5	-4	-3	-2

8.
x	0	1	2	3	4	5
y = -8x	0	-8	-16	-24	-32	-40

Make a table of values for each equation. Use 0, 1, 2, 3, 4, and 5.

9. $y = x + 10$ **10.** $y = -3x$

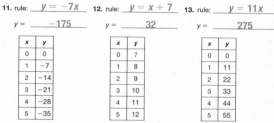

x	0	1	2	3	4	5
y	10	11	12	13	14	15

x	0	1	2	3	4	5
y	0	-3	-6	-9	-12	-15

Find a rule that relates x and y in each table. Then find y when $x = 25$.

11. rule: $\underline{y = -7x}$ **12.** rule: $\underline{y = x + 7}$ **13.** rule: $\underline{y = 11x}$

$y = \underline{-175}$ $y = \underline{32}$ $y = \underline{275}$

x	y
0	0
1	-7
2	-14
3	-21
4	-28
5	-35

x	y
0	7
1	8
2	9
3	10
4	11
5	12

x	y
0	0
1	11
2	22
3	33
4	44
5	55

14. Science Every spider has 8 legs. Make a table relating the number of spiders to the number of legs.

Spiders	0	1	2	3	4	5
Legs	0	8	16	24	32	40

Solutions of Two-Variable Equations

Determine whether each ordered pair is a solution of the equation.

1. $y = x + 9$ **a.** $(4, 13)$ **b.** $(5, -4)$ **c.** $(-8, 1)$

$\underline{Yes}$ $\underline{No}$ $\underline{Yes}$

2. $y = 4x$ **a.** $(3, 12)$ **b.** $(16, 4)$ **c.** $(6, 10)$

$\underline{Yes}$ $\underline{No}$ $\underline{No}$

3. $y = -\frac{1}{3}x$ **a.** $(-3, 9)$ **b.** $(6, -2)$ **c.** $(-15, -5)$

$\underline{No}$ $\underline{Yes}$ $\underline{No}$

4. $x = y + 4$ **a.** $(-2, 2)$ **b.** $(-2, -6)$ **c.** $(12, 8)$

$\underline{No}$ $\underline{Yes}$ $\underline{Yes}$

5. $x + 2y = 10$ **a.** $(2, 8)$ **b.** $(4, 3)$ **c.** $(3, 4)$

$\underline{No}$ $\underline{Yes}$ $\underline{No}$

Give two solution pairs for each equation.   **Possible answers**

6. $y = x + 8$ **7.** $y = x - 3$ **8.** $y = 7x$

$\underline{(2, 10), (3, 11)}$ $\underline{(2, -1), (3, 0)}$ $\underline{(2, 14), (3, 21)}$

9. $y = 3x - 2$ **10.** $y = \frac{1}{4}x + 8$ **11.** $y = -3x + 7$

$\underline{(2, 4), (3, 7)}$ $\underline{(0, 8), (4, 9)}$ $\underline{(0, 7), (1, 4)}$

12. $x - y = 5$ **13.** $2x + y = 11$ **14.** $x - 4y = 10$

$\underline{(5, 0), (6, 1)}$ $\underline{(3, 5), (4, 3)}$ $\underline{(10, 0), (14, 1)}$

15. The equation $y = 0.23x + 0.09$ gives the cost, in dollars, of mailing a letter weighing x ounces, where x is a positive integer. Make a table showing the number of ounces and the price, for letters weighing 1 to 6 ounces.

Weight (oz)	1	2	3	4	5	6
Price ($)	0.32	0.55	0.78	1.01	1.24	1.47

Graphing Two-Variable Relationships

Graph each equation. Use 0, 1, 2, and 3 as x-values.

1. $y = x - 2$ **2.** $y = -\frac{1}{3}x$ **3.** $y = -x + 1$

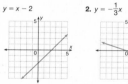

4. $y = \frac{1}{2}x + \frac{3}{2}$ **5.** $y = 3x - 4$ **6.** $y = -2x + 3$

Graph the ordered pairs in each table. Connect the points to determine if the graphs are linear. Write linear or not linear.

7. $\underline{Not\ linear}$ **8.** $\underline{Linear}$

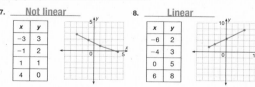

x	y
-3	3
-1	2
1	1
4	0

x	y
-6	2
-4	3
0	5
6	8

9. Consumer Adeshima plans to order some fabric from a mail-order catalog. The price is $0.75 per yard, plus $2.00 for shipping. Use x for the number of yards, and y for the price she will pay. Graph the price that she will pay.

Section 4A Review

Find the value of y for $x = -4$ in each equation.

1. $y = x + 21$ **2.** $y = x - 5$ **3.** $y = -\frac{3}{4}x$ **4.** $y - x = 5$

    17   −9   3   1

5. Make a table of values for the equation $y = -1.5x + 3$. Use 0, 1, 2, 3, and 4 as x-values.

x	0	1	2	3	4
y	3	1.5	0	−1.5	−3

Determine whether each ordered pair is a solution of the equation.

6. $y = x - 3$ **a.** (2, 5)   No   **b.** (−4, −7)   Yes

7. $y = -10x$ **a.** (30, −3)   No   **b.** (−4, 40)   Yes

8. a. Find a rule that relates x and y in the table. $y = x - 8$

x	0	1	2	3	4	5
y	−8	−7	−6	−5	−4	−3

   b. Find the value of y when $x = 32$.   24

Graph each equation.

9. $y = -x - 2$ **10.** $y = 3x + 2$ **11.** $y = \frac{1}{2}x - 1$

12. In 1994, the top ten best selling prerecorded videos sold 27.0, 21.5, 12.0, 11.5, 9.1, 8.2, 7.5, 5.2, 5.1, and 4.2 million copies, respectively. Make a box-and-whisker plot showing the number of millions of videos sold. [Lesson 1-3]

13. The sum of the natural numbers 1 through n is given by $\frac{1}{2}n(n + 1)$. Find the sum of the natural numbers 1 through 85. [Lesson 3-2]   3655

Understanding Slope

Give the slope of each of these items.

1. $\dfrac{6}{7}$ **2.** $-\dfrac{3}{4}$ **3.** $\dfrac{7}{5}$

Find the slope of each line on the graph.

4. Line through A and B 0

5. Line through B and C 1

6. Line through B and D $\frac{3}{2}$

7. Line through A and E $-\frac{1}{3}$

Draw a line through the origin with each of the given slopes.

8. −1   **9.** $\frac{2}{3}$ **10.** 4

11. The steepest street in the world is Baldwin St. in Dunedin, New Zealand, which rises 1 m in a horizontal distance of 1.266 m. Find the slope of Baldwin St. Round to the nearest hundredth if necessary.   0.79

12. **Industry** A roofing manufacturer says its product is suitable for roofs that rise at least $2\frac{1}{2}$ in. for every 12 horizontal in. What is the minimum positive slope of a roof that can use this product? $\frac{5}{24}$

Patterns in Linear Equations and Graphs

For each line, find the slope, the x-intercept, and the y-intercept.

1. Line through A and B **2.** Line through B and C

slope: $-\frac{1}{2}$ slope: 3

x-intercept: 4 x-intercept: $-\frac{2}{3}$

y-intercept: 2 y-intercept: 2

3. Line through C and D **4.** Line through A and D

slope: $-\frac{1}{2}$ slope: −1

x-intercept: −3 x-intercept: 0

y-intercept: $-\frac{3}{2}$ y-intercept: 0

5. Which lines in Exercises 1–4 are parallel? Explain.

1 and 3
They have the same slope.

Graph each equation. Find the slope, the x-intercept, and the y-intercept.

6. $y = -x + 2$ **7.** $y = \frac{1}{2}x + 3$ **8.** $y = 2x - 4$

slope: −1   slope: $\frac{1}{2}$ slope: 2

x-intercept: 2 x-intercept: −6 x-intercept: 2

y-intercept: 2 y-intercept: 3 y-intercept: −4

9. Which lines in Exercises 6–8 are parallel? Explain.

None. The lines all have different slopes.

Pairs of Linear Equations

Solve each system of equations by graphing.

1. $y = x + 2$
$y = 2x + 1$
Solution: (1, 3)

2. $y = -2x + 2$
$y = 3x + 2$
Solution: (0, 2)

3. $y = -\frac{1}{2}x - 1$
$y = x - 4$
Solution: (2, −2)

4. $y = 2x + 3$
$y = \frac{1}{2}x$
Solution: (−2, −1)

5. $y = -\frac{3}{2}x + 2$
$y = \frac{1}{2}x - 2$
Solution: (2, −1)

6. $y = 2x - 5$
$y = \frac{1}{4}x + 2$
Solution: (4, 3)

7. Tomatoes are $0.80 per pound at Rob's Market, and $1.20 per pound at Sal's Produce. You have a coupon for $1.40 off at Sal's. (Assume that you buy at least $1.40 worth of tomatoes.)

   a. Write an equation relating the cost, y, to the number of pounds, x, at each market.

     Rob's: $y = 0.8x$ Sal's: $y = 1.2x - 1.4$

   b. Use a graph to estimate the number of pounds for which the cost is the same at either store.

     $x = 3.5$ pounds

140

Linear Inequalities

Practice
4-7

Test whether each point is a solution of the inequality.

1. $y \geq -2x + 5$ a. $(2, -1)$ No   b. $(3, -1)$ Yes   c. $(4, -1)$ Yes

2. $y < 3x - 4$ a. $(2, 1)$ Yes   b. $(2, 2)$ No   c. $(3, 2)$ Yes

Graph each inequality.

3. $y \leq \frac{1}{2}x + 2$

4. $y > -x + 3$

5. $y \geq 2x$

6. $y < x - 2$

7. $y \leq \frac{2}{3}x - 1$

8. $y > -\frac{1}{2}x$

9. "The number of women is at least half the number of men." Express this statement as an inequality, using x for the number of men.

$y \geq \frac{1}{2}x$

10. Harold is making soup. He wants the soup to have at least twice as many ounces of broccoli as ounces of carrots. Graph the number of ounces of broccoli, y, for x ounces of carrots.

Section 4B Review

Practice

Find the slope of each line. Then find the x-intercept and the y-intercept for each line.

1. Line through R and S

slope: 2

x-intercept: -1

y-intercept: 2

2. Line through S and T

slope: $-\frac{2}{3}$

x-intercept: 3

y-intercept: 2

3. Graph a line through the origin having a a slope of $-\frac{4}{3}$.

4. Graph $y = \frac{2}{3}x + 2$. Find the following:

slope: $\frac{2}{3}$

x-intercept: -3

y-intercept: 2

5. Solve the following system of equations by graphing.

$y = \frac{1}{2}x + 3$

$y = -\frac{3}{2}x - 1$

Solution: $(-2, 2)$

Graph each inequality.

6. $y \leq 2x + 3$

7. $y > x - 3$

8. $y < -\frac{1}{3}x + 2$

9. **Geography** Mt. McKinley in Alaska is 5,826 ft taller than Mt. Whitney in California. If Mt. McKinley is 20,320 ft tall, how tall is Mt. Whitney? *[Lesson 3-4]*

14,494 ft

Cumulative Review Chapters 1–4

Practice

State the range and draw a stem-and-leaf diagram for each data set. *[Lesson 1-1]*

1. 38, 51, 42, 23, 40, 23, 31, 53, 47, 33, 41, 27, 36, 41, 29, 30, 58

Range: 35

stem	leaf
2	3 3 7 9
3	0 1 3 6 8
4	0 1 1 2 7
5	1 3 8

2. 107, 91, 83, 110, 87, 86, 91, 95, 104, 83, 113, 83, 96, 89, 90, 106, 112, 91

Range: 30

stem	leaf
8	3 3 3 6 7 9
9	0 1 1 1 5 6
10	4 6 7
11	0 2 3

Evaluate. *[Lesson 2-7]*

3. 3^5 243   4. $(-2)^6$ 64   5. 17^1 17   6. $(-4)^3$ -64

Solve each equation. *[Lesson 3-6]*

7. $7x - 4 = 73$ 8. $-53 = 5c + 7$ 9. $\frac{u}{3} + 8 = 5$ 10. $23 = -3m + 2$

$x = $ 11 $c = $ -12 $u = $ -9 $m = $ -7

Determine whether each ordered pair is a solution of the equation. *[Lesson 4-2]*

11. $y = -2x + 5$ a. $(2, 1)$ Yes   b. $(-3, 11)$ Yes   c. $(1, 2)$ No

12. $y = -x + 3$ a. $(2, 5)$ No   b. $(-1, 4)$ Yes   c. $(4, -1)$ Yes

Graph each inequality.

13. $y \geq x + 1$

14. $y < \frac{3}{4}x - 2$

15. $y \leq 3x + 2$

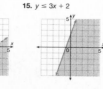

Exploring and Estimating Ratios and Rates

Practice
5-1

Write each ratio or rate as a fraction.

1. 8 : 7 $\frac{8}{7}$

2. 5 to 21 $\frac{5}{21}$

3. 120 beats per second $\frac{120 \text{ beats}}{1 \text{ second}}$

Draw a picture to show each ratio.

4. squares to circles 3 : 5   Possible answer: ■ ■ ■ ● ● ● ● ●

5. circles to stars 1 : 4   Possible answer: ● ★ ★ ★ ★

Write all the ratios that can be made using the figure.

6.

Ratio of shaded area to total area is 3 : 8.

Ratio of total area to shaded area is 8 : 3.

Ratio of unshaded area to total area is 5 : 8.

Ratio of total area to unshaded area is 8 : 5.

Ratio of shaded area to unshaded area is 3 : 5.

Ratio of unshaded area to shaded area is 5 : 3.

Language Arts Write a ratio comparing the number of vowels to the number of consonants in each word.

7. algebra
$\frac{3 \text{ vowels}}{4 \text{ consonants}}$

8. calculator
$\frac{4 \text{ vowels}}{6 \text{ consonants}}$ or $\frac{2 \text{ vowels}}{3 \text{ consonants}}$

9. literature
$\frac{5 \text{ vowels}}{5 \text{ consonants}}$ or $\frac{1 \text{ vowel}}{1 \text{ consonant}}$

10. Yesterday the fax machine at Shambles Realty handled 38 incoming faxes and 49 outgoing faxes. Estimate each ratio:

a. incoming faxes to outgoing faxes   About 4 : 5

b. total faxes to incoming faxes   About 9 : 4

Proportions and Equal Ratios

Complete each table to create ratios equal to the given ratio.

1.

3	6	9	12	15
5	10	15	20	25

2.

1	2	3	4	5
2	4	6	8	10

3.

7	14	21	28	35
3	6	9	12	15

4.

8	16	24	32	40
7	14	21	28	35

5.

4	8	12	16	20
9	18	27	36	45

6.

11	22	33	44	55
5	10	15	20	25

Check each pair of ratios to see if a proportion is formed. Use = or ≠ .

7. $\frac{13}{20} \neq \frac{3}{5}$ **8.** $\frac{9}{11} \neq \frac{17}{20}$ **9.** $\frac{2}{1} = \frac{4}{2}$ **10.** $\frac{12}{9} = \frac{8}{6}$

11. $\frac{11}{7} \neq \frac{5}{3}$ **12.** $\frac{3}{19} \neq \frac{1}{8}$ **13.** $\frac{45}{40} = \frac{18}{16}$ **14.** $\frac{10}{2} = \frac{25}{5}$

15. $\frac{1.8}{0.5} = \frac{7.2}{2.0}$ **16.** $\frac{1.6}{1.4} \neq \frac{1.3}{1.1}$ **17.** $\frac{30}{1.5} = \frac{20}{1.0}$ **18.** $\frac{2.4}{1.5} = \frac{3.2}{2.0}$

19. $\frac{\left(\frac{2}{3}\right)}{10} = \frac{1}{15}$ **20.** $\frac{\left(\frac{1}{2}\right)}{6} = \frac{4}{24}$ **21.** $\frac{\left(\frac{4}{7}\right)}{9} = \frac{4}{63}$ **22.** $\frac{\left(\frac{3}{4}\right)}{5} = \frac{6}{40}$

23. Measurement Fill in the table of equal rates.

Gallons	2	4	6	8	10
Pints	16	32	48	64	80

24. Social Science In 1990, Wyoming had about 7,650 foreign-born residents and a total population of about 454,000. North Carolina had about 115,000 foreign-born residents and a total population of about 6,630,000. Did these states have about the same ratio of foreign-born residents to total residents? Explain.

Possible answer: Yes, $\frac{7,650}{454,000}$ and $\frac{115,000}{6,630,000}$ are both

approximately equal to 0.017.

25. Career Use cross products to test whether the typing rates are equal: 30 words in 6 minutes and 440 words in 8 minutes.

Not equal

Relating Proportions and Graphs

Is each table an equal ratio table? If so find the value of *k*.

1. Yes   *k* = __8__

x	3	4	5	10
y	24	32	40	80

2. No   *k* = None

x	9	12	15	20
y	6	8	10	15

3. No   *k* = None

x	4	6	8	10
y	9	12	15	18

4. Yes   *k* = $\frac{1}{4}$

x	4	12	20	28
y	1	3	5	7

5. If the value of *k* in $\frac{y}{x} = k$ is 18 and *x* = 5, what is the value of *y*?   90

6. If the value of *k* in $\frac{y}{x} = k$ is 11 and *y* = 33, what is the value of *x*?   3

7. Use a cm-ruler to measure the width and height of each rectangle. Graph the width on the *x*-axis and the height on the *y*-axis. Are the ratios of height to width equal?   No

Width (cm)	1.6	1.2	0.8	0.4
Height (cm)	1.9	1.4	1.0	0.5

8. Science An object is suspended on a spring. The graph shows the relationship between the weight *F* of the object and the distance *x* that the spring is stretched by the weight.

a. Find the slope using any two points on the line. $\frac{2}{5}$

b. Make a table of values for the graph. Find the value of *k*. $k = \frac{2}{5}$

x	2.5	5	7.5	10
F	1	2	3	4

c. Write a rate equation describing this relationship. $\frac{F}{x} = \frac{2}{5}$

d. What is the weight of an object that stretches the spring 18 in.?   7.2 lb

---

Section 5A Review

Write a ratio comparing the number of vowels to the number of consonants in each word.

1. Washington $\frac{3 \text{ vowels}}{7 \text{ consonants}}$ **2.** Roosevelt $\frac{4 \text{ vowels}}{5 \text{ consonants}}$

Check each pair of ratios to see if a proportion is formed. Use = or ≠ .

3. $\frac{9}{4} \neq \frac{7}{3}$ **4.** $\frac{15}{25} = \frac{6}{10}$ **5.** $\frac{17}{18} \neq \frac{14}{15}$ **6.** $\frac{3.5}{4} \neq \frac{1.4}{1.6}$

Complete each table to create ratios equal to the given ratio.

7.

7	14	21	28	35
3	6	9	12	15

8.

6	12	18	24	30
10	20	30	40	50

9. The bar graph shows the number of thousands of miles of railroad tracks in each country.

a. Estimate the ratio of the lengths of the railway networks in India and the former USSR.

About $\frac{1}{4}$

b. For what countries is the ratio about 5 to 4?

Canada to China

Railway Networks

Is the table an equal ratio table? If so, find the value of *k*.

10. No   *k* = None

x	3	6	9	11
y	15	25	35	45

11. Yes   *k* = 7

x	1	3	5	7
y	7	21	35	49

12. If the value of *k* in $\frac{y}{x} = k$ is 15 and *y* = 45, what is the value of *x*?   3

13. The Bitter Nut Company sells pecans for $4.50 per pound, plus $3.00 for shipping and handling. Use *x* for the number of pounds. Graph the relationship between the total cost and the number of pounds. *[Lesson 4-3]*

Solving Proportions

Write a proportion for each situation. Do not solve.   Possible answers:

1. How much should 5 pounds of potatoes cost if 2 pounds cost $0.88? $\frac{5}{x} = \frac{2}{0.88}$

2. A recipe for 30 cookies uses 2 cups of flour. How much flour would you use to make 54 cookies? $\frac{30}{2} = \frac{54}{x}$

Solve each proportion. Which method did you use? Why?

3. $\frac{18}{x} = \frac{9}{8}$ *x* = 16; Possible answer: Mental math. It is easy to see that 18 is 2 × 9, so *x* should be 2 × 8.

4. $\frac{16}{28} = \frac{x}{7}$ *x* = 4; Possible answer: Equivalent ratios. $\frac{16}{28}$ in lowest terms is $\frac{4}{7}$.

5. $\frac{32}{44} = \frac{48}{x}$ *x* = 66; Possible answer: Cross products. The numbers are difficult to work mentally.

Which is the best estimate for *x* in each proportion? Explain your choice.

6. $\frac{6.2}{5.41} = \frac{51}{x}$ (A) 4.5   (B) 36   (C) 45   (D) 61

(C); Possible explanation: $\frac{6.0}{5.4}$ is about $\frac{51}{45}$

7. $\frac{2134}{769} = \frac{x}{22}$ (A) 60   (B) 75   (C) 120   (D) 600

(A); Possible explanation: $\frac{2100}{770} = \frac{60}{22}$

Solve each proportion.

8. $\frac{12}{10} = \frac{42}{u}$ *u* = 35

9. $\frac{10}{5} = \frac{14}{y}$ *y* = 7

10. $\frac{n}{28} = \frac{21}{12}$ *n* = 49

11. $\frac{18}{66} = \frac{t}{11}$ *t* = 3

12. A typical paint roller uses 5 gallons of paint to cover 3250 square feet. How much paint would be used to cover 5850 square feet?   9 gallons

Practice 5-5

Name _____

Using Unit Rates

For each of the following, find the unit rate and create a rate formula.

Possible formula answers:

1. $408 for 24 months — _$17 per month; $C = 17t$_
2. $38.50 for 7 hours of work — _$5.50 per hour; $C = 5.5t$_
3. 160 students for 8 teachers — _20 students per teacher; $S = 20t$_
4. $18.00 for 12 pounds — _$1.50 per pound; $C = 1.5w$_
5. 360 miles in 8 hours — _45 mi/hr; $d = 45t$_
6. $80 for 5 dictionaries — _$16 per dictionary; $C = 16d$_
7. 42 meters in 7 seconds — _6 m/sec; $d = 6t$_

8. Hong Kong has a population of about 5,550,000 and an area of about 402 sq mi. Estimate the number of people per square mile. — _About 14,000_

9. **Consumer** An insurance policy is advertised with the phrase "only 75¢ per day!" What is the cost for one year? — _$273.75_

Which is a better buy? (Underline the correct choice.)

10. A 24-exposure roll of film for $5.50, or a 36-exposure roll for $9.00
11. 8 binder clips for $0.88, or 10 binder clips for $1.00
12. 4 pounds of bananas for $1.00, or 1 pound for $0.22
13. A 3 hour equipment rental for $210, or 5 hours for $335
14. A 20-lb bag of dog food for $14, or a 25-lb bag for $18
15. 28 oz of honey for $6.30, or 16 oz for $3.76
16. A 2-lb watermelon for $0.37, or a 3-lb watermelon for $0.48

17. In 1992, the Disney Channel set a record by unveiling a jar containing 2,910 lb of jelly beans. If there were 378,000 jelly beans in the jar, how many jelly beans would be in a 1-lb jar? — _About 130_

Practice 5-6

Name _____

Problem Solving Using Rates and Proportions

1. A 7-inch record turns 165 times to play a song lasting $3\frac{2}{3}$ minutes. How many times would a 7-inch record turn to play a song lasting $4\frac{1}{15}$ minutes? Explain how you solved this problem.
   183; Possible answer: by solving $\frac{165}{3\frac{2}{3}} = \frac{x}{4\frac{1}{15}}$

2. For which two figures do the ratios of shaded area to unshaded area form a proportion? — _(B) and (D)_

(A)   (B)   (C)   (D)

3. The World Trade Center is about 240 m tall, and the Citicorp Center is about 280 m tall. If a scale model of New York includes a 33-cm tall replica of the World Trade Center, how tall is the replica of the Citicorp Center? Explain how you solved this problem.
   About 38.5 cm; Possible answer: by solving $\frac{280}{240} = \frac{x}{33}$

4. **Social Science** In San Francisco, about 27% of residents (that is, 27 out of every 100 residents) speak a foreign language at home. If there were about 195,500 foreign language speakers in 1990, what was the population? Explain how you solved this problem.
   About 724,000; Possible answer: by solving $\frac{27}{100} = \frac{195,500}{x}$

5. Use the numbers 3, 6, 9, 12, and 18 to write as many true proportions as you can. (Use a number only once in each proportion.)
   $\frac{3}{6} = \frac{9}{18}, \frac{3}{9} = \frac{6}{18}, \frac{3}{18} = \frac{6}{9}, \frac{9}{9} = \frac{12}{12}, \frac{6}{18} = \frac{9}{18}, \frac{9}{3} = \frac{18}{6}, \frac{6}{6} = \frac{18}{18}$
   $\frac{12}{6} = \frac{18}{9}, \frac{3}{6} = \frac{6}{12}, \frac{6}{3} = \frac{12}{6}$ (Additional proportions can be found by switching the left and right sides of each of the proportions.)

6. **Social Science** The ratio of men to women in the United Arab Emirates is about 3 to 2. If there are about 1,680,000 men, how many women are there? Explain how you solved this problem.
   About 1,120,000; Possible answer: by solving $\frac{3}{2} = \frac{1,680,000}{x}$

Practice 5-7

Name _____

Scale, Scale Drawings, and Models

Geography Use the map and a ruler. What is the approximate distance from

1. Seattle to Miami — _2600 mi_
2. New York to Miami — _1100 mi_
3. Denver to Dallas — _660 mi_
4. Seattle to New Orleans — _2000 mi_
5. Dallas to Milwaukee — _800 mi_

Use the scale 3 cm = 10 km to find each missing measure.

	6.	7.	8.	9.	10.
Scaled dimension	2.7 cm	15 cm	21 cm	72.9 cm	13.5 cm
Actual dimension	9 km	50 km	70 km	243 km	45 km

Geometry Find the missing measures in each pair of similar figures.

11. $x =$ _18_

12. $y =$ _7_

13. $a =$ _8_ $b =$ _18_

14. $c =$ _4.5_ $d =$ _4_ $e =$ _3.5_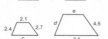

15. Suppose you need to make a map of a 35 mi by 45 mi region. The map needs to fit in an 8 in. by 10 in. frame. What is the largest scale you could use? — _1 in. = 4.5 mi_

16. The Renaissance Tower in Dallas is 216 m tall. If a drawing of the Renaissance Tower is made using a scale of 5 cm = 27 m, how tall will the drawing be? — _40 cm_

Practice

Name _____

Section 5B Review

Write and solve a proportion for each of the following situations.

1. How much should 22 notebooks cost if 4 cost $11? — _$\frac{22}{x} = \frac{4}{11}$; $60.50_

2. Monte's Music Store has 7 jazz CDs for every 4 classical CDs. If there are 1001 jazz CDs, how many classical CDs are there? — _$\frac{7}{4} = \frac{1001}{x}$; 572_

Solve each proportion. Which method did you use? Why? **Possible answers:**

3. $\frac{4}{12} = \frac{6}{u}$ — _$u = 18$; mental math; the numbers are easy_

4. $\frac{s}{21} = \frac{24}{18}$ — _$s = 28$; cross products; the numbers are difficult_

For each of the following, find the unit rate and create a rate formula.

5. $180 for 4 tires — _$45 per tire; $C = 45t$_

6. 45 children for 9 adults — _5 children per adult; $C = 5a$_

Find the missing values for each pair of similar figures.

7. $u =$ _44_ $v =$ _21_

8. $w =$ _20_ $x =$ _21_ $y =$ _15_

9. A building is 56 ft wide and 378 ft tall. If a model of this building is made with scale 3 in. = 28 ft, what are the width and height of the model? — _6 in.; 40.5 in._

10. **Consumer** Henry can buy ink cartridges for his computer printer for $7.50 each at a local store, or he can order them by mail for $4.75 each. If he orders by mail, he will have to pay $8.25 for shipping and handling. *[Lesson 4-6]*

   a. Write a system of equations showing the total cost y for each method of purchasing x cartridges.
      _$y = 7.5x$; $y = 4.75x + 8.25$_

   b. Graph the equations. For how many cartridges is the price the same either way? — _3 cartridges_

Name

Cumulative Review Chapters 1–5

Compute the following. *[Lessons 2-2, 2-3, and 2-4]*

1. 132 + (−18)   **2.** 22 × (−8)   **3.** −37 − 18   **4.** 38 ÷ (−2)

__114__   __−176__   __−55__   __−19__

5. 47 − (−15)   **6.** −16 + 142   **7.** $\frac{-275}{-11}$ **8.** −12 × (−4)

__62__   __126__   __25__   __48__

Write an expression for each situation. *[Lesson 3-3]*

9. The number of feet in *d* miles   **10.** the number of eyes on *c* cats

__5280d__   __2c__

11. the number of gallons in *b* quarts   **12.** the number of cans in *t* twelve-packs

__$\frac{b}{4}$__   __12t__

For each line, find the slope, the *x*-intercept, and the *y*-intercept.
[Lesson 4-5]

13. Line through   **14.** Line through   **15.** Line through
A and *B*   *A* and *D*   *B* and *C*

slope: __$\frac{1}{2}$__   slope: __−2__   slope: __$\frac{3}{2}$__

x-intercept: __−4__   *x*-intercept: __1__   *x*-intercept: __$1\frac{1}{3}$__

y-intercept: __2__   *y*-intercept: __2__   *y*-intercept: __−2__

Complete each table to create ratios equal to the given ratio.
[Lesson 5-2]

16.

3	6	9	12	15
7	14	21	28	35

17.

5	10	15	20	25
2	4	6	8	10

Solve each proportion. *[Lesson 5-4]*

18. $\frac{7}{4} = \frac{x}{28}$ **19.** $\frac{4}{z} = \frac{6}{18}$ **20.** $\frac{h}{9} = \frac{7}{3}$ **21.** $\frac{16}{22} = \frac{56}{u}$

x = __49__   *z* = __12__   *h* = __21__   *u* = __77__

Use with page 269. **53**

Name

Percents, Decimals, and Fractions

1. Draw a diagram to show 60%.   Possible answer:

2. Use the circle graph to answer the questions about music sales in 1994.

1994 Music Sales

Other 7%, Classical/jazz 12%, Rock 36%, Pop 10%, Country 17%, Urban/rap 18%

   a. What percent of music sold was classical or jazz?   __7%__

   b. What percent of music sold was rock?   __36%__

   c. What percent of music sold was *not* rock, country, or pop?   __37%__

Write each fraction or decimal as a percent.

3. $\frac{2}{5}$ **4.** 0.53   **5.** $\frac{1}{4}$ **6.** 0.014

__40%__   __53%__   __25%__   __1.4%__

7. $\frac{3}{8}$ **8.** 0.0051   **9.** $\frac{5}{4}$ **10.** 1.39

__37.5%__   __0.51%__   __125%__   __139%__

Write each percent as a fraction in lowest terms and as a decimal.

11. 50%   **12.** 23%   **13.** 78%   **14.** 87.5%

__$\frac{1}{2}$; 0.5__   __$\frac{23}{100}$; 0.23__   __$\frac{39}{50}$; 0.78__   __$\frac{7}{8}$; 0.875__

15. 64%   **16.** 0.1%   **17.** 300%   **18.** 175%

__$\frac{16}{25}$; 0.64__   __$\frac{1}{1000}$; 0.001__   __$\frac{3}{1}$; 3__   __$\frac{7}{4}$; 1.75__

19. A bag contains 8 green marbles, 7 blue marbles, and 5 clear marbles. What percent of the marbles are

   a. green? __40%__   **b.** blue? __35%__   **c.** not green? __60%__

20. The House of Representatives has 435 members, of whom 52 are from California. What percent of the members are from California?   __About 12%__

54   Use with pages 274–279.

Name

Solving Problems with Percent

Solve.

1. What number is 85% of 560?   **2.** What percent of 120 is 36?

__476__   __30%__

3. 75 out of 500 is what percent?   **4.** 46 is $66\frac{2}{3}$% of what number?

__15%__   __69__

5. 150% of 84 is what number?   **6.** What percent of 64 is 36?

__126__   __56.25%__

7. What number is 180% of 90?   **8.** 250 is what percent of 400?

__162__   __62.5%__

9. About 15% of prime time television is devoted to commercials. How many minutes of commercials are broadcast each hour?   __9 minutes__

10. About 40% of the waste in American landfills is paper. This paper waste amounts to 420 lb per person, per year. How much garbage is generated by the average person each year?   __1050 lb__

11. 800 households were surveyed to determine how many children lived in each household.

Number of Children in Households

20% 1 child, 50% No children, 19% 2 children, 8% 3 children, 3% 4 or more children

   a. How many households had no children? __400__

   b. How many households had 3 children? __64__

   c. How many households had at least 2 children? __240__

12. You can make a delicious peanut sauce by combining the ingredients shown in the order given, and then adding a dash of cayenne pepper. Complete the table to show how much of each ingredient you would use to make $1\frac{1}{2}$ cups (24 tablespoons) of sauce.

Ingredient	Peanut butter	Hot water	Cider vinegar	Soy sauce	Molasses
Percent	$33\frac{1}{3}$	$33\frac{1}{3}$	$16\frac{2}{3}$	$8\frac{1}{3}$	$8\frac{1}{3}$
Amount (tbls.)	8	8	4	2	2

Use with pages 280–285. **55**

Name

Estimating Percents

Estimate each percent.

1. 83 out of 201   **2.** 43 out of 126   **3.** 73 out of 139

__About 42%__   __About 33%__   __About 50%__

4. 408 out of 991   **5.** 5 out of 485   **6.** 119 out of 121

__About 40%__   __About 1%__   __About 98%__

Estimate.

7. 91% of 385   **8.** 6% of 158   **9.** 32% of 1190

__About 360__   __About 8__   __About 360__

Estimate the percent that each shaded region represents.

10. __About 33%__   **11.** __About 38%__   **12.** __About 89%__

Use mental math. Insert >, <, or =. Explain your answer.

13. 33% of 682 ⬡ $\frac{1}{3}$ of 682   Possible answer: 33% < $33\frac{1}{3}$%

14. 6% of 518 ⬡ 0.006 · 518   Possible answer: 0.06 > 0.006

15. 14% of 82 ⬡ 28% of 41   Possible answer:
14% · (2 · 41) = (14% · 2) · 41

16. Health A serving of granola contains 38 g of carbohydrate, which is 13% of the daily requirement. What is the daily requirement for carbohydrate?   __About 300 g__

17. The average per capita income in America was $20,800 in 1993. The city with the highest per capita income was New York, NY, where the per capita income was 251.3% of the national average. What was the average per capita income in New York?   __About $52,300__

56   Use with pages 286–290.

144

Section 6A Review

For each figure, write the fraction, decimal, and percent that tells how much of the figure is shaded.

1. fraction: $\dfrac{7}{25}$

   decimal: _0.28_

   percent: _28%_

2. fraction: $\dfrac{5}{8}$

   decimal: _0.625_

   percent: _62.5%_

Write each fraction, mixed number, or decimal as a percent.

3. $1\dfrac{7}{20}$ _135%_   4. 0.025 _2.5%_   5. $\dfrac{11}{16}$ _68.75%_   6. 2.35 _235%_

Write each percent as a decimal and as a fraction or mixed number in lowest terms.

7. 4% _0.04; $\dfrac{1}{25}$_   8. 21% _0.21; $\dfrac{21}{100}$_   9. 270% _2.7; $2\dfrac{7}{10}$_

For Exercises 10–13, estimate each percent.

10. 17 out of 32   11. 154 out of 445   12. 63% of 144   13. 76% of 540

   About 50%   _About 34%_   _About 90_   _About 405_

14. What number is 18% of 360? _64.8_   15. 32 is 16% of what number? _200_

16. 94.5 is what percent of 525? _18%_   17. 117 is 180% of what number? _65_

18. Without evaluating, insert >, <, or =: 36% of 842 ◯ 35% of 842

19. In 1960, 56.1% of the U.S. civilian labor force was employed. If 65,778,000 civilians were employed, estimate the civilian labor force.   _About 117,000,000_

20. **Health** The recommended daily allowance for vitamin C is 60 mg. How much vitamin C is in a serving of fruit juice which provides 18% of the daily allowance?   _10.8 mg_

21. **Science** The maximum depth of the Atlantic Ocean is 30,246 ft. This is 5,049 ft deeper than the maximum depth of the Caribbean Sea. What is the maximum depth of the Caribbean Sea? *[Lesson 3-4]*   _25,197 ft_

22. Hal typed 385 words in 7 minutes. Val typed 495 words in 9 minutes. Use cross products to test whether the rates are equal. *[Lesson 5-2]*   _Yes_

Percent Increase

For Exercises 1–8, find the percent of increase. Round to the nearest whole percent.

1. Old: 360 New: 392   _9%_
2. Old: 35 New: 105   _200%_
3. Old: 72 New: 100   _39%_
4. Old: 365 New: 521   _43%_

5. Old: $63.95 New: $75.60   _18%_
6. Old: $18.00 New: $24.95   _39%_
7. Old: $168 New: $195   _16%_
8. Old: $3820 New: $5160   _35%_

9. The average speed of a horse-drawn carriage was 8 mi/hr in 1900. In New York City, the average speed for traffic was 9.9 mi/hr in 1988. Find the percent increase.   _23.75%_

10. What is the wholesale price of a product if the percent of increase is 35% and the amount of increase is $14.70?   _$42.00_

11. **Consumer** Find the total cost of a $22 toaster whose price is increased 18%.   _$25.96_

12. The price of an average movie ticket increased 1880% between 1940 and 1990. The average price was $0.24 in 1940. What was the average price in 1990?   _$4.75_

13. In 1993, the average cost for four people to go to a major league baseball game was $90.81. This was an increase of 4.7% over the average cost in 1992. What was the average cost in 1992?   _$86.73_

14. The circulation of *YM* magazine increased 13.26% from 1993 to 1994. If the 1993 circulation was 1,707,377, find the 1994 circulation.   _1,933,775_

15. **Social Science** The fastest-growing major city in the U.S. from 1980 to 1990 was Mesa, AZ, which grew 89% to a population of 288,091. What was the 1980 population?   _About 152,400_

16. **Consumer** The wholesale cost of a computer is $2250. Find the retail cost after an increase of 18%.   _$2655_

Percent Decrease

For Exercises 1–8 find the percent decrease. Round to the nearest whole percent.

1. Old: 50 New: 47   _6%_
2. Old: 275 New: 230   _16%_
3. Old: 460 New: 240   _48%_
4. Old: 220 New: 98   _55%_

5. Old: $36.75 New: $32.50   _12%_
6. Old: $165 New: $94   _43%_
7. Old: $1.99 New: $1.25   _37%_
8. Old: $374 New: $197   _47%_

9. **Consumer** What is the sale price of a $200 removable computer disk drive that has been discounted 25%?   _$150_

10. There were 470 "top 40" radio stations in September, 1994. This is 43% fewer than there were in September, 1990. How many "top 40" stations were there in 1990?   _825_

11. **Consumer** You want to buy a $128 tape player that is supposed to go on sale for 15% off next month. How much will you save if you wait until the sale to buy it?   _$19.20_

12. **Social Science** The population of Detroit, Michigan, declined 14.6% from 1980 to 1990. The 1980 population was 1,203,368. What was the 1990 population?   _About 1,028,000_

13. Sarah invests in stocks. Unfortunately, she made some poor decisions last year, and the value of her stock portfolio fell from $24,638 to $13,874. What was the percent decrease?   _About 43.7%_

14. The number of American daily evening papers dropped 12.6% from 1990 to 1994. There were 1084 evening papers in 1990. How many were there in 1994?   _947_

15. **Consumer** An advertisement for a bicycle reads "22% off, this week only! Your price $265.20." What is the regular price for the bicycle?   _$340_

16. The enrollment at Valley High School fell 18% from 1265 students last year. What is the enrollment now?   _1037 students_

Applications of Percent Change

Start with 100. Find each result (+ means increase, − means decrease).

1. +40% followed by +40%   _196_
2. +40% followed by −40%   _84_
3. −40% followed by +40%   _84_
4. −40% followed by −40%   _36_
5. −40% followed by +60%   _96_
6. +75% followed by −60%   _70_
7. −37.5% followed by +60%   _100_
8. +600% followed by −100%   _0_
9. −50% followed by +300%   _200_
10. +400% followed by −75%   _125_

11. **Consumer** A $180 ring is discounted 20%, but you must pay 8% sales tax on the purchase. Find the total cost if

   a. you take off the discount first, then add the tax.   _$155.52_

   b. you add the tax first, then calculate the discount.   _$155.52_

12. In Houston, Texas, the median price for a pre-owned home was $78,600 in 1985. This amount fell 10.0% from 1985 to 1990, and increased 13.8% from 1990 to 1994. What was the median price in 1994?   _About $80,500_

Find the simple interest.

13. Savings Account Principal: $1275 Rate: 7% Time: 3 years   Interest: _$267.75_
14. Loan Principal: $540 Rate: 13% Time: 1.5 years   Interest: _$105.30_
15. Retirement Account Principal: $8450 Rate: 8% Time: 5 years   Interest: _$3380_

16. **Consumer** Before traveling to France, Scott could have exchanged his 100 U.S. dollars for French francs, and the bank would have given him 4.60 francs for each dollar. But, when he arrived in France, he found that the franc had dropped 10%. Scott exchanged his francs there. How many francs did he receive?   _414_

17. **History** During the late 1970s and early 1980s, interest rates were very high by today's standards. Cecelia opened a savings account which paid 11.5% simple interest for 4 years. If her interest amounted to $386.40, what was her principal?   _$840_

Top Left

Name _____

Practice

Section 6B Review

Find the percent of increase or decrease. Round to the nearest whole percent.

1. Old: 814
New: 675
17% decrease

2. Old: 381
New: 461
21% increase

3. Old: 625
New: 419
33% decrease

4. Old: $31.60
New: $35.95
14% increase

5. Old: $142
New: $119
16% decrease

6. Old: $949
New: $325
66% decrease

7. A sign in a music store reads, "15% off—You save $2.70!" What is the regular price? **$18**

8. A stereo priced at $385.00 costs $406.18 after the sales tax is added. What is the tax rate? **5.5%**

9. A suit is normally $364.95. Find its cost during a 25%-off sale. **$273.71**

10. Connie took some friends out to dinner. The meal's regular price was $48. Connie had a 30%-off coupon, and she left a tip of 15% of the discounted amount. How much did she pay for the meal? **$38.64**

11. Shares of stock in *XYZ* Corporation fell 42% from last year's price of $83.00 per share. What percent of increase would bring them back to last year's price? **About 72.4%**

12. Find the simple interest earned in 3 years on a savings account that started at $1820.00 if the interest rate is 7.5%. **$409.50**

13. The value of a home increased 10%, and then fell 5%. Find the total percent increase or decrease from the original price. **4.5% increase**

14. **Social Science** The population of Rome, Italy, is about 3274 times the population of the Vatican City. If 2,688,000 people live in Rome, what is the population of the Vatican City? *[Lesson 3-5]* **About 821**

15. Tom is making miniature models of Chicago skyscrapers for a movie set. His model of the 700-ft Leo Burnett building is 63 in. tall. How tall is his model of the 900-ft building at Two Prudential Center? *[Lesson 5-6]* **81 in.**

Use with page 314. **61**

Top Right

Name _____

Practice

Cumulative Review Chapters 1–6

Plot each point on the coordinate grid. *[Lesson 2-6]*

1. $A(0, 2)$
2. $B(-1, -3)$
3. $C(0, 0)$
4. $D(2, 4)$
5. $E(-3, 0)$
6. $F(4, -2)$

Solve each equation. *[Lesson 3-6]*

7. $3x + 4 = 52$ $x = \underline{16}$
8. $7x - 5 = 51$ $x = \underline{8}$
9. $6x - 10 = -76$ $x = \underline{-11}$
10. $11x + 18 = 62$ $x = \underline{4}$
11. $\frac{1}{2}y - 5 = 21$ $y = \underline{52}$
12. $\frac{n}{12} + 6 = 8$ $n = \underline{24}$
13. $2.5x - 5 = -10$ $x = \underline{-2}$
14. $16 = \frac{5}{7}x - 19$ $x = \underline{49}$

Determine whether each ordered pair is a solution of the equation. *[Lesson 4-2]*

15. $y = x - 5$ a. (7, 2) **Yes**   b. (2, −7) **No**   c. (2, 7) **No**
16. $y = 7x$ a. (6, 42) **Yes**   b. (6, 13) **No**   c. (42, 6) **No**
17. $y = 3x - 7$ a. (17, 8) **No**   b. (8, 17) **Yes**   c. (5, 8) **Yes**
18. $2x - 5y = 7$ a. (8, 3) **No**   b. (6, 1) **Yes**   c. (1, 6) **No**

Write each fraction or decimal as a percent. *[Lesson 6-1]*

19. $\frac{3}{5}$ **60%**   20. 0.61 **61%**   21. $\frac{7}{8}$ **87.5%**   22. 0.84 **84%**

23. 0.162 **16.2%**   24. $\frac{5}{6}$ **$83\frac{1}{3}$%**   25. 2.87 **287%**   26. $\frac{21}{4}$ **525%**

Find the percent of increase or decrease. Round to the nearest whole percent. *[Lessons 6-4 and 6-5]*

27. old: 614
new: 321
48% decrease

28. old: 163
new: 184
13% increase

29. old: 217
new: 365
68% increase

62 Use with page 319.

Bottom Left

Name _____

Practice
7-1

Divisibility Patterns and Prime Factorization

Determine whether each given number is divisible by 2, 3, 4, 5, 6, 8, 9, or 10.

1. 290 **2, 5, 10**
2. 420 **2, 3, 4, 5, 6, 7, 10**
3. 156 **2, 3, 4, 6**
4. 4547 **None**
5. 3576 **2, 3, 4, 6, 8**
6. 8379 **3, 9**

List all of the factors for each number and identify the prime factors.

7. 110
Factors **±1, ±2, ±5, ±10, ±11, ±22, ±55, ±110**
Prime factors: **2, 5, 11**

8. 72
Factors **±1, ±2, ±3, ±4, ±6, ±8, ±9, ±12, ±18, ±24, ±36, ±72**
Prime factors: **2, 3**

Use a factor tree to determine the prime factorization of each number. Express your answer using exponents.   **Possible factor trees:**

9. 182 **$2 \times 7 \times 13$**

10. 735 **$3 \times 5 \times 7^2$**

11. 198 **$2 \times 3^2 \times 11$**

The equations below involve prime factorization. Solve for the variable in each equation.

12. $y = 2^5$ $y = \underline{32}$
13. $c = 11 \times 5^3$ $c = \underline{1375}$
14. $k = 2^2 \times 5$ $k = \underline{20}$
15. $m = 2^4 \times 7$ $m = \underline{112}$

16. A *perfect number* is a whole number that is equal to the sum of its positive factors (excluding itself). For example, 6 is a perfect number because 6 = 1 + 2 + 3. Find a perfect number between 20 and 30. **28**

Use with pages 324–329. **63**

Bottom Right

Name _____

Practice
7-2

Greatest Common Factors (GCF)

Find the GCF of each group of numbers.

1. 16, 40 **8**
2. 9, 12 **3**
3. 40, 112 **8**
4. 42, 48 **6**
5. 154, 147 **7**
6. 35, 54 **1**
7. 49, 91, 168 **7**
8. 90, 50, 10 **10**
9. 16, 72, 104 **8**

Use prime factorization to find the GCF of each group of numbers.

10. 125 = **5^3**
440 = **$2^3 \times 5 \times 11$**
GCF = **5**

11. 24 = **$2^3 \times 3$**
60 = **$2^2 \times 3 \times 5$**
GCF = **12**

12. 120 = **$2^3 \times 3 \times 5$**
165 = **$3 \times 5 \times 11$**
GCF = **15**

13. 156 = **$2^2 \times 3 \times 13$**
54 = **2×3^3**
GCF = **6**

14. 100 = **$2^2 \times 5^2$**
84 = **$2^2 \times 3 \times 7$**
GCF = **4**

15. 90 = **$2 \times 3^2 \times 5$**
72 = **$2^3 \times 3^2$**
GCF = **18**

16. 216 = **$2^3 \times 3^3$**
144 = **$2^4 \times 3^2$**
180 = **$2^2 \times 3^2 \times 5$**
GCF = **36**

17. 132 = **$2^2 \times 3 \times 11$**
60 = **$2^2 \times 3 \times 5$**
252 = **$2^2 \times 3^2 \times 7$**
GCF = **12**

18. 96 = **$2^5 \times 3$**
90 = **$2 \times 3^2 \times 5$**
175 = **$5^2 \times 7$**
GCF = **1**

Write each fraction in lowest terms.

19. $\frac{19}{38}$ **$\frac{1}{2}$**
20. $\frac{58}{64}$ **$\frac{29}{32}$**
21. $\frac{68}{114}$ **$\frac{34}{57}$**
22. $\frac{10}{120}$ **$\frac{1}{12}$**
23. $\frac{14}{18}$ **$\frac{7}{9}$**
24. $\frac{85}{90}$ **$\frac{17}{18}$**
25. $\frac{20}{196}$ **$\frac{5}{49}$**
26. $\frac{112}{175}$ **$\frac{16}{25}$**
27. $\frac{28}{62}$ **$\frac{14}{31}$**
28. $\frac{42}{122}$ **$\frac{21}{61}$**
29. $\frac{76}{236}$ **$\frac{19}{59}$**
30. $\frac{56}{100}$ **$\frac{14}{25}$**

31. The number of students in Mrs. Folsom's art classes are 28, 36, and 32. She wants to divide each class into groups for a class project. If all of the groups are to be the same size, what is the largest group size that will work? **4**

64 Use with pages 330–334.

Practice 7-3

Least Common Multiples (LCM)

Find the LCM for each pair of numbers.

1. 16, 12 __48__ 2. 12, 8 __24__ 3. 8, 3 __24__ 4. 20, 45 __180__

5. 27, 15 __135__ 6. 34, 18 __306__ 7. 12, 15 __60__ 8. 6, 75 __150__

9. 64, 20 __320__ 10. 12, 6 __12__ 11. 28, 8 __56__ 12. 36, 24 __72__

Use prime factorization to find the LCM for each group of numbers.

13. $45 = \underline{3^2 \times 5}$ 14. $22 = \underline{2 \times 11}$ 15. $39 = \underline{3 \times 13}$

$50 = \underline{2 \times 5^2}$ $26 = \underline{2 \times 13}$ $36 = \underline{2^2 \times 3^2}$

LCM = __450__   LCM = __286__   LCM = __468__

16. $24 = \underline{2^3 \times 3}$ 17. $30 = \underline{2 \times 3 \times 5}$ 18. $80 = \underline{2^4 \times 5}$

$20 = \underline{2^2 \times 5}$ $18 = \underline{2 \times 3^2}$ $105 = \underline{3 \times 5 \times 7}$

LCM = __120__   LCM = __90__   LCM = __1680__

19. $20 = \underline{2^2 \times 5}$ 20. $33 = \underline{3 \times 11}$ 21. $60 = \underline{2^2 \times 3 \times 5}$

$15 = \underline{3 \times 5}$ $18 = \underline{2 \times 3^2}$ $56 = \underline{2^3 \times 7}$

$35 = \underline{5 \times 7}$ $12 = \underline{2^2 \times 3}$ $35 = \underline{5 \times 7}$

LCM = __420__   LCM = __396__   LCM = __840__

Rewrite each group of fractions with the LCD.

22. $\frac{1}{3}$ and $\frac{7}{12}$ $\underline{\frac{4}{12}, \frac{7}{12}}$ 23. $\frac{7}{10}$ and $\frac{2}{15}$ $\underline{\frac{21}{30}, \frac{4}{30}}$

24. $\frac{2}{3}, \frac{3}{5}$, and $\frac{5}{7}$ $\underline{\frac{70}{105}, \frac{63}{105}, \frac{75}{105}}$ 25. $\frac{5}{12}, \frac{4}{9}, \frac{5}{16}$ $\underline{\frac{60}{144}, \frac{64}{144}, \frac{45}{144}}$

26. A carousel has two rows of plastic ponies going at different speeds. Ralph is riding a pony that goes around every 135 seconds, and Lucy is riding a pony that goes around every 150 seconds. If Ralph and Lucy start on the east side of the carousel at the same time, how soon will they again meet on the east side of the carousel?

After 1350 seconds (22.5 minutes)

Practice

Section 7A Review

Use divisibility rules. State whether the given number is divisible by 2, 3, 4, 5, 6, 8, 9, or 10. Indicate when the number is prime.

1. 1792 __2, 4, 8__   2. 2748 __2, 3, 4, 6__   3. 1492 __2, 4__

4. 1947 __3__   5. 331 __Prime__   6. 4494 __2, 3, 6__

Find the prime factorization of each number.

7. $150 \; \underline{2 \times 3 \times 5^2}$ 8. $360 \; \underline{2^3 \times 3^2 \times 5}$ 9. $96 \; \underline{2^5 \times 3}$

10. $168 \; \underline{2^3 \times 3 \times 7}$ 11. $555 \; \underline{3 \times 5 \times 37}$ 12. $378 \; \underline{2 \times 3^3 \times 7}$

Find the GCF and the LCM of each group of numbers.

13. 20, 6   14. 15, 2   15. 28, 36   16. 15, 25, 40

GCF: __2__   GCF: __1__   GCF: __4__   GCF: __5__

LCM: __60__   LCM: __30__   LCM: __252__   LCM: __600__

Write each fraction in lowest terms.

17. $\frac{28}{140}$ __$\frac{1}{5}$__   18. $\frac{25}{45}$ __$\frac{5}{9}$__   19. $\frac{320}{380}$ __$\frac{16}{19}$__   20. $\frac{54}{126}$ __$\frac{3}{7}$__

Find the LCD for each group of fractions.

21. $\frac{5}{6}$ and $\frac{17}{18}$ __18__   22. $\frac{9}{10}$ and $\frac{4}{25}$ __50__   23. $\frac{3}{16}, \frac{7}{20}$, and $\frac{11}{24}$ __240__

24. Do you think the LCM of an odd and even number is always even? Explain your answer.

Possible answer: Yes, because the multiples of an even number are always even.

25. The Thrifty Copy Shop charges $0.10 per copy, plus a service charge of $0.50 for the entire order. Use x for the number of copies made, and graph the price paid. *[Lesson 4-3]*

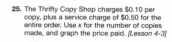

26. The population of Glendale, Arizona, increased from about 97,000 in 1980 to 148,000 in 1990. Find the percent increase. *[Lesson 6-4]*

About 52.6%

Practice 7-4

Defining Rational Numbers

Use >, <, or = to compare each pair of numbers.

1. $\frac{7}{8}$ ⊘ 0.82   2. 1.03 ⊘ 1.029   3. $\frac{-3}{16}$ ⊘ 0.4   4. $\frac{3}{5}$ ⊘ $\frac{4}{7}$

5. $\frac{8}{3}$ ⊘ 2.6   6. 0.4 ⊘ $\frac{2}{5}$ 7. 2.34 ⊘ 2.43   8. 0.4 ⊘ $\frac{5}{12}$

9. -0.63 ⊘ $\frac{-5}{8}$ 10. $\frac{8}{25}$ ⊘ 0.32   11. $\frac{-3}{16}$ ⊘ -0.2 12. 1.333 ⊘ $\frac{4}{3}$

Write each fraction as a decimal and state whether it is repeating or terminating.

13. $\frac{5}{8}$ __0.625; terminating__   14. $-\frac{7}{10}$ __-0.7; terminating__

15. $\frac{16}{33}$ __$0.\overline{48}$; repeating__   16. $\frac{6}{7}$ __$0.\overline{857142}$, repeating__

17. $\frac{21}{80}$ __0.2625; terminating__   18. $-\frac{5}{6}$ __$-0.8\overline{3}$; repeating__

Write each decimal as a fraction or mixed number in lowest terms.

19. 0.36 __$\frac{9}{25}$__   20. 0.375 __$\frac{3}{8}$__   21. 1.24 __$1\frac{6}{25}$__   22. $0.\overline{8}$ __$\frac{8}{9}$__

23. $0.\overline{54}$ __$\frac{6}{11}$__   24. 0.13 __$\frac{13}{100}$__   25. $2.\overline{4}$ __$2\frac{4}{9}$__   26. $7.\overline{6}$ __$7\frac{2}{3}$__

Compare each group of numbers and order them on a number line.

27. $0.7, 0.\overline{7}, \frac{3}{4}, \frac{7}{8}$ 28. $\frac{3}{5}, 1.2, \frac{5}{3}, 0.\overline{3}$ 29. $-0.\overline{5}, -\frac{2}{3}, -\frac{1}{2}, -\frac{3}{8}$

30. $8.2, 8.\overline{25}, 8.\overline{3}, 8\frac{1}{4}$ 31. $0.6, -0.5, \frac{1}{2}, -\frac{4}{5}$ 32. $-2\frac{2}{3}, -2\frac{2}{5}, -2.1, -2.25$

33. During the 1992 Summer Olympic Games, the top three scorers for the women's long jump were Inessa Kravets ($23\frac{3}{8}$ ft), Jackie Joyner-Kersee ($23\frac{5}{24}$ ft), and Heike Drechsler ($23\frac{7}{16}$ ft). Write these women's names in order from the longest jump to the shortest.

Heike Drechsler, Inessa Kravets, Jackie Joyner-Kersee

34. **Social Science** In 1990, 21.5% of the world's population lived in China. What fraction is this? __$\frac{43}{200}$__

Practice 7-5

Add and Subtract Rational Numbers

Add or subtract each of the following. Write each answer in lowest terms.

1. $0.1465 + 0.28$ __0.4265__   2. $2.73 - 1.2496$ __1.4804__   3. $28.4167 + 7.9$ __36.3167__

4. $8.63 - (-4.721)$ __13.351__   5. $-3.6017 + 8.85$ __5.2483__   6. $35.6408 - 8.59$ __27.0508__

7. $2.384 + (-12.9)$ __-10.516__   8. $-3.8712 - 6.84$ __-10.7112__   9. $12.63821 + 7.38$ __20.01821__

10. $\frac{3}{5} + \frac{1}{5}$ __$\frac{4}{5}$__   11. $\frac{15}{11} - \frac{7}{11}$ __$\frac{8}{11}$__   12. $\frac{5}{4} + \frac{7}{4}$ __3__

13. $9\frac{9}{16} - 2\frac{1}{24}$ __$7\frac{25}{48}$__   14. $2\frac{4}{5} + 20\frac{1}{4}$ __$23\frac{1}{20}$__   15. $5\frac{7}{8} - 2\frac{3}{8}$ __$3\frac{1}{2}$__

16. $18\frac{3}{4} - 16\frac{1}{5}$ __$2\frac{11}{20}$__   17. $6\frac{4}{11} + \left(-2\frac{1}{2}\right)$ __$3\frac{19}{22}$__   18. $5\frac{9}{20} + 1\frac{3}{5}$ __$7\frac{1}{20}$__

Find n.

19. $n - 1\frac{1}{3} = 9\frac{4}{5}$ $n = \underline{11\frac{2}{15}}$ 20. $n + 7\frac{4}{11} = 21\frac{1}{33}$ $n = \underline{13\frac{2}{3}}$ 21. $n - \frac{1}{3} = 5\frac{1}{6}$ $n = \underline{5\frac{1}{2}}$

22. $n + 6\frac{1}{6} = 7\frac{5}{21}$ $n = \underline{1\frac{1}{14}}$ 23. $n + \left(-2\frac{1}{22}\right) = 5\frac{5}{11}$ $n = \underline{7\frac{1}{2}}$ 24. $n + 3\frac{2}{3} = 5\frac{2}{5}$ $n = \underline{1\frac{11}{15}}$

25. $n - 7\frac{2}{5} = \frac{6}{35}$ $n = \underline{7\frac{4}{7}}$ 26. $n + 8\frac{5}{7} = 13\frac{4}{35}$ $n = \underline{4\frac{2}{5}}$ 27. $n - \left(-7\frac{1}{22}\right) = 20\frac{10}{11}$ $n = \underline{13\frac{19}{22}}$

28. In 1970, $\frac{13}{25}$ of the funding for U.S. public elementary and secondary schools came from local sources, and $\frac{2}{5}$ of the funding came from state governments. The remaining funds came from the federal government. What fraction of funding came from the federal government? __$\frac{2}{25}$__

29. Miguel bought some stock that was priced at $14\frac{3}{8}$ per share. Find the value of the stock after it went up $2\frac{3}{4}$. __$17\frac{1}{8}$__

Multiply and Divide Rational Numbers

Multiply or divide each of the following. Write each answer in lowest terms.

1. $97.98 \times (-0.2)$ __−19.596__   2. 7.039×0.04 __0.28156__   3. $-0.1 \times (-4.1)$ __0.41__   4. -0.05×0.014 __−0.0007__

5. $0.17)\overline{8.126}$ __47.8__   6. $-3.6)\overline{32.256}$ __−8.96__   7. $-0.5)\overline{-423.55}$ __847.1__   8. $2.7)\overline{-19.899}$ __−7.37__

9. -0.06×5.89 __−0.3534__   10. 4×0.478 __1.912__   11. $-5.8 \times (-7.2)$ __41.76__   12. $0.008 \times (-12.22)$ __−0.09776__

13. $-5.5)\overline{-34.1}$ __6.2__   14. $8.58)\overline{-0.1716}$ __−0.02__   15. $0.091)\overline{8.6541}$ __95.1__   16. $-0.87)\overline{-4.524}$ __5.2__

17. $\frac{3}{8} \times \frac{5}{6}$ __$\frac{5}{16}$__   18. $\frac{4}{9} \times \frac{6}{7}$ __$\frac{8}{21}$__   19. $\frac{4}{5} \times \frac{11}{12}$ __$\frac{11}{15}$__

20. $\frac{1}{2} \div \frac{7}{9}$ __$\frac{9}{14}$__   21. $\frac{3}{5} \div \frac{7}{8}$ __$\frac{24}{35}$__   22. $\frac{5}{7} \div \frac{15}{28}$ __$1\frac{1}{3}$__

23. $\frac{1}{5} \times 7\frac{1}{8}$ __$1\frac{17}{40}$__   24. $3 \times 6\frac{5}{9}$ __$19\frac{2}{3}$__   25. $2 \times 2\frac{1}{5}$ __$4\frac{2}{5}$__

26. $1\frac{2}{3} \div 3\frac{4}{5}$ __$\frac{25}{57}$__   27. $1\frac{2}{5} \div 2\frac{6}{7}$ __$\frac{49}{100}$__   28. $1 \div 14\frac{1}{2}$ __$\frac{2}{29}$__

29. $4\frac{3}{7} \times 1\frac{1}{4}$ __$5\frac{15}{28}$__   30. $1\frac{6}{7} \times (-5)$ __$-9\frac{2}{7}$__   31. $\frac{2}{5} \times 6\frac{3}{10}$ __$2\frac{13}{25}$__

32. $1\frac{1}{2} \div (-8)$ __$-\frac{3}{16}$__   33. $3\frac{1}{2} \div \frac{5}{7}$ __$4\frac{9}{10}$__   34. $-8\frac{1}{2} \div 9$ __$-\frac{17}{18}$__

35. $-3 \times 7\frac{2}{3}$ __-23__   36. $1\frac{1}{5} \times 5\frac{1}{6}$ __$6\frac{1}{5}$__   37. $6\frac{1}{4} \times 4\frac{1}{10}$ __$25\frac{5}{8}$__

38. $1\frac{11}{14} \div 2\frac{1}{7}$ __$\frac{5}{6}$__   39. $16 \div 1\frac{2}{5}$ __$11\frac{3}{7}$__   40. $2\frac{5}{8} \div 7\frac{1}{2}$ __$\frac{7}{20}$__

41. **Social Science** In 1994, about $\frac{27}{140}$ of the federal budget was spent on national defense. About $\frac{7}{25}$ of the money spent on defense was used for military personnel. What fraction of the federal budget was spent on military personnel?

About __$\frac{27}{500}$__

42. **Geography** The area of Colombia is about $1\frac{1}{4}$ times the area of Venezuela, which is about 352,000 square miles. What is the area of Colombia?

__About 440,000 mi^2__

Section 7B Review

Compare each group of numbers and order them on a number line.

1. $\frac{3}{4}, \frac{5}{6}, 0.\overline{8}, 0.8$ 2. $5\frac{1}{3}, 5\frac{1}{5}, 5.25, 5.\overline{4}$ 3. $-\frac{5}{8}, -\frac{3}{7}, -0.\overline{6}, -0.5$

Write each fraction as a decimal and determine whether it's terminating or repeating.

4. $\frac{5}{7}$ __0.714285; repeating__   5. $-\frac{7}{8}$ __−0.875; terminating__

Write each decimal as a fraction or mixed number.

6. 0.68 __$\frac{17}{25}$__   7. $0.\overline{6}$ __$\frac{2}{3}$__   8. $-8.\overline{36}$ __$-8\frac{4}{11}$__

Calculate.

9. $5.63 + 2.073$ __7.703__   10. $9.6 - 3.176$ __6.424__   11. 8.36×7.4 __61.864__

12. $7\frac{5}{8} + 3\frac{5}{6}$ __$11\frac{11}{24}$__   13. $1\frac{2}{3} \times 2\frac{1}{6}$ __$3\frac{11}{18}$__   14. $10\frac{2}{3} - 8\frac{1}{5}$ __$2\frac{7}{15}$__

Solve.

15. $\frac{8}{9} = \frac{1}{6} + x$ 16. $x - \frac{3}{8} = \frac{9}{10}$ 17. $3\frac{1}{2} = x - \left(-7\frac{3}{5}\right)$

$x =$ __$\frac{13}{18}$__ $x =$ __$1\frac{11}{40}$__ $x =$ __$-4\frac{1}{10}$__

18. For a party, a caterer needs to prepare twice as many chicken sandwiches as vegetarian sandwiches. There are to be 24 sandwiches altogether. Write a system of equations, using x for the number of vegetarian sandwiches and y for the number of chicken sandwiches. Then solve the system using a table or a graph to find the number of each kind of sandwich. *[Lesson 4-6]*

__$y = 2x, x + y = 24$; 8 vegetarian, 16 chicken__

19. **Social Science** The population of Chattanooga, Tennessee, was about 120,000 in 1970. The population increased 42% from 1970 to 1980, and decreased 11% from 1980 to 1990. What was the population in 1990? *[Lesson 6-6]*

__About 152,000__

Perfect Squares and Square Roots

State whether or not each number is a perfect square.

1. 20 __No__   2. 16 __Yes__   3. 60 __No__   4. 110 __No__

5. 76 __No__   6. 4 __Yes__   7. 64 __Yes__   8. 9 __Yes__

9. 36 __Yes__   10. 32 __No__   11. 50 __No__   12. 200 __No__

13. 160 __No__   14. 625 __Yes__   15. 1 __Yes__   16. 144 __Yes__

17. 45 __No__   18. 25 __Yes__   19. 12 __No__   20. 400 __Yes__

Find the two consecutive integers that each is between.

21. $\sqrt{175}$ __13, 14__   22. $\sqrt{30}$ __5, 6__   23. $\sqrt{135}$ __11, 12__

24. $\sqrt{6}$ __2, 3__   25. $\sqrt{53}$ __7, 8__   26. $\sqrt{21}$ __4, 5__

27. $\sqrt{111}$ __10, 11__   28. $\sqrt{3}$ __1, 2__   29. $\sqrt{580}$ __24, 25__

30. $\sqrt{90}$ __9, 10__   31. $\sqrt{200}$ __14, 15__   32. $\sqrt{12}$ __3, 4__

33. $\sqrt{42}$ __6, 7__   34. $\sqrt{408}$ __20, 21__   35. $\sqrt{910}$ __30, 31__

Determine each square root and write in lowest terms.

36. $\sqrt{\frac{25}{36}}$ __$\frac{5}{6}$__   37. $\sqrt{\frac{25}{400}}$ __$\frac{1}{4}$__   38. $\sqrt{\frac{4}{36}}$ __$\frac{1}{3}$__   39. $\sqrt{\frac{9}{64}}$ __$\frac{3}{8}$__

40. $\sqrt{\frac{81}{144}}$ __$\frac{3}{4}$__   41. $\sqrt{\frac{1}{4}}$ __$\frac{1}{2}$__   42. $\sqrt{\frac{64}{25}}$ __$\frac{8}{5}$__   43. $\sqrt{\frac{81}{36}}$ __$\frac{3}{2}$__

44. $\sqrt{\frac{4}{100}}$ __$\frac{1}{5}$__   45. $\sqrt{\frac{4}{9}}$ __$\frac{2}{3}$__   46. $\sqrt{\frac{64}{400}}$ __$\frac{2}{5}$__   47. $\sqrt{\frac{121}{400}}$ __$\frac{11}{20}$__

48. $\sqrt{\frac{16}{49}}$ __$\frac{4}{7}$__   49. $\sqrt{\frac{81}{225}}$ __$\frac{3}{5}$__   50. $\sqrt{\frac{36}{121}}$ __$\frac{6}{11}$__   51. $\sqrt{\frac{49}{144}}$ __$\frac{7}{12}$__

52. A square cake pan has an area of 529 cm^2. How long is each side of the pan?   __23 cm__

53. In the Japanese art of origami, square paper is folded to create animals and other objects. If a sheet of origami paper has area 324 cm^2, what is the length of each edge of the paper?   __18 cm__

Square Roots and Irrational Numbers

Identify each number as rational or irrational.

1. $2.717711777 \ldots$ __Irrational__   2. 75 __Rational__   3. $\sqrt{36}$ __Rational__

4. $6.18181818 \ldots$ __Rational__   5. 18.7 __Rational__   6. $\frac{4}{7}$ __Rational__

7. 13.61324 __Rational__   8. $\sqrt{21}$ __Irrational__   9. $\sqrt{\frac{49}{64}}$ __Rational__

Use a calculator to find each of the square roots and round to the nearest thousandth.

10. $\sqrt{35}$ __5.916__   11. $\sqrt{23}$ __4.796__   12. $\sqrt{50}$ __7.071__   13. $\sqrt{44}$ __6.633__

14. $\sqrt{27}$ __5.196__   15. $\sqrt{18}$ __4.243__   16. $\sqrt{69}$ __8.307__   17. $\sqrt{56}$ __7.483__

18. $\sqrt{79}$ __8.888__   19. $\sqrt{39}$ __6.245__   20. $\sqrt{314}$ __17.720__   21. $\sqrt{73}$ __8.544__

22. $\sqrt{62}$ __7.874__   23. $\sqrt{108}$ __10.392__   24. $\sqrt{48}$ __6.928__   25. $\sqrt{1200}$ __34.641__

Geometry Find the side length of each of the squares with the given area.

26. 150 in^2 $\approx$ __12.247 in.__   27. 144 m^2 __12 m__   28. 14 cm^2 $\approx$ __3.742 cm__

29. 18.49 ft^2 __4.3 ft__   30. 2.89 km^2 __1.7 km__   31. 94.09 yd^2 __9.7 yd__

32. 49 mm^2 __7 mm__   33. 0.2025 mi^2 __0.45 mi__   34. 85 cm^2 $\approx$ __9.220 cm__

35. 40.96 in^2 __6.4 in.__   36. 111 m$^2 \approx$ __10.536 m__   37. 169 ft^2 __13 ft__

38. A square card table has a tabletop with area 1350 in^2. Find the length of each side.   __About 36.7 in.__

39. **Science** The formula $t = \sqrt{\frac{d}{4.9}}$ gives the time (t), in seconds, for an object to free fall a distance (d), in meters. A rock is dropped from a 35-m-high cliff. How soon will it hit the beach below?   __About 2.67 sec__

Top-left quadrant

Name _____

The Pythagorean Theorem

Find the length of the missing side for each right triangle.

1. x = 25

2. x = 65

3. x = 150

4. x = 117

5. x = 28

6. x = 13

7. x ≈ 38.48

8. x = 35

9. x = 5

10. x = 8

11. x = 65

12. x = 48

13. x = 6.4

14. x = 85

15. x ≈ 43.87

16. An 8-ft ladder is leaning against a building. If the base of the ladder is 3 ft from the base of the building, how far is it up the building from the base of the ladder to the top of the ladder?

About 7.4 ft

17. Geography Washington, DC, is 494 miles east of Indianapolis, Indiana. Birmingham, Alabama, is 433 miles south of Indianapolis. How far is Birmingham from Washington, DC?

About 657 mi

Use with pages 374–378. **73**

Top-right quadrant

Name _____

Section 7C Review

Use your calculator to determine whether each is a perfect square.

1. 3823 __No__ **2.** 7245 __No__ **3.** 1849 __Yes__ **4.** 5916 __No__

Determine each square root and write in lowest terms.

5. $\sqrt{\frac{25}{81}}$ $\frac{5}{9}$ **6.** $\sqrt{49}$ __7__ **7.** $\sqrt{441}$ __21__ **8.** $\sqrt{\frac{100}{144}}$ $\frac{5}{6}$

9. $-\sqrt{81}$ __−9__ **10.** $\sqrt{30.25}$ __5.5__ **11.** $\pm\sqrt{169}$ __±13__ **12.** $\sqrt{68.89}$ __8.3__

Identify each number as rational or irrational.

13. 2.141414 ... __Rational__ **14.** $\frac{5}{11}$ __Rational__ **15.** 5.8$\overline{3}$ __Rational__

Find the side length of a square with the given area.

16. 196 ft² __14 ft__ **17.** 75 m² ≈ __8.66 m__ **18.** 116 yd² ≈ __10.77 yd__

19. 7.84 in² __2.8 in.__ **20.** 8.4 cm² ≈ __2.90 cm__ **21.** 12.8 km² ≈ __3.58 km__

Find the missing side of each right triangle.

22. 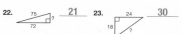 21 **23.** 30 **24.** 48

25. This graph shows the price to item ratio for oranges. How many oranges could you buy for $9? Explain your reasoning. *[Lesson 5-3]*

22 oranges; Possible explanation: (22.5, 9) is on the graph, but you can't buy half an orange.

26. In 1994, 36,521,700 Americans age 25 or older had completed at least 4 years of college. This was 22.2% of all Americans age 25 or older. How many Americans were at least 25 years old in 1994? *[Lesson 6-2]*

About 164,512,000

74 Use with page 380.

Bottom-left quadrant

Name _____

Cumulative Review Chapters 1–7

For each line, find the slope, the x-intercept, and the y-intercept. *[Lesson 4-5]*

1. Line through A and B   slope: $\frac{2}{3}$
   x-intercept: __−3__   y-intercept: __2__

2. Line through B and C   slope: __2__
   x-intercept: __1__   y-intercept: __−2__

3. Line through C and D   slope: __−1__
   x-intercept: __4__   y-intercept: __4__

Complete each table to create ratios equal to the given ratio. *[Lesson 5-2]*

4.

3	6	9	42	66
7	14	21	98	154

5.

8	16	32	64	88
11	22	44	88	121

6.

9	18	27	54	81
5	10	15	30	45

7.

6	12	18	30	2
15	30	45	75	5

Estimate. *[Lesson 6-3]*

8. 63% of 12 ≈ __8__ **9.** 80% of 365 ≈ __290__ **10.** 35% of 67 ≈ __22__

11. 12% of 582 ≈ __70__ **12.** 28% of 737 ≈ __200__ **13.** 125% of 89 ≈ __112__

Calculate. *[Lessons 7-5 and 7-6]*

14. $6\frac{3}{4} + 7\frac{1}{3}$ $14\frac{1}{12}$ **15.** $12\frac{3}{7} - 4\frac{5}{8}$ $7\frac{45}{56}$ **16.** $3\frac{5}{6} \times 3$ $11\frac{1}{2}$ **17.** $\frac{3}{8} \div 1\frac{1}{5}$ $\frac{5}{16}$

18. $3\frac{5}{6} + 8\frac{3}{8}$ $12\frac{5}{24}$ **19.** $23\frac{4}{5} - 8\frac{1}{4}$ $15\frac{11}{20}$ **20.** $4\frac{3}{8} \times 7\frac{2}{3}$ $33\frac{13}{24}$ **21.** $8\frac{3}{4} \div 2\frac{3}{8}$ $3\frac{13}{19}$

Determine the following square roots and write in lowest terms. *[Lesson 7-7]*

22. $\sqrt{361}$ __19__ **23.** $\sqrt{1024}$ __32__ **24.** $\sqrt{\frac{9}{16}}$ $\frac{3}{4}$ **25.** $\sqrt{\frac{36}{49}}$ $\frac{6}{7}$

26. $\sqrt{\frac{64}{121}}$ $\frac{8}{11}$ **27.** $\sqrt{\frac{100}{36}}$ $\frac{5}{3}$ **28.** $\sqrt{\frac{49}{144}}$ $\frac{7}{12}$ **29.** $\sqrt{\frac{100}{169}}$ $\frac{10}{13}$

Use with page 385. **75**

Bottom-right quadrant

Name _____

Units of Measurement

What U.S. customary unit would you use for each measurement?

1. The weight of a whale   __ton__
2. The length of a freeway   __mile__
3. The capacity of a punch bowl   __quart__
4. The area of a window   __square inch__

What metric unit would you use for each measurement?

5. The width of a computer monitor   __centimeter__
6. The amount of gasoline in a car   __liter__
7. The mass of a feather   __gram__
8. The volume of a closet   __cubic meter__

Convert each measurement.

9. 38 min to sec   __2280 sec__
10. 72 ft to in.   __864 in.__
11. 684 m to cm   __68,400 cm__

12. 25 lb to oz   __400 oz__
13. 46.3 kg to g   __46,300 g__
14. 384 mL to L   __0.384 L__

15. 64 qt to cups   __256 cups__
16. 84 mi to ft   __443,520 ft__
17. 1632 m to km   __1.632 km__

18. 3000 lb to T   __1.5 T__
19. 14.86 g to kg   __0.01486 kg__
20. 2136 min to hr   __35.6 hr__

21. A group of students ran one lap around a track. Their times were 132 sec, 1.83 min, 118 sec, 1.97 min, and 101 sec. Give the average time in seconds.   __115.8 sec__

22. The smallest street-legal car in the United States is 7 ft 4.75 in. long. Convert this length to inches.   __88.75 in.__

76 Use with pages 390–395.

Worksheet 8-2

Name _____

Practice 8-2

Significant Digits and Precision

Determine the number of significant digits in each measurement.

1. 1.063 in. **4** **2.** 12,000 g **2** **3.** 634 yd **3** **4.** 8300 qt **2**

5. 0.0037 sec **2** **6.** 10.9 kg **3** **7.** 2.030 pt **4** **8.** 4.87 hr **3**

Underline the more precise measurement.

9. 23 oz, <u>20.7 oz</u>   **10.** <u>1830 g</u>, 2.5 kg   **11.** 160 qt, <u>137 qt</u>

12. 63.7 L, <u>63.70 L</u>   **13.** 3.7 T, <u>5610 lb</u>   **14.** 47 qt, <u>83 pt</u>

15. <u>58.3 cm</u>, 4.6 m   **16.** 12 L, <u>1735 mL</u>   **17.** 61 lb, <u>63.7 lb</u>

18. <u>3.008 pt</u>, 0.95 pt   **19.** 7.3 min, <u>516 sec</u>   **20.** <u>2.7 mL</u>, 12 mL

Calculate each and give the answer with the correct number of significant digits.

21. 6.35 oz + 4.2 oz **10.6 oz**
22. 83 g − 1.8 g **81 g**
23. 6.25 in. × 15.85 in. **99.1 in²**

24. 4.20 yd × 8.64 yd **36.3 yd²**
25. 21 cm × 5360 cm **110,000 cm²**
26. 8137 hr − 500 hr **7600 hr**

27. 5.382 m × 8 m **40 m²**
28. 6.4 ft × 4300 ft **28,000 ft²**
29. 30 mi × 165 mi **5000 mi²**

30. 2.713 mL + 8.4 mL **11.1 mL**
31. 50 lb − 4.6 lb **45 lb**
32. 6.83 km × 10.3 km **70.3 km²**

33. Geography Boundary Peak in Nevada is 13,000 ft high. Guadalupe Peak in Texas is 8749 ft high. How much higher than Guadalupe Peak is Boundary Peak? Use the correct number of significant digits. **4000 ft**

34. A rectangular swimming pool has length 98 ft and width 33.5 ft. Use significant digits to express the area of the pool. **3300 ft²**

Use with pages 396–400. **77**

Name _____

Practice 8-3

Position

1. What city is located at 24°N and 104.5°W? **Durango**

2. What is the position of Ciudad Mante relative to Mexico City? **About 230 mi north**

3. What is the position of Guadalajara relative to Veracruz? **About 480 mi northwest**

4. What is the absolute position of Monterrey using latitude and longitude? **About 25.5°N, 100.5°W**

5. How many degrees of latitude are between Durango and Veracruz? **About 5°**

6. How many degrees of longitude are between San Pedro and Mexico City? **About 4°**

7. Locate the position 23°N, 95°W, on the map. Is this location in Mexico, in the Pacific Ocean, or in the Gulf of Mexico? **Gulf of Mexico**

Tell what state contains each location.

8. 40°N, 105°W **Colorado**
9. 32°N, 100°W **Texas**
10. 47°N, 110°W **Montana**
11. 45°N, 100°W **South Dakota**
12. 35°N, 95°W **Oklahoma**

78 Use with pages 401–406.

Name _____

Practice

Section 8A Review

What metric unit would you use for each measurement?

1. The mass of a television set **kilogram**
2. The area of a football field **square meters**

Convert each measurement.

3. 75 in. to ft **6.25 ft**
4. 21 hr to min **1260 min**
5. 258 cm to m **2.58 cm**
6. 3.8 T to lb **7600 lb**

Determine the number of significant digits in each measurement.

7. 5.360 mL **4** **8.** 748 lb **3** **9.** 21,000 ft **2** **10.** 0.0075 hr **2**

Underline the more precise measurement.

11. 26.4 cm, <u>8.39 cm</u>   **12.** 216 ft, <u>3106 in.</u>   **13.** 4100 lb, <u>6123 lb</u>

Calculate each and give the answer with the correct number of significant digits.

14. 2100 cm − 418 cm **1700 cm**   **15.** 41.3 in. × 84 in. **3500 in²**

Geography Tell what country contains each location.

16. 30° N, 5° E **Algeria**
17. 15° N, 20° E **Chad**
18. 20° N, 5° W **Mali**
19. 10° N, 8° E **Nigeria**

20. The American International Building is 950 ft tall, and the Statue of Liberty is 152 ft tall. If a scale model of New York City includes a 75 in. replica of the America International Building, how tall is the model Statue of Liberty? *[Lesson 5-6]* **12 in.**

21. Explain the difference between the GCF and the LCM. *[Lessons 7-2 and 7-3]*
Possible answer: The GCF of two numbers is the greatest number that is a factor of both numbers, and the LCM is the smallest positive number that is a multiple of both numbers.

Use with page 408. **79**

Name _____

Practice 8-4

Lines and Angles

Classify each angle measurement as right, straight, obtuse, or acute.

1. 27° **Acute** **2.** 90.2° **Obtuse** **3.** 100° **Obtuse**
4. 89° **Acute** **5.** 153° **Obtuse** **6.** 180° **Straight**
7. 74° **Acute** **8.** 90° **Right** **9.** 4° **Acute**

Find the measure of the complement of each angle measure.

10. 82° **8°** **11.** 31° **59°** **12.** 7° **83°** **13.** 64° **26°**
14. 35° **55°** **15.** 0.7° **89.3°** **16.** 50° **40°** **17.** 12° **78°**

Find the measure of the supplement of each angle measure.

18. 34° **146°** **19.** 100° **80°** **20.** 67° **113°** **21.** 125° **55°**
22. 2.3° **177.7°** **23.** 53° **127°** **24.** 176° **4°** **25.** 84° **96°**

Use a protractor to measure each angle.

26. ∠ABC **127°** **27.** ∠CDE **75°**
28. ∠BDE **110°** **29.** ∠BCD **92°**
30. ∠EDF **70°** **31.** ∠BDC **35°**
32. ∠CBD **53°** **33.** ∠BDF **180°**

Identify each as a ray, line, or line segment and draw each.

Possible drawings:

34. $\overleftrightarrow{JK}$ **Line** $\overleftrightarrow{J\ \ K}$
35. $\overrightarrow{ML}$ **Ray** $\overrightarrow{L\ \ M}$
36. $\overline{PQ}$ **Line segment** $\overline{P\ \ Q}$

37. a. Measure ∠WXY and ∠XYZ in the parallelogram shown at the right.
m∠WXY = **104°** m∠XYZ = **76°**

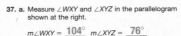

b. Are these angles complementary, supplementary, or neither? **Supplementary**

80 Use with pages 410–415.

150

Parallel and Perpendicular Lines

In the figure shown at right, $\overleftrightarrow{PQ} \parallel \overleftrightarrow{RS}$. Use the figure for Exercises 1–7.

1. Name all interior angles. $\angle 2, \angle 3, \angle 6, \angle 7$

2. Name all exterior angles. $\angle 1, \angle 4, \angle 5, \angle 8$

3. Name the transversal. $\overleftrightarrow{TU}$

4. Name two pairs of alternate interior angles. $\angle 2$ and $\angle 7$, $\angle 3$ and $\angle 6$

5. Name two pairs of alternate exterior angles. $\angle 1$ and $\angle 8$, $\angle 4$ and $\angle 5$

6. Name four pairs of corresponding angles.

$\angle 1$ and $\angle 3$, $\angle 2$ and $\angle 4$, $\angle 5$ and $\angle 7$, $\angle 6$ and $\angle 8$

7. If $m\angle 6 = 75°$, find each angle measure.

$m\angle 1 = \underline{75°}$ $m\angle 2 = \underline{105°}$ $m\angle 3 = \underline{75°}$ $m\angle 4 = \underline{105°}$

$m\angle 5 = \underline{105°}$ $m\angle 7 = \underline{105°}$ $m\angle 8 = \underline{75°}$

In the figure on the right, $\overleftrightarrow{VW} \parallel \overleftrightarrow{XY}$. Use the figure to find the measure of each angle.

8. $m\angle 1 = \underline{138°}$ 9. $m\angle 2 = \underline{42°}$

10. $m\angle 4 = \underline{42°}$ 11. $m\angle 5 = \underline{138°}$

12. $m\angle 7 = \underline{138°}$ 13. $m\angle 8 = \underline{42°}$

Complete each statement to make it true.

14. When a transversal crosses __parallel__ lines, the alternate exterior angles are congruent.

15. Two pairs of congruent angles called __vertical__ angles are formed whenever two lines intersect.

The map shows some streets in downtown San Francisco. Use it for Exercises 16–17.

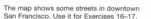

16. Name the streets that are parallel to Market. __Mission, Howard__

17. Name the streets that are perpendicular to Market. __5th, 6th, 7th__

Polygons

Identify each polygon. Be as specific as possible.

1. __Rectangle__   2. __Regular hexagon__   3. __Trapezoid__

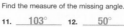

4. __Regular pentagon__   5. __Parallelogram__   6. __Irregular octagon__

Decide whether each statement is true or false.

7. All squares are parallelograms.   8. All quadrilaterals are parallelograms.

__True__   __False__

9. Some rhombuses are rectangles.   10. Some scalene triangles are isosceles.

__True__   __False__

Find the measure of the missing angle.

11. __103°__   12. __50°__   13. __59°__   14. __35°__

Determine the sum of all angles in each polygon.

15. nonagon (9-sided polygon)   16. decagon (10-sided polygon)   17. dodecagon (12-sided polygon)

__1260°__   __1440°__   __1800°__

18. Name the polygon that describes the shape of a stop sign.

__Regular octagon__

3-D Views

1. Draw the right, front, and top views for the 3-D object shown.

Right view   **Front view**   **Top view**

Draw a base plan for the cube towers shown.

2.

2	3	3
1	2	3
1	1	2

3.

| 4 | 4 | 2 | 2 |
| 4 | 3 | 2 | 1 |

Draw a net for the following objects: **Possible answers:**

4. a rectangular prism

5. a regular triangular prism

6. Draw a net for the number cube shown. Show the dots in the correct position.

Possible answer:

Section 8B Review

Use a protractor to measure each angle. Classify each angle as right, straight, obtuse, or acute.

1. $\angle UVX$ __58°; acute__   2. $\angle XVZ$ __90°; right__

3. $\angle WVY$ __67°; acute__   4. $\angle UVW$ __180°; straight__

5. $\angle UVY$ __113°; obtuse__   6. $\angle XVW$ __122°; obtuse__

7. Find the angle measure complementary to 23.8°. __66.2°__

8. Find the angle measure supplementary to 81°. __99°__

Use figure at right to answer Exercises 9–16. $\overleftrightarrow{JK} \parallel \overleftrightarrow{LM}$. If $m\angle 2 = 70°$, find each angle measure.

9. $m\angle 4$ __70°__   10. $m\angle 7$ __70°__

11. $m\angle 5$ __70°__   12. $m\angle 3$ __110°__

Match each pair of angles with the angle classification.

13. $\angle 6$ and $\angle 8$ __C__   A. alternate interior angles

14. $\angle 3$ and $\angle 6$ __A__   B. alternate exterior angles

15. $\angle 4$ and $\angle 7$ __D__   C. corresponding angles

16. $\angle 1$ and $\angle 8$ __B__   D. vertical angles

Identify each polygon. Be as specific as possible.

17. __Rhombus__   18. __Irregular pentagon__   19. __Isosceles triangle__

20. The largest hotel lobby is the 160 ft by 350 ft lobby at the Hyatt Regency in San Francisco. What is the largest scale that could be used to make a scale drawing of this lobby on an 8-in. by 10-in. sheet of paper? *[Lesson 5-7]*   __1 in. = 35 ft__

21. **Geography** Tucson, Arizona, is about 75 miles south and 70 miles east of Phoenix. What is the distance from Phoenix to Tucson? *[Lesson 7-9]*   __About 103 mi__

Cumulative Review Chapters 1–8

Practice

Solve each proportion. *[Lesson 5-4]*

1. $\frac{15}{21} = \frac{x}{35}$
   x = **25**

2. $\frac{33}{t} = \frac{48}{64}$
   t = **44**

3. $\frac{45}{33} = \frac{105}{p}$
   p = **77**

4. $\frac{k}{54} = \frac{36}{81}$
   k = **24**

5. $\frac{n}{26} = \frac{40}{65}$
   n = **16**

6. $\frac{85}{51} = \frac{15}{r}$
   r = **9**

7. $\frac{30}{48} = \frac{u}{104}$
   u = **65**

8. $\frac{45}{c} = \frac{27}{66}$
   c = **110**

Find the percent of increase or decrease. Round to the nearest whole percent. *[Lessons 6-4 and 6-5]*

9. old: 7.3 new: 11.4 — **56% increase**
10. old: 27.6 new: 21.8 — **21% decrease**
11. old: 384 new: 400 — **4% increase**
12. old: $129.95 new: $113.60 — **13% decrease**

13. old: 16.4 new: 12.8 — **22% decrease**
14. old: $84.30 new: $89.90 — **7% increase**
15. old: 57 new: 42 — **26% decrease**
16. old: 38 new: 157 — **313% increase**

Determine whether the given number is divisible by 2, 3, 4, 5, 6, 8, 9, or 10. *[Lesson 7-1]*

17. 532 **2, 4**
18. 817 **None**
19. 486 **2, 3, 6, 9**
20. 860 **2, 4, 5, 10**
21. 178 **2**
22. 135 **3, 5, 9**

Use a protractor to measure each angle. Classify each angle as right, straight, obtuse, or acute. *[Lesson 8-4]*

23. ∠BAD **65°; acute**
24. ∠BCD **65°; acute**
25. ∠ABC **90°; right**
26. ∠ABD **35°; acute**
27. ∠ADC **140°; obtuse**
28. ∠BDC **60°; acute**

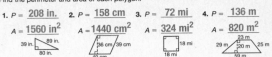

Identify each polygon. Be as specific as possible. *[Lesson 8-6]*

29. **Trapezoid**
30. **Regular pentagon**
31. **Scalene triangle**

Perimeter and Area of Polygons

Practice
9-1

Find the perimeter and area of each polygon.

1. P = **208 in.** A = **1560 in²** (39 in., 89 in., 80 in.)
2. P = **158 cm** A = **1440 cm²** (36 cm/39 cm, 40 cm)
3. P = **72 mi** A = **324 mi²** (18 mi, 18 mi)
4. P = **136 m** A = **820 m²** (23 m, 29 m, 20 m, 25 m, 59 m)

5. P = **50 cm** A = **115.5 cm²** (16.5 cm, 18.7 cm, 17.3 cm, 14 cm)
6. P = **$7\frac{3}{4}$ in.** A = **$3\frac{7}{16}$ in²** ($1\frac{3}{8}$ in, $2\frac{1}{2}$ in)
7. P = **13.6 m** A = **9.86 m²** (2.9 m, 3.4 m, 3.4 m)
8. P = **196 ft** A = **1777 ft²** (55 ft, 43 ft, 21 ft, 15 ft, x)

9. P = **$21\frac{3}{4}$ ft** A = **$23\frac{3}{4}$ ft²** ($7\frac{3}{4}$ ft, $7\frac{1}{4}$ ft, 5 ft, $2\frac{1}{8}$ ft)
10. P = **12.2 km** A = **7.98 km²** (2.3 km, 2.1 km, 3.8 km)
11. P = **$11\frac{1}{2}$ in.** A = **$6\frac{5}{32}$ in²** ($1\frac{3}{8}$ in, $1\frac{1}{4}$ in, 1 in, $3\frac{1}{2}$ in)
12. P = **30.0 cm** A = **35.28 cm²** (7.8 cm, 7.3 cm, 4.8 cm, 6.9 cm, 8 cm)

Use the figure to the right for Exercises 13–15.

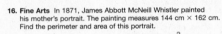

13. Give the value of x and the value of y.
   x = **28 cm** y = **24 cm**

(80 cm, 36 cm, 48 cm, 36 cm, 108 cm)

14. Find each area.
   Square: **1296 cm²** Rectangle: **1536 cm²**
   Triangle: **1536 cm²** Total: **4368 cm²**

15. Find the perimeter of the figure. **368 cm**

16. **Fine Arts** In 1871, James Abbott McNeill Whistler painted his mother's portrait. The painting measures 144 cm × 162 cm. Find the perimeter and area of this portrait.
   Perimeter: **612 cm** Area: **23,328 cm²**

Scale and Area

Practice
9-2

Find the perimeter and area of each polygon after the given dilation.

1. Scale factor = $\frac{1}{3}$
   P = **20 cm** A = **25 cm²** (15 cm, 15 cm)
2. Scale factor = 2
   P = **252 ft** A = **2520 ft²** (45 ft, 53 ft, 28 ft)
3. Scale factor = 0.8
   P = **112 m** A = **604.8 m²** (25 m, 21 m, 45 m)

4. Scale factor = 3.6
   P = **75.6 ft** A = **272.16 ft²** ($7\frac{1}{2}$ ft, 7 ft, 6 ft, $6\frac{3}{4}$ ft)
5. Scale factor = 0.4
   P = **8.32 cm** A = **4.032 cm²** (6.5 cm, 3.2 cm, 4.8 cm, 6.3 cm)
6. Scale factor = 1.8
   P = **180 yd** A = **1620 yd²** (25 yd, 20 yd, 25 yd)

7. Scale factor = 4
   P = **18 in.** A = **$19\frac{1}{4}$ in²** ($1\frac{3}{8}$ in, $\frac{7}{8}$ in)
8. Scale factor = 7.5
   P = **252 cm** A = **2646 cm²** (8.4 cm, 14 cm, 11.2 cm)
9. Scale factor = $\frac{1}{2}$
   P = **$28\frac{1}{4}$ in.** A = **$41\frac{1}{4}$ in²** ($2\frac{3}{8}$ in, $18\frac{3}{4}$ in, $19\frac{1}{2}$ in, 18 in, $15\frac{1}{2}$ in)

10. Carolyn's construction business has been hired to provide new carpet and baseboard for a rectangular hotel lobby. A floor plan, drawn at a scale factor of $\frac{1}{20}$, measures 3 ft × $1\frac{3}{4}$ ft.

   a. What is the area of the carpet for the lobby? **2100 ft²**

   b. The length of baseboard required is equal to the perimeter of the lobby. How much baseboard is needed? **190 ft**

Circles

Practice
9-3

Sketch each figure.

1. Octagon inscribed in a circle
2. Hexagon circumscribed about a circle

Find the circumference of each circle. Use π = 3.14.

3. **25.12 cm** (r = 4 cm)
4. **34.54 in.** (d = 11 in.)
5. **52.752 m** (r = 8.4 m)
6. **19.625 ft** (d = $6\frac{1}{4}$ ft)

Find the area of each circle. Use π = 3.14.

7. **226.865 mi²** (d = 17 mi)
8. **530.66 in²** (r = 13 in.)
9. **70.84625 ft²** (d = $9\frac{1}{2}$ ft)
10. **162.7776 km²** (r = 7.2 km)

11. **75.3914 cm²** (r = 4.9 cm)
12. **≈ 0.4416 ft²** (d = $\frac{3}{4}$ ft)
13. **0.5024 cm²** (r = 0.4 cm)
14. **≈ 371.354 in²** (d = $21\frac{1}{2}$ in.)

15. **Science** Saturn is surrounded by hundreds of rings of tiny particles in orbit about the planet. The innermost rings have a circumference of about 260,000 mi. Find the radius. **About 41,400 mi**

16. A round clock face has a diameter of 15 in. Find the area. **About 177 in²**

Name _____

Surface Area of Prisms and Cylinders

Practice 9-4

Sketch a net for each, then find the surface area. **Nets may vary**

1. SA = **292 cm²**

 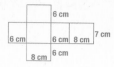

8 cm   7 cm   6 cm
6 cm   6 cm   8 cm   7 cm
6 cm   6 cm
8 cm   6 cm

2. SA ≈ **123.6 in²**

$r = 2\frac{1}{4}$ in.

≈14.13 in. $6\frac{1}{2}$ in.

$6\frac{1}{2}$ in.

3. SA = **413.34 cm²**

 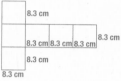

8.3 cm   8.3 cm   8.3 cm   8.3 cm   8.3 cm
8.3 cm   8.3 cm
8.3 cm

4. SA = **324 ft²**

6 ft   15 ft
9 ft
9 ft
12 ft

9 ft
12 ft   15 ft   9 ft   6 ft
9 ft

5. A birthday present is packaged in a tube that has length 8 in. and diameter 3 in. How much paper is needed to wrap the present? (Ignore any overlap.)   **About $89\frac{1}{2}$ in²**

6. A shoebox is 4 in. tall with a 6-in. × 10-in. base. If there is no lid, how much cardboard is needed to make this box?   **188 in²**

Use with pages 461–465. **89**

Name _____

Surface Area of Pyramids and Cones

Practice 9-5

For each figure, find **a.** the slant height; **b.** the surface area.

1. a. **41 cm**
   b. **1800 cm²**

h = 40 cm
18 cm
18 cm

2. a. **Given**
   b. **≈ 332.4 in²**

15 in.
12 in.
12 in.   12 in.

3. a. **19.3 m**
   b. **≈ 859.1 m²**

h = 16.8 m
r = 9.5 m

4. a. **Given**
   b. **≈ 36.93 cm²**

5 cm
4 cm   4 cm
4 cm

5. a. **$15\frac{1}{4}$ in.**
   b. **155.43 in²**

15 in.
$5\frac{1}{2}$ in.

6. a. **15.7 m**
   b. **822.8 m²**

h = 13.2 m
17 m   17 m

7. a. **65 mm**
   b. **≈ 10,155 mm²**

r = 33 mm
56 mm

8. a. **29 ft**
   b. **3920 ft²**

h = 21 ft
40 ft
40 ft

9. a. **Given**
   b. **≈ 177.8 cm²**

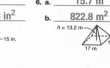

8.6 cm   11.3 cm
8.6 cm   8.6 cm

10. **History** The largest of the Egyptian pyramids was built almost 5000 years ago. Its square base has sides of length 755 ft, and it was originally about 482 ft tall. Find the slant height and the surface area (do not include the base).

   Slant height: **About 612.2 ft**   Surface area: **About 924,000 ft²**

11. A circular cone has a surface area of 282.6 cm². The base of the cone has radius 5 cm. Find the slant height. Then use the Pythagorean Theorem to find the height of the cone.

   Slant height: **13 cm**   Height: **12 cm**

90 Use with pages 466–471.

Name _____

Section 9A Review

Practice

Fill in the appropriate vocabulary term for each sentence.

1. A **(circular) cone** is a 3-D figure with a single vertex and a circular base.

2. The circumference of a circle is 2π times the **radius**.

3. The **surface area** of a polyhedron can be found by adding the areas of all the faces.

Find the perimeter/circumference and area for each figure.

4. P = **50.8 cm**
   A = **161.29 cm²**

12.7 cm
12.7 cm

5. P = **$13\frac{3}{4}$ in.**
   A = **$10\frac{5}{16}$ in²**

$2\frac{3}{4}$ in. $3\frac{1}{8}$ in.
$3\frac{3}{4}$ in.

6. P = **15.6 m**
   A = **10.14 m²**

6.5 m   5.2 m
3.9 m

7. P = **47.6 m**
   A = **122.85 m²**

7.3 m
13.7 m   10.5 m
16.1 m

8. P = **51 km**
   A = **115.08 km²**

14.3 km
11.2 km   6.6 km
x   y
4.5 km

9. C = **≈ 17.27 ft**
   A = **≈ 23.75 ft²**

$d = 5\frac{1}{2}$ ft

Find the surface area of each figure.

10. **≈ 1413 cm²**

40 cm
9 cm

11. **118 in²**

4 in.
6 in. $3\frac{1}{2}$ in.

12. **≈ 119.4 m²**

6.2 m
4.5 m

13. The population of Cleveland, Ohio, decreased 11.9% from 1980 to 1990. If the 1990 population was 505,600, what was the 1980 population? [Lesson 6-5]   **About 573,890**

14. Tell what metric unit you would use to measure the height of a cathedral. [Lesson 8-1]   **Possible answer: meter**

Use with page 474. **91**

Name _____

Volume of Rectangular Prisms

Practice 9-6

Find the volume of each figure.

1. **16,422 in³**

42 in.   17 in.
23 in.

2. **1728 cm³**

12 cm
12 cm   12 cm

3. **21 ft³**

$3\frac{1}{2}$ ft
2 ft   3 ft

4. **24 yd³**

2 yd   6 yd
2 yd

5. **1881 in³**

$8\frac{1}{2}$ in.   24 in.

6. **389.017 cm³**

7.3 cm
7.3 cm   7.3 cm

7. **32.487 m³**

1.6 m
3.1 m   5.6 m
2.1 m
3.7 m

8. **1840 in³**

8 in.
9 in.
8 in.
7 in.   10 in.

9. **56,862 mm³**

26 mm   22 mm
48 mm   65 mm
27 mm

Sketch the figure, then find its volume.   **Drawings will vary.**

10. A cassette box that measures 1.7 cm by 7 cm by 10.9 cm

   V = **129.71 cm³**

7 cm
1.7 cm   The Best of Bubba
10.9 cm

11. A recycling bin that is 15 in. wide, $20\frac{1}{2}$ in. long and 13 in. tall

   V = **$3997\frac{1}{2}$ in³**

Newspapers Only
13 in.
15 in.
$20\frac{1}{2}$ in.

12. The lobby of the Hyatt Regency Hotel in San Francisco, California measures 350 ft by 160 ft. Its ceiling is 170 ft tall. Find the volume of a rectangular prism with these dimensions.

   9,520,000 ft³

92 Use with pages 476–480.

153

Practice 9-7

Scale and Volume

Find the volume of each prism after scaling one dimension by the indicated scale factor.

1. Scale factor = 3

$V = \underline{2016 \ cm^3}$

14 cm, 6 cm, 8 cm

2. Scale factor = $\frac{1}{16}$

$V = \underline{32 \ in^3}$

8 in., 8 in., 8 in.

3. Scale factor = $\frac{3}{7}$

$V = \underline{126 \ m^3}$

7 m, 14 m, 3 m

Find the volume of each figure after the dilation.

4. Scale factor = $\frac{1}{2}$

$V = \underline{259.47 \ cm^3}$

18 cm, 12.4 cm, 9.3 cm

5. Scale factor = $\frac{2}{3}$

$V = \underline{333\frac{1}{3} \ in^3}$

$7\frac{1}{2}$ in., 20 in., $7\frac{1}{2}$ in.

6. Scale factor = 10

$V = \underline{804,357 \ cm^3}$

9.3 cm, 9.3 cm, 9.3 cm

7. Scale factor = $\frac{1}{10}$

$V = \underline{91 \ mm^3}$

65 mm, 40 mm, 35 mm

8. Scale factor = 3

$V = \underline{1012\frac{1}{2} \ ft^3}$

2 ft, $2\frac{1}{2}$ ft, $7\frac{1}{2}$ ft

9. Scale factor = $\frac{1}{7}$

$V = \underline{30 \ cm^3}$

42 cm, 35 cm, 7 cm

10. Some sponges expand when they become wet. A dry sponge measures $\frac{3}{8}$ in. by $1\frac{3}{4}$ in. by $2\frac{3}{4}$ in. If water dilates this sponge by a scale factor of 2, find the volume of the wet sponge.

$\underline{14\frac{7}{16} \ in^3}$

11. **Science** Every cubic foot of air weighs about 0.26 lb. Find the weight of the air in a 11-ft by 13-ft room with an 8-ft ceiling.

$\underline{About \ 297 \ lb}$

Practice 9-8

Volume of Prisms and Cylinders

Find the volume of each solid. Use 3.14 for π.

1. $\underline{1552.5 \ cm^3}$

15 cm, 9 cm, 23 cm

2. $\underline{693 \ in^3}$

7 in., 9 in., 11 in.

3. $\underline{\approx 773,325 \ mm^3}$

143 mm, 83 mm

4. $\underline{\approx 4786 \ cm^3}$

38.4 cm, r = 6.3 cm

5. $\underline{244\frac{3}{8} \ in^3}$

10 in., $5\frac{3}{4}$ in., $8\frac{1}{2}$ in.

6. $\underline{36,192 \ mm^3}$

26 mm, 48 mm, 29 mm

7. $\underline{38.88 \ m^3}$

5.4 m, 4.8 m, $\frac{3}{?}$ m

8. $\underline{2400 \ ft^3}$

12 ft, 20 ft, 8 ft, 18 ft

9. $\underline{\approx 2111 \ cm^3}$

r = 9 cm, 8.3 cm

10. $\underline{39.69 \ m^3}$

6.3 m, 2.8 m, 4.5 m, 5.3 m

11. $\underline{\approx 45.73 \ yd^3}$

d = $3\frac{3}{?}$ yd, $4\frac{1}{3}$ yd

12. $\underline{879.06 \ cm^3}$

Pentagon area: 48.3 cm²
18.2 cm

13. The attic of Karen's house has the shape of the triangular prism shown at the right. Find the volume of the attic.

$\underline{6075 \ ft^3}$

9 ft, 45 ft, 30 ft

14. A cylindrical cookie tin has a diameter of 10 in. and a height of $3\frac{1}{2}$ in. How many cubic inches of cookies can it hold? Round your answer to the nearest cubic inch.

$\underline{275 \ in^3}$

Practice 9-9

Volume of Pyramids and Cones

Find the volume of each solid. Use 3.14 for π.

1. $\underline{2601 \ ft^3}$

h = 27 ft, 17 ft, 17 ft

2. $\underline{484.5 \ cm^3}$

h = 17 cm, 19 cm, 9 cm

3. $\underline{28.26 \ in^3}$

h = 12 in., r = $1\frac{1}{2}$ in.

4. $\underline{1205.76 \ ft^3}$

h = 18 ft, 16 ft

5. $\underline{\approx 114.7 \ cm^3}$

h = 11.5 cm, 7.3 cm, 8.2 cm

6. $\underline{\approx 21.1 \ in^3}$

h = $4\frac{1}{2}$ in., $3\frac{3}{4}$ in., $3\frac{3}{4}$ in.

7. $\underline{\approx 3538 \ ft^3}$

r = 13 ft, h = 20 ft

8. $\underline{1650 \ cm^3}$

h = 22 cm, 15 cm

9. $\underline{136\frac{7}{8} \ in^3}$

h = $7\frac{1}{2}$ in., 12 in., $9\frac{3}{8}$ in.

10. $\underline{110,592 \ ft^3}$

h = 81 ft, 64 ft, 64 ft

11. $\underline{7728 \ mm^3}$

h = 46 mm, 24 mm, 42 mm

12. $\underline{\approx 362.9 \ in^3}$

h = $8\frac{7}{8}$ in., r = $6\frac{1}{4}$ in.

13. The base of a square pyramid has sides of length 15 in. If the pyramid has volume 1050 in³, what is the height?

$\underline{14 \ in.}$

14. A special cushion designed to go in a corner is shaped like a triangular pyramid. The base is a right triangle with sides of length 42 cm, 56 cm, and 70 cm. If the height of the pillow is 64 cm, what is the volume?

$\underline{25,088 \ cm^3}$

Practice

Section 9B Review

Find the volume of each solid. Use 3.14 for π.

1. $\underline{660 \ ft^3}$

11 ft, 8 ft, 15 ft

2. $\underline{110.592 \ cm^3}$

4.8 cm, 4.8 cm, 4.8 cm

3. $\underline{\approx 78.28 \ in^3}$

h = $5\frac{1}{2}$ in., $7\frac{3}{8}$ in.

4. $\underline{1309 \ ft^3}$

$8\frac{1}{2}$ ft, 14 ft, 11 ft

5. $\underline{9847.04 \ m^3}$

r = 14 m, 16 m

6. $\underline{\approx 7.29 \ in^3}$

h = $3\frac{1}{2}$ in., $2\frac{1}{2}$ in.

Find the volume for each after the given dilation.

7. Scale factor = 4

$V = \underline{24\frac{1}{16} \ in^3}$

$\frac{5}{16}$ in., $\frac{7}{8}$ in., $1\frac{3}{8}$ in.

8. Scale factor = $\frac{2}{3}$

$V = \underline{7.68 \ cm^3}$

3 cm, 2.4 cm, 3.6 cm

9. Scale factor = 0.75

$V = \underline{216 \ in^3}$

8 in., 8 in., 8 in.

10. Which has the greater volume: a cone with radius 8 in. and height 12 in. or a cylinder with diameter 9 in. and height 12 in.?

$\underline{Cone}$

11. A decorative pedestal has the shape of a prism with a square pyramid on top, as shown. What is the volume of the pedestal?

$\underline{960 \ in^3}$

Total height 32 in., 24 in., 6 in., 6 in.

12. **Geography** Springfield, Illinois, is 193 mi due west of Indianapolis, Indiana. Jeanette drove due north from Indianapolis until she was 215 mi from Springfield. How far did she drive? [Lesson 7-9]

$\underline{About \ 94.7 \ miles}$

215 mi, x, Springfield, 193 mi, Indianapolis

13. **Geography** A portion of Utah is shown. Name all cities in 2B. If none, write "None." [Lesson 8-3]

$\underline{Knolls, \ Delle}$

Cumulative Review Chapters 1–9

Write each percent as a fraction in lowest terms and as a decimal. *[Lesson 6-1]*

1. 82% $\frac{41}{50}$; 0.82   **2.** 60% $\frac{3}{5}$; 0.60   **3.** 13% $\frac{13}{100}$; 0.13

4. 25% $\frac{1}{4}$; 0.25   **5.** 8% $\frac{2}{25}$; 0.08   **6.** 35% $\frac{7}{20}$; 0.35

Identify each number as rational or irrational. *[Lesson 7-8]*

7. $\sqrt{36}$ Rational   **8.** $\sqrt{0.64}$ Rational   **9.** $\sqrt{28}$ Irrational

10. $\sqrt{\frac{49}{81}}$ Rational   **11.** $\sqrt{12}$ Irrational   **12.** $\sqrt{\frac{144}{25}}$ Rational

In the figure shown at right, $\overleftrightarrow{VW} \parallel \overleftrightarrow{XY}$. *[Lesson 8-5]*   **Possible answers:**

13. Name a pair of alternate interior angles. $\angle 4, \angle 6$

14. Name a pair of corresponding angles. $\angle 3, \angle 7$

15. Name a pair of vertical angles. $\angle 1, \angle 3$

16. Name the angles that are congruent to $\angle 3$. $\angle 1, \angle 5, \angle 7$

Find the perimeter and area of each polygon after the given dilation. *[Lesson 9-2]*

17. Scale factor = 4   **18.** Scale factor = 2   **19.** Scale factor = $\frac{1}{5}$

$P = $ __184 cm__ $P = $ __250 in.__ $P = $ __3.2 m__

$A = $ __2112 cm^2__ $A = $ __$2062\frac{1}{2}$ in^2__ $A = $ __0.5504 m^2__

Find the volume of each solid. Use 3.14 for π. *[Lesson 9-9]*

20. __246.96 cm^3__   **21.** __$143\frac{11}{16}$ in^3__   **22.** __≈151.0 m^3__

Functions

For the function machine shown, find the output value for each input value.

1. Input of 20 __1__   **2.** Input of 5 __−2__

3. Input of −35 __−10__   **4.** Input of 13 __−0.4__

[Input → Divide by 5 and subtract 3 → Output]

For the function machine shown, find the input value for each output value.

5. Output of 6 __−1__   **6.** Output of 12 __5__

7. Output of −28 __−35__   **8.** Output of −13 __−20__

[Input → Add 7 → Output]

What is a possible rule for the input and output shown in each table?

9.

Input	1	3	5	9
Output	16	18	20	24

Add 15.

10.

Input	−1	0	1	2
Output	−5	−2	1	4

Multiply by 3 and subtract 2.

11.

Input	−8	−3	2	7
Output	7	7	7	7

Output is always 7.

12.

Input	64	4	−4	−8
Output	16	1	−1	−2

Divide by 4.

13. At Roy's Donut Shop, if you buy 1 to 4 donuts, you pay $0.50 per donut. If you buy 5 to 8 donuts, the price is $0.40 each. Roy limits each customer to 8 donuts.

a. Complete the table by finding the *total* purchase price for each number of donuts.

Number of donuts	0	1	2	3	4	5	6	7	8
Total price ($)	0.00	0.50	1.00	1.50	2.00	2.00	2.40	2.80	3.20

b. Is the price a function of the number of donuts? Explain. __Yes. For each number of donuts, there is only one price.__

c. Is the number of donuts a function of the price? Explain. __No. For the input $2.00, there are two possible outputs (4 or 5 donuts).__

Linear Functions

Given the following function rules, complete the table of values.

1. $y = 4x - 8$

Input (x)	Output (y)
−1	−12
0	−8
1	−4
2	0
3	4

2. $y = -2x + 3$

Input (x)	Output (y)
−1	5
0	3
1	1
2	−1
3	−3

3. $y = -5x - 2$

Input (x)	Output (y)
−1	3
0	−2
1	−7
2	−12
3	−17

Graph each linear equation. Does the equation describe a function?

4. $y = -2$ __Yes__   **5.** $y = x - 3$ __Yes__   **6.** $x = 1$ __No__

Does each table of values represent a function? Explain your answer.

7.

Input (x)	−1	3	1	5	3
Output (y)	3	4	7	2	8

No; There are two possible outputs for an input of 3.

8.

Input (x)	−4	2	6	7	8
Output (y)	3	5	1	5	7

Yes; For each input value, there is only one output value.

9. Science The speed of sound in air is about 1088 ft/sec.

a. Write an equation to show the relationship between distance d and time t. $d = 1088t$

b. Use your equation to find how far a sound travels in 2 seconds, 5 seconds, and 10 seconds.

2 seconds __2,176 ft__   5 seconds __5,440 ft__   10 seconds __10,880 ft__

Quadratic Functions

Graph each set of functions.

1. $y = x^2 - 2$, $y = x^2$, and $y = x^2 + 2$

2. $y = x^2$, $y = -2x^2$ and $y = 3x^2$

3. $y = -x^2$, $y = -x^2 + 2$ and $y = -x^2 + 5$

Match each graph with the function that describes it.

4. __B__   **5.** __C__   **6.** __A__

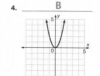

7. __E__   **8.** __D__   **9.** __F__

  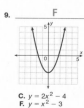

A. $y = -2x^2$ **B.** $y = 2x^2$ **C.** $y = 2x^2 - 4$
D. $y = -2x^2 + 4$ **E.** $y = -x^2 + 3$ **F.** $y = x^2 - 3$

10. For a group of n people, the formula $h = \frac{1}{2}(n^2 - n)$ gives the number of handshakes that would occur if each person shook hands once with each other person. Find the number of handshakes for each number of people.

a. $n = 1$ __0__   **b.** $n = 4$ __6__   **c.** $n = 9$ __36__   **d.** $n = 25$ __300__

Other Functions

Graph each function.

1. $y = 3x$

2. $y = 3^x$

3. $y = 0.4x$

4. $y = 0.4^x$

5. $y = \left(\frac{4}{3}\right)^x$

6. $y = \left(\frac{3}{4}\right)^x$

Identify each function as linear, quadratic, exponential, or step.

7. $y = 2x + 5$ __Linear__

8. $y = 5^x$ __Exponential__

9. $y = $ round up to the next hundred __Step__

10. $y = 0.3^x$ __Exponential__

11. $y = 4x^2$ __Quadratic__

12. $y = $ multiply by 7 __Linear__

13. $y = x + 8$ __Linear__

14. $y = -x^2 + 3$ __Quadratic__

15. $y = $ round to the nearest 0.1 __Step__

16. Consumer A mail-order catalog lists the following charges for shipping and handling:

Price of Order ($)	Under 10	10 to 25	Over 25
Shipping Charge ($)	2.50	4.00	7.00

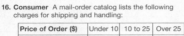

a. Graph the function.

b. What kind of function is this? __Step function__

Section 10A Review

For the function machine shown, find each missing value.

1. Input 3, output __3__   **2.** Input __9__, output 5

3. Input −9, output __−1__   **4.** Input __−15__, output −3

Sketch an example of a graph for each kind of function.

Possible answers:

5. Exponential

6. Step

7. Quadratic

8. Is y a function of x? Explain.

x	1	0	1	2	3
y	−2	−1	0	1	2

No; There are two possible outputs for an input value of 1.

9. Graph $y = 2$, $y = 2x$, $y = x^2$, and $y = 2^x$. Describe the similarities and differences.

__Answers will vary.__

10. Science An elephant can run about 25 mi/hr at maximum speed. If distance is a function of time, write an equation to show the relationship between distance and time. Use your equation to show how far the elephant could travel in 3 hours at this speed.

$d = 25t$; 75 mi

11. The population of San Francisco, California, was about 716,000 in 1970. It decreased 5.2% from 1970 to 1980, and increased 6.6% from 1980 to 1990. What was the population in 1990? *[Lesson 6-6]*

About 724,000

12. The floor plan of a home shows a kitchen that is $6\frac{2}{3}$ in. by 8 in. If the scale factor is 18, what is the area of the actual kitchen? *[Lesson 9-2]*

17,280 in² or 120 ft²

Polynomials

Identify each expression as a monomial, binomial, or trinomial.

1. $2x^3$ __Monomial__   **2.** $5y - 7$ __Binomial__   **3.** $x^5 - 3x^2 + 2$ __Trinomial__

4. $c^3 - 5$ __Binomial__   **5.** $8d + 2 - d^5$ __Trinomial__   **6.** $215k$ __Monomial__

Write each polynomial expression in descending order. Then find the degree of each polynomial.

7. $7 - 5x + 2x^3$ Deg.: __3__   **8.** $12 + 3x$ Deg.: __1__   **9.** $3x + 2 + x^2$ Deg.: __2__

$2x^3 - 5x + 7$ $3x + 12$ $x^2 + 3x + 2$

10. $-x^3 + 2x^7$ Deg.: __7__   **11.** $7x^4 - 2x^3$ Deg.: __4__   **12.** $4x - 3 + x^5$ Deg.: __5__

$2x^7 - x^3$ $7x^4 - 2x^3$ $x^5 + 4x - 3$

Evaluate each polynomial for $x = -5$.

13. $4x + 7$ __−13__   **14.** $-7x + 3$ __38__   **15.** $4x^2 + 18x$ __10__

16. $x^2 - 3x + 8$ __48__   **17.** x^3 __−125__   **18.** $x^2 - 5x + 7$ __57__

Evaluate each polynomial for $t = 3$ and for $t = 8$.

19. $t^3 - 5$ **20.** $-3t^2 + 12t$ **21.** $56 - 9t$

$t = 3$: __22__ $t = 3$: __9__ $t = 3$: __29__

$t = 8$: __507__ $t = 8$: __−96__ $t = 8$: __−16__

22. $5 + 8t^2 - t$ **23.** $8t - 4 + t^2$ **24.** $t^3 - 2t - 12$

$t = 3$: __74__ $t = 3$: __29__ $t = 3$: __9__

$t = 8$: __509__ $t = 8$: __124__ $t = 8$: __484__

25. Science A ball is thrown upward at a speed of 48 ft/sec. Its height h, in feet, after t seconds, is given by $h = 48t - 16t^2$. Find the height after 2 seconds.

__32 ft__

26. Geometry The formulas $S = 4\pi r^2$ and $V = \frac{4}{3}\pi r^3$ give the surface area S and volume V of a sphere with radius r. The moon has radius 1080 mi. Find the surface area and volume. Use 3.14 for π.

Surface area: __≈ 14,650,000 mi²__   Volume __≈ 5,274,000,000 mi³__

Adding Polynomials

Simplify each if possible. If the expression cannot be simplified, write "simplified." Write answers in descending order.

1. $5p^2 + 7p^2$ __12p²__   **2.** $3x^4 - 3x + 4x^2 + 8x$ __3x⁴ + 4x² + 5x__

3. $9t^3 - 5t^2 - 4t^3$ __5t³ − 5t²__   **4.** $6w^3 - 4w^2 + 6w - 4$ __Simplified__

5. $7x + 9x^2 - 12x + 3$ __9x² − 5x + 3__   **6.** $4u^3 + 7u - 21u^3$ __−17u³ + 7u__

7. $8g^5 + 3g^3 - 2g + 3$ __Simplified__   **8.** $3k - 9 - 2k + 35$ __k + 26__

Find each polynomial sum. Write the answers in simplest form.

9. $(3x^2 + 4x) + (x^2 + 7x - 3)$

$4x^2 + 11x - 3$

10. $(2j - 5) + (3j^2 - 7j + 14)$

$3j^2 - 5j + 9$

11. $(-z^3 + 8z - 2) + (2z^2 - 3z + 2)$

$-z^3 + 2z^2 + 5z$

12. $(5s^2 - 4s + 7) + (3s^2 + 4s + 11)$

$8s^2 + 18$

13. $(7g^2 - 5g + 4)$ $+ (4g^2 + 7g - 6)$

$11g^2 + 2g - 2$

14. $(-4y^2 + 2y - 3)$ $+ (-6y - 7)$

$-4y^2 - 4y - 10$

15. $(m^2 + 4m + 3)$ $+ (2m^2 - m + 4)$

$3m^2 + 3m + 7$

Find the total floor area of each birdhouse.

16. $3x^2 - 3x + 7$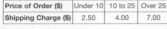

17. $5x^3 + 23x + 7$

18. $3x^2 - 21x + 22$

19. A tabletop is $4x^2 - 2x + 7$ in. above the floor. A computer monitor with height $7x - 3$ in. is on the table. Write a polynomial in simplest form to represent the distance from the top of the monitor to the floor. What is the distance if $x = 3$?

$4x^2 + 5x + 4$; 55 in.

20. If you know x^2, the square of an even number x, you can find the square of the next even number by adding $4x + 4$ to x^2. The square of 46 is 2116. Show how you can add polynomials and evaluate to find 48^2.

Possible answer: $x^2 + 4x + 4 = 2116 + 4 \cdot 46 + 4 = 2304$

Subtracting Polynomials

Find the additive inverse of each polynomial.

1. $3x + 7$ ___ $-3x - 7$ 2. $4x^2 - (-2x) - 7$ ___ $-4x^2 - 2x + 7$

3. $x^2 + 2x + (-9)$ ___ $-x^2 - 2x + 9$ 4. $3x^3 - 7x + 5$ ___ $-3x^3 + 7x - 5$

Subtract. Write your answers in simplest form.

5. $(4x - 3) - (9x + 4)$

___ $-5x - 7$

6. $(3x^2 - 2x + 7) - (x^2 + 2x + 5)$

___ $2x^2 - 4x + 2$

7. $(4p + 7) - (p^2 + 8p - 3)$

___ $-p^2 - 4p + 10$

8. $(7t^2) - (3t^2 + 5t + 8)$

___ $4t^2 - 5t - 8$

9. $\begin{array}{r} (8k^2 + 2k + 3) \\ -(3k^2 - 6k + 4) \end{array}$
$5k^2 + 8k - 1$

10. $\begin{array}{r} (5u^2 + 7u + 9) \\ -(2u^2 + 3u + 9) \end{array}$
$3u^2 + 4u$

11. $\begin{array}{r} (c^3 - 2c^2 + 4) \\ -(c^3 + 3c^2 + 8) \end{array}$
$-5c^2 - 4$

Find an expression for the area of each shaded region, given the total area A of each figure.

12. $x^2 - 7x + 15$ 13. $x^2 - 4x - 13$ 14. $x^2 - 8x + 7$

$A = x^2 - 3x + 6$

$A = 3x^2 - 7x - 2$

$A = 4x^2 - 8x + 2$

Find the missing side length, based on the perimeter of each figure.

15. $3x^2 - 4x - 4$ 16. $x^2 - 3x - 7$ 17. $x^2 + 3x - 9$

$p = 5x^2 + 3x - 2$ $p = 3x^2 + 10x - 6$ $p = 4x^2$

18. **Physics** A ball is dropped from the top of a 128-foot building at the same time that Sam begins riding up on the elevator. The ball's height, in feet, is given by $-16t^2 + 128$, and Sam's height, in feet, is given by $4t$, where t is the number of seconds. Find a polynomial that tells how far above Sam that ball is after t seconds.

$-16t^2 - 4t + 128$ ft

Multiplying Polynomials and Monomials

Multiply.

1. $3^7 \cdot 3^4$ ___ 3^{11} 2. $x^3 \cdot x^5$ ___ x^8 3. $3t^6 \cdot t^8$ ___ $3t^{14}$

4. $(5c^8)(7c^{12})$ ___ $35c^{20}$ 5. $(11u^2)(3u^0)$ ___ $33u^2$ 6. $(7p)(5p^3)$ ___ $35p^4$

7. $(12y^2)(3y^9)$ ___ $36y^{11}$ 8. $(-5g^3)(2g)$ ___ $-10g^4$ 9. $(6k^2)(-8k^4)$ ___ $-48k^6$

10. $4x(x^2 + 5x - 3)$

$4x^3 + 20x^2 - 12x$

11. $-7r(4r^7 - 8r^3 + 9)$

$-28r^8 + 56r^4 - 63r$

12. $\frac{1}{3}h^2(6h^3 - 12h^2 + 15)$

$2h^5 - 4h^4 + 5h^2$

13. $8v^3(-2v^2 + 7v - 3)$

$-16v^5 + 56v^4 - 24v^3$

14. $-2n^6(5n^4 + 3n^2 + 4)$

$-10n^{10} - 6n^8 - 8n^6$

15. $b^2(5b^2 - 8b + 3)$

$5b^4 - 8b^3 + 3b^2$

16. $-\frac{3}{4}q^3(-8q^2 + 64)$

$6q^5 - 48q^3$

17. $20w^6(6w^8 - 3w^6 + w^4)$

$120w^{14} - 60w^{12} + 20w^{10}$

Multiply each of the following. Write your answers in scientific notation.

18. $(2.3 \times 10^3)(1.7 \times 10^4)$ 3.91×10^7 19. $(4.6 \times 10^{11})(3.9 \times 10^9)$ 1.794×10^{21}

20. $(3.2 \times 10^3)(1.4 \times 10^3)$ 4.48×10^6 21. $(1.6 \times 10^6)(4.1 \times 10^5)$ 6.56×10^{11}

22. $(6.8 \times 10^7)(1.1 \times 10^1)$ 7.48×10^8 23. $(8.3 \times 10^{10})(7.9 \times 10^8)$ 6.557×10^{19}

24. $(3.0 \times 10^2)(1.9 \times 10^7)$ 5.7×10^9 25. $(2.4 \times 10^4)(3.1 \times 10^9)$ 7.44×10^{13}

26. $(6.3 \times 10^9)(1.4 \times 10^6)$ 8.82×10^{15} 27. $(8.4 \times 10^8)(1.0 \times 10^5)$ 8.4×10^{13}

28. **Social Science** Japan has about 3.35×10^2 people per square kilometer of land. The area of Japan is about 3.78×10^5 km². Find the population of Japan. Give your answer in scientific notation.

About 1.27×10^8 people

29. Multiply to find an expression for the volume of the aquarium. Simplify if possible.

$30x^7 - 90x^6 + 120x^5$

Section 10B Review

Identify each polynomial expression as a monomial, binomial, trinomial, or polynomial. Explain your choice.

1. $3x^5 + 2x - 4$

Trinomial; 3 terms

2. $7x^3$

Monomial; 1 term

3. $x^7 - 2$

Binomial; 2 terms

4. $-4x^3 + 2x - x + 3$

Polynomial; more than 3 terms

Find the degree of each polynomial expression. Write the polynomial expression in descending order.

5. $4x + 3x^5 - 6$ Deg.: 5   6. $-7 + 3x^2 - 5x$ Deg.: 2   7. $8x^3 - 5x^2 + x^4$ Deg.: 4

$3x^5 + 4x - 6$ $3x^2 - 5x - 7$ $x^4 + 8x^3 - 5x^2$

Simplify each if possible. If the expression cannot be simplified, write "simplified." Write your answer in descending order.

8. $5x + x^2 - 8x + x^2$ $2x^2 - 3x$ 9. $-7k^3 - 6k^2 + 2k - 3$ Simplified

10. $\begin{array}{r} (c^2 - 7c + 11) \\ +(4c^2 + 4c + 5) \end{array}$
$5c^2 - 3c + 16$

11. $\begin{array}{r} (15x^2 + 4x + 12) \\ -(7x^2 + 5x - 3) \end{array}$
$8x^2 - x + 15$

12. A rectangle has length $3x$ and width $2x + 1$. After a dilation of scale factor x, the area of the new rectangle is $x^2(3x)(2x + 1)$. Simplify this expression.

$6x^4 + 3x^3$

13. Multiply to find an expression for each area. Simplify if possible.

a. $24x^2 - 12x$ b. $6x^2 + 3x$

c. $9x^2$ d. $21x^2 - 15x$

$3x$	a.	b.	c.	d.
	$8x - 4$	$2x + 1$	$3x$	$7x - 5$

14. Four students were asked their heights. The answers were 4 ft, 51 in., 55 in., and $4\frac{1}{2}$ ft. What was the average height? [Lesson 8-1]

52 in. or $4\frac{1}{3}$ ft

15. A 1.44-megabyte computer disk uses a circular piece of magnetic media with radius $1\frac{11}{16}$ in. Find the circumference and the area. [Lesson 9-3]

Circumference: About 10.6 in.   Area: About 8.94 in²

Cumulative Review Chapters 1–10

Add, subtract, multiply or divide each of the following. Write each answer in simplest form. [Lessons 7-5, 7-6]

1. $3\frac{1}{5} + 2\frac{1}{4}$ $5\frac{9}{20}$ 2. $5\frac{1}{3} - 2\frac{1}{2}$ $2\frac{5}{6}$ 3. $4\frac{3}{7} + 8\frac{1}{2}$ $12\frac{13}{14}$ 4. $6\frac{1}{5} - \frac{5}{8}$ $5\frac{23}{40}$

5. $\frac{3}{4} \times \frac{5}{7}$ $\frac{15}{28}$ 6. $2\frac{1}{2} \div 3\frac{1}{3}$ $\frac{3}{4}$ 7. $2\frac{5}{8} \times 3\frac{3}{7}$ 9 8. $8\frac{2}{3} \div 2\frac{3}{5}$ $3\frac{1}{3}$

Identify each polygon. Be as specific as possible. [Lesson 8-6]

9. Regular pentagon   10. Trapezoid

11. Octagon   12. Equilateral triangle

Find the surface area of each figure. [Lesson 9-4]

13. $821\frac{3}{4}$ in²   14. 675.36 cm²   15. ≈ 25,321 ft²   16. ≈ 253.2 mm²

Graph each linear equation. Does the equation describe a function? [Lesson 10-2]

17. $x = -4$ No   18. $y = 3x$ Yes   19. $y = -2x + 1$ Yes

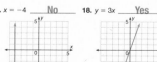 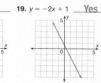

Add or subtract. Write the answers in simplest form. [Lesson 10-6]

20. $\begin{array}{r} (x^2 - 5x - 6) \\ -(3x^2 + 2x - 4) \end{array}$
$-2x^2 - 7x - 2$

21. $\begin{array}{r} (2x^2 + 7) \\ +(-x^2 - 2x + 3) \end{array}$
$x^2 - 2x + 10$

22. $\begin{array}{r} (5x - 3) \\ -(4x^2 + x - 7) \end{array}$
$-4x^2 + 4x + 4$

Practice 11-1

Name _____

Similar Figures

Decide whether each pair of figures is similar.

1. **Similar**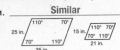

2. **Not similar**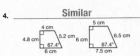

3. **Not similar**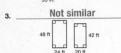

4. **Similar**

5. The two triangles are similar.
   a. Find x. **45 ft**
   b. Find the measure of $\angle 1$. **62°**

6. The two parallelograms are similar.
   a. Find y. **1.8 m**
   b. Find the measure of $\angle 2$. **72°**

7. The two trapezoids are similar.
   a. Find z. **44 in.**
   b. Find the measure of $\angle 3$. **134°**

8. The two car drawings are similar. Find x, the length of the larger car.
   85 cm

9. The Society Tower in Cleveland, Ohio, is 271 m tall. A scale drawing shows the tower at 10.84 cm. What is the scale factor of the drawing? $\dfrac{1}{2500}$

Practice 11-2

Name _____

Congruent Figures

The two quadrilaterals are congruent.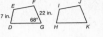

1. Find $m\angle JKH$. **68°**
2. Find $m\overline{HI}$. **17 in.**

The two hexagons are congruent.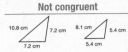

3. Find $m\angle STU$. **115°**
4. Find $m\overline{MN}$. **1.2 cm**

Determine whether each pair of figures is congruent.

5. **Not congruent**

6. **Not congruent**

7. **Congruent**

8. **Congruent**

9. **Algebra** In the figure, the polygons are congruent. Find the values of x and y.
   $x = $ **12** $y = $ $\dfrac{25}{6}$

10. Construct a polygon congruent to the one shown. Label the vertices and complete the statements. **Possible answers:**

   $\overline{AB}$ corresponds to **$\overline{GH}$**
   $\overline{AF}$ corresponds to **$\overline{GL}$**
   $\overline{DE}$ corresponds to **$\overline{JK}$**

Practice 11-3

Name _____

Triangle Congruence

For each pair, what rule tells you that the two triangles are congruent?

1. **Angle-Side-Angle**

2. **Side-Side-Side**

3. **Side-Angle-Side**

4. **Side-Angle-Angle**

State whether each pair of triangles has congruence; if it does, give the rule that justifies your answer.

5. **No**

6. **Yes; Side-Angle-Side**

7. **Yes; Side-Angle-Angle**

8. **No**

9. A craftsman building a stained glass window determines that BC and CD are the same length. State the rule used to determine this.
   Angle-Side-Angle

Practice 11-4

Name _____

Trigonometry

Use the lengths of the sides to evaluate the sine, cosine, and tangent ratios for each of the labeled angles.

1. $\sin \angle A = \dfrac{4}{5} = 0.8$
   $\cos \angle A = \dfrac{3}{5} = 0.6$
   $\tan \angle A = \dfrac{4}{3} \approx 1.333$

2. $\sin \angle B = \dfrac{12}{13} \approx 0.923$
   $\cos \angle B = \dfrac{5}{13} \approx 0.385$
   $\tan \angle B = \dfrac{12}{5} = 2.4$

3. $\sin \angle C = \approx 0.707$
   $\cos \angle C = \approx 0.707$
   $\tan \angle C = 1$

4. $\sin \angle D = \dfrac{45}{53} \approx 0.849$
   $\cos \angle D = \dfrac{28}{53} \approx 0.528$
   $\tan \angle D = \dfrac{45}{28} \approx 1.607$

5. $\sin \angle E = \dfrac{36}{85} \approx 0.424$
   $\cos \angle E = \dfrac{77}{85} \approx 0.906$
   $\tan \angle E = \dfrac{36}{77} \approx 0.468$

6. $\sin \angle F = \approx 0.883$
   $\cos \angle F = \approx 0.469$
   $\tan \angle F = \approx 1.881$

7. $\sin \angle G = \dfrac{48}{73} \approx 0.658$
   $\cos \angle G = \dfrac{55}{73} \approx 0.753$
   $\tan \angle G = \dfrac{48}{55} \approx 0.873$

8. $\sin \angle H = \dfrac{56}{65} \approx 0.862$
   $\cos \angle H = \dfrac{33}{65} \approx 0.508$
   $\tan \angle H = \dfrac{56}{33} \approx 1.697$

Find the length represented by x.

9. $x \approx 2.463$

10. $x \approx 19.178$

11. The top of the Landmark Tower in Yokohama, Japan, forms a 72° angle with a point $315\frac{1}{2}$ ft away from the tower's base, as shown. How tall is the Landmark Tower?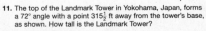
    About 971 ft

158

Indirect Measurement

1. Find the length of side $\overline{YZ}$.

_____ ≈ **3.30 cm**

2. The two triangles are similar. If $\overline{UW}$ measures 6.3 m, find $m\overline{UV}$.

_____ **4.05 m**

3. Fine Arts Giorgione's 1508 painting, *The Tempest*, is about 82 cm tall. A 16-cm-tall reproduction of this painting in a book features a bridge that is about 5.3 cm long. How long is the bridge on the actual painting?

_____ **About 27.2 cm**

4. Eve is 55 in. tall. Find the length of her shadow if the sun makes an angle of 38° as shown.

_____ **About 70.4 in.**

5. Larry wants to know the distance between two trees, *A* and *B*, on the opposite side of a river. He knows the river is 25 m wide. He marks off and measures a right triangle as shown. The two triangles are similar. How far apart are the trees?

_____ **40 m**

6. Geography Santa Fe, New Mexico, is about 480 mi from Fort Worth, Texas. Find the distance from Fort Worth to Oklahoma City, Oklahoma, if the three cities form a right triangle as shown.

_____ **About 188 mi**

7. Harold is 4 ft tall. When he stands 9 ft away from the base of a streetlight, his shadow is 3 ft long. How tall is the streetlight? (Start by finding the length of the base of the larger triangle.)

_____ **16 ft**

Section 11A Review

1. The pentagons are similar. Find the length represented by *x*.

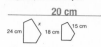

20 cm

2. Measure to determine if the two quadrilaterals are congruent.

Congruent

State whether each pair of triangles has congruence; if it does, give the rule that justifies your answer.

3.

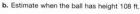

No

4.

Yes; Side-Angle-Side

5. A small table is supported by diagonal legs as shown. If $\triangle ABC \sim \triangle EDC$, find the width $m\overline{AB}$ of the table.

_____ **14.4 in.**

6. Kelly is flying a kite. If the kite string is 24 m long and makes an angle of 55° with the ground, how high is the kite? **About 19.66 m**

7. A cone-shaped container for a crushed ice drink is 5 in. tall and has a $3\frac{1}{2}$-in. diameter. How many cubic inches of crushed ice can the container hold? *[Lesson 9-5]*

About 16.0 in³

8. A ball is thrown upwards at a speed of 96 ft/sec. Its height, in feet, after *t* seconds is given by $h = 96t - 16t^2$. *[Lesson 10-3]*

a. Graph the function $h = 96t - 16t^2$.

b. Estimate when the ball has height 108 ft.

At $t = 1.5$ sec and $t = 4.5$ sec

c. When does the ball hit the ground?

At $t = 6$ sec

Transformations and Congruence

Tell what transformation of the lightly shaded figure produced the dark one.

1. **Reflection**

2. **Rotation**

3. **Translation**

Across which axis was each figure reflected?

4. _____ *x*-axis

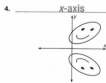

5. _____ *y*-axis

6. Find the coordinates of points *P* and *Q* on the triangle that has been translated 4 units to the right and 2.5 units up.

P **(1, −0.5)**   *Q* **(3, 2.5)**

7. Find the coordinates of points *R* and *S* on the trapezoid that has been rotated 90° clockwise about the origin.

R **(2, 5)**   *S* **(5, −1)**

8. a. Name each polygon, if any, that is a translation of 1.

_____ **3**

b. Name each polygon, if any, that is a reflection of 4.

_____ **None**

c. Name each polygon, if any, that is a rotation of 6.

_____ **1, 2, 3, 5**

Transformations and Similarity

1. Hexagon 2 is a dilation of hexagon 1. Classify the dilation as a reduction or enlargement, and find the scale factor.

_____ **Reduction; 0.75**

2. The larger dinosaur is a dilation of the smaller one. Classify the dilation as a reduction or enlargement, and find the scale factor.

_____ **Enlargement; 1.6**

3. a. Use a scale factor of 1.5 to dilate trapezoid *ABCD*. Find the coordinates of the vertices of the dilation.

A' **(0, 4.5)**   *B'* **(3, 1.5)**
C' **(1.5, −1.5)**   *D'* **(−4.5, −4.5)**

b. Graph trapezoid *A'B'C'D'*.

4. Complete the sentence: The scale factor of a(n) **reduction** is less than 1.

5. Draw a reduction of this envelope. Use a scale factor of $\frac{1}{3}$.

6. Draw an enlargement of this paper clip. Use a scale factor of 1.75.

7. An APS camera uses a 1.6-cm by 2.8-cm negative to produce a photograph measuring 10.16 cm by 17.78 cm. Think of the photograph as a dilation of the negative. What is the scale factor? **6.35**

Name _____

Symmetry

1. **a.** What kinds of symmetry does this figure have?
   Line, rotational, point

   b. Identify any lines of symmetry and rotation points.

Rotation point

2. **a.** What kinds of symmetry does this figure have?
   Rotational, point

   b. Identify any lines of symmetry and rotation points.

Rotation point

3. **a.** How many degrees can this figure be turned and end up unchanged? **60°**

   b. Does the figure have rotational symmetry? **Yes**

4. **a.** How many degrees can this figure be turned and end up unchanged? **360°**

   b. Does the figure have rotational symmetry? **No**

5. How many lines of symmetry does the flower pattern have? **8**

For each letter shown, draw any and all lines of symmetry.

6.   7.   8.   9.

10. **Language Arts** The word BED has a horizontal line of symmetry. Find at least three other words that have horizontal lines of symmetry.
    Possible answer: BOX, CODE, CHECK, DOCK

11. An adapter like the one shown can be used to make a 45-rpm record ("single") play on a standard record player.

    a. Draw all lines of symmetry, if any.

    b. How many degrees can this figure be turned and end up unchanged? **120°**

Name _____

Covering the Plane

1. Use 8 translations of the figure to produce a tessellation.

Possible answer:

2. What transformation would have to be used for the tessellation of triangles shown?
   Rotation

3. How many square tiles with 8-in. sides would it take to cover a wall with area 108 ft²?
   243 tiles

4. Is this pattern a tessellation of octagons? Explain.
   No; There are gaps.

5. Sketch a tessellation of a figure that is not a polygon.
   Possible answer:

6. How many square tiles with 3-in. sides would it take to cover a floor with area 45 ft²? **720 tiles**

7. What polygon is used for the tessellation shown?
   Pentagon

8. Could the pattern in Exercise **7** be created using

   a. Only translations? **No**   **b.** Only rotations? **Yes**

   c. Only reflections? **No**   **d.** A combination? **Yes**

Name _____

Section 11B Review

1. What transformation is used in each of the two pairs of figures?

   a. _____**Dilation**_____   **b.** _____**Reflection**_____

2. The shape is reflected across the x-axis. What are the corresponding vertex coordinates of the reflected figure?

   W' **(3, −3)** X' **(5, 1)**

   Y' **(2, 0)** Z' **(1, −1)**

W (3, 3)
Z (1, 1)
Y (2, 0)
X (5, −1)

3. What is the general rule for reflecting point (x, y) across the x-axis?
   Possible answer: Change to $(x, -y)$.

4. A parallelogram with vertices $P(3, 3)$, $Q(0, −3)$, $R(−4, −2)$, and $S(−1, 4)$ is dilated with respect to the origin, by a factor of $\frac{4}{5}$. What are the new coordinates of the vertices?

   P' **(2.4, 2.4)** Q' **(0, −2.4)** R' **(−3.2, −1.6)** S' **(−0.8, 3.2)**

5. **a.** How many degrees can this figure be turned and look just as it did before? **90°**

   b. What kind or kinds of symmetry does it have?
   Line, rotational, point

6. **Geography** What is the absolute position of Mexico City using latitude and longitude? *[Lesson 8-3]*
   About 19.4° N, 99.2° W

7. **Science** The heaviest door in the world is designed to protect people from radiation at the Natural Institute for Fusion Science in Japan. It is 11.7 m high, 11.4 m wide, and 2.0 m thick. Find the volume of the door. *[Lesson 9-6]*
   266.76 m³

Name _____

Cumulative Review Chapters 1–11

Use a protractor to measure each angle. *[Lesson 8-4]*

1. $\angle FBC$ **45°**   2. $\angle BFE$ **72°**   3. $\angle BGC$ **70°**

4. $\angle BCF$ **27°**   5. $\angle DCG$ **115°**   6. $\angle ECD$ **153°**

Find the volume of each figure after the dilation. *[Lesson 9-7]*

7. Scale factor = $\frac{2}{3}$ Volume = **125 cm³**

7.5 cm
7.5 cm 7.5 cm

8. Scale factor = 6   Volume = **36,504 in³**

$6\frac{1}{2}$ in.
$3\frac{1}{4}$ in.
8 in.

Graph each function. *[Lesson 10-4]*

9. $y = \left(\frac{2}{3}\right)^x$

10. $y = $ round to the nearest even number

State whether each pair of triangles has congruence; if it does, give the rule that justifies your answer. *[Lesson 11-3]*

11. **Yes; Side-Angle-Angle**

12. **Yes; Side-Side-Side**
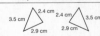
3.5 cm 2.4 cm 2.4 cm 3.5 cm
2.9 cm 2.9 cm

13. **a.** What polygon is used to produce the tessellation shown? *[Lesson 11-9]*
    Hexagon

   b. Can the pattern be produced using:

   Only translations? **No**   Only rotations? **Yes**

   Only reflections? **No**   A combination? **Yes**

160

Tree Diagrams and the Counting Principle

Practice 12-1

Name _____

1. A restaurant offers a choice of apple pie or pecan pie. Each slice of pie can be ordered with whipped cream, ice cream, or fresh fruit.

   a. How many choices of pie are there? **2**

   How many choices of garnish or topping are there? **3**

   b. Use the Counting Principle to find the number of different ways to order a slice of pie with topping or garnish. You may want to check it by drawing a tree diagram. **6**

2. Make a tree diagram to show the possible results of spinning both spinners.

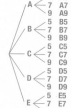

```
        5  A5
A <     7  A7
        9  A9
        5  B5
B <     7  B7
        9  B9
        5  C5
C <     7  C7
        9  C9
        5  D5
D <     7  D7
        9  D9
        5  E5
E <     7  E7
        9  E9
```

3. How many choices do you have in each situation?

   a. 4 types of muffin, 3 types of spread **12**

   b. 5 t-shirt color choices, 4 sizes **20**

   c. 12 ice cream flavors, cone or cup, with or without sprinkles **48**

The early bird special from the Mighty Cafe is shown. Use it to answer Exercises 4 and 5.

> **Early Bird Special $6.49**
> • Soup or Salad
> • Quiche, Casserole, or Pasta
> • Potatoes, Peas, Broccoli, or Carrots
> • Milk, Juice, or Soda

4. How many different early bird specials can be ordered? **72**

5. If the Mighty Café runs out of soup and pasta, how many different early bird specials can be ordered? **24**

6. **Geography** Rich is trying to get from San Francisco to San Jose, California. He needs to stop in San Bruno on the way. There are 3 major roads or freeways from San Francisco to San Bruno, and 3 major roads or freeways from San Bruno to San Jose. How many routes can Rich take? **9**

Use with pages 626–630. **121**

Permutations and Arrangements

Practice 12-2

Name _____

1. Show all arrangements of the letters R, E, A, and D.

ADER, ADRE, AEDR, AERD, ARDE, ARED, DAER, DARE, DEAR, DERA, DRAE, DREA, EADR, EARD, EDAR, EDRA, ERAD, ERDA, RADE, RAED, RDAE, RDEA, READ, REDA

Evaluate.

2. 4! **24**   3. (5!)(3!) **720**   4. (8 − 5)! **6**   5. $\frac{6!}{3!}$ **120**

6. 7(6!) **5,040**   7. 7! **5,040**   8. $\frac{12!}{9!}$ **1,320**   9. (11 − 6)! **120**

10. (6 − 2)! **24**   11. $\frac{7!}{2!}$ **2,520**   12. (4!)(6!) **17,280**   13. $\frac{8!}{(8-2)!}$ **56**

How many ways can the letters of each of these words be arranged? (No letter is used twice.) The letters do not have to form a word.

14. WORDS **120**

15. THE **6**

16. EQUATION **40,320**

17. SALE **24**

18. SWITZERLAND **39,916,800**

19. NATURE **720**

20. A librarian has 7 books to arrange on a shelf. How many ways can he order them? **5,040**

21. Five runners are competing in the 100-yard dash. In how many orders can the runners finish? Assume there are no ties. **120**

22. Jill bought 4 new CD singles. In how many orders can she play them? **24**

23. An 18-member club is choosing its president, vice president, secretary, and treasurer. In how many ways can these four officers be chosen? **73,440**

24. **Geography** On vacation in Hawaii, Kevin wants to visit the islands of Maui, Kauai, Hawaii, Molokai, and Oahu. He only has time to visit 3 islands. In how many ways can he select and order the islands he will visit? **60**

122 Use with pages 631–636.

Combinations and Groups

Practice 12-3

Name _____

Evaluate.

1. $\frac{8!}{3! \times 5!}$ **56**   2. $\frac{5!}{4! \times 1!}$ **5**   3. $\frac{7!}{5! \times 2!}$ **21**   4. $\frac{11!}{8! \times 3!}$ **165**

5. $\frac{6!}{5!(6-5)!}$ **6**   6. $\frac{4!}{2!(4-2)!}$ **6**   7. $\frac{9!}{5!(9-6)!}$ **84**   8. $\frac{5!}{3!(5-3)!}$ **10**

9. In how many ways can 9 Senators be selected from among 100 Senators to serve on a committee? Write in factorial notation. $\frac{100!}{9! \times 91!}$

10. In how many ways can a used car lot manager choose 12 of his 45 cars to feature in a newspaper advertisement? Write in factorial notation. $\frac{45!}{12! \times 33!}$

11. Becky wants to buy 12 of the posters at a poster shop, but she only has enough money for 3 posters. How many ways can she select 3 out of 12 posters? **220**

12. A test instructs you to "answer 2 of the next 5 questions." How many ways can you choose 2 questions to answer? **10**

13. A teacher wants 5 of her 25 students to write solutions on the board. How many ways can she select a group of 5 students? **53,130**

14. **Social Science** In 1995, President Clinton had 20 men and women on his cabinet. How many ways could he select 4 cabinet members to consult regarding a particular issue? **4,845**

15. Patrick read 10 short stories for his English class. He needs to write an essay describing 3 of the stories. How many ways can he choose 3 stories to write about? **120**

16. A pancake restaurant has 8 different syrups, jams, and honeys. Tammy wants to put a different topping on each of her 4 pancakes. How many ways can she choose 4 toppings? **70**

17. Chih is joining a music club. He needs to choose 4 out of 65 compact discs for his first shipment. How many ways can he choose? Write in factorial notation. $\frac{65!}{4! \times 61!}$

18. A computer drawing program has 256 colors available, but you can only use 16 colors at a time. How many ways can you choose 16 out of 256 colors? Write in factorial notation. $\frac{256!}{16! \times 240!}$

Use with pages 637–642. **123**

Section 12A Review

Practice

Name _____

Evaluate.

1. 9! **362,880**   2. 11! **39,916,800**   3. (15 − 8)! **5,040**

4. 8(7!) **40,320**   5. $\frac{12!}{7!}$ **95,040**   6. $\frac{14!}{4!(14-4)!}$ **1,001**

7. A bag contains many blue, green, and red marbles. Make an organized list showing the possible outcomes of removing two marbles, one after the other.

Blue-blue, blue-green, blue-red, green-blue, green-green, green-red, red-blue, red-green, red-red

8. Suppose you remove one marble from the bag in Exercise 7, then flip a coin twice. Make a tree diagram to show the possible outcomes.

```
        H < H = blue - heads - heads
          < T = blue - heads - tails
B <
        T < H = blue - tails - heads
          < T = blue -tails - tails

        H < H = green - heads - heads
          < T = green - heads - tails
G <
        T < H = green - tails - heads
          < T = green - tails - tails

        H < H = red - heads - heads
          < T = red - heads - tails
R <
        T < H = red - tails - heads
          < T = red - tails - tails
```

How many ways can the letters of each of these words be arranged if no letter is used twice? The letters do not have to form a word.

9. SQUARE **720**   10. IOWA **24**   11. SURVEY **720**

12. At an amusement park, Faye and Gary have chosen 5 rides they want to go on. In how many different orders can they go on the rides? **120**

13. A group of friends plan to share 6 of the 36 dishes on the menu at a Chinese restaurant. How many ways can they choose what dishes to order? Write in factorial notation. $\frac{36!}{6! \times 30!}$

14. **Science** A ball is thrown upward at a speed of 48 ft/sec from a height of 12 ft. After t seconds, the height (in feet) is given by the sum of $-16t^2$ and $48t + 12$. What is the height of the ball after 2.5 sec? *[Lesson 10-6]* **32 ft**

15. The Renaissance Tower in Dallas, Texas, is 216 m tall. A scale model of it is 54 cm tall. What is the scale factor of the model? *[Lesson 11-1]* $\frac{1}{400}$

124 Use with page 644.

161

Probability

List all outcomes in each sample space.

1. Tossing a coin   **Heads, tails**

2. Choosing one of 7 cards labeled with the days of the week

   _____ **Sun., Mon., Tue., Wed., Thu., Fri., Sat.** _____

3. Asking a student at your school what grade he or she is in

   _____ **Answers will vary.** _____

Express the probability as a fraction, decimal, and percent.

4. Tossing a coin that lands heads $\frac{1}{2}$; 0.5; 50%

5. Having 60 minutes in the next hour   1; 1.0; 100%

6. Having a birthday that is *not* in January $\frac{11}{12}$; ≈0.917; ≈91.7%
   (assuming that all months are equally likely)

7. Drawing a white marble out of a bag that contains $\frac{3}{10}$; 0.3; 30%
   3 white and 7 black marbles

The blue, gold, and white sectors of the spinner are each $\frac{1}{5}$ of the spinner area.

8. Which color or colors have the same   **Blue, white**
   probability as gold?

9. What is the probability of spinning black? $\frac{2}{5}$

10. What is the probability of spinning blue? $\frac{1}{5}$

11. What is the probability of *not* spinning black? $\frac{3}{5}$

12. Suppose you choose someone at random from your
    school. What is the probability that he or she was
    born on the same day of the week as you? $\frac{1}{7}$

13. In the game of Monopoly™, the probability of going to
    jail in any one turn is about 4.5%. What is the probability
    of *not* going to jail?   **About 95.5%**

Experimental and Geometric Probability

1. Toss 4 coins 40 times and complete the table to record   **Answers will vary.**
   your results. Use the data to find the experimental
   probability of each event. Give each probability as a percent.

Outcome	4 heads	3 heads 1 tails	2 heads 2 tails	1 heads 3 tails	4 tails
Frequency					
Experimental Probability					

2. Compare the experimental probability of tossing 4 tails and
   no heads with the theoretical probability.

   Answers will vary. (Theoretical probability is 6.25%.)

3. Helen works in an ice cream shop. For the last
   three hours, she has recorded what flavor each
   customer purchased. Her data is shown.

Outcome	Customers
Vanilla	27
Chocolate	14
Strawberry	16
Other	13

   a. What is the probability that a
      customer purchased chocolate?   **20%**

   b. What is the probability that a
      customer purchased vanilla or
      strawberry?   **About 61.4%**

   c. What is the probability that the next customer
      will *not* purchase strawberry?   **About 77.1%**

4. A player tosses a coin onto the game board.

   a. What is the probability that
      the coin lands in the circle?   **About 24.7%**

   b. What is the probability that
      the coin lands outside the circle? **About 75.3%**

5. **Social Science** The stem-and-leaf diagram shows the ages of
   U.S. Presidents at inauguration.

   ```
   stem | leaf
     4  | 2366899
     5  | 00111122444455556667778
     6  | 0111244589
   ```

   a. What is the probability that a President was 57?   **About 9.8%**

   b. What is the probability that a President was over 59? **About 24.4%**

Conditional Probability

Suppose that a fly lands on the 7 by 7 game board shown.
What is the probability that it lands:

1. On a white square? $\frac{24}{49}$

2. In the fifth row? $\frac{1}{7}$

3. On a white square in the fifth row? $\frac{3}{49}$

4. On a shaded square in the first row? $\frac{4}{49}$

5. If you know that the fly landed on a shaded square, what is
   the probability that it landed on the top right corner square? $\frac{1}{25}$

6. You roll a pair of number cubes. If the first one comes up 3,
   find the probability that the sum of the 2 number cubes is:

   a. 6 $\frac{1}{6}$ ≈ 16.7%   b. less than 7 $\frac{1}{2}$ = 50%   c. 5 or 8 $\frac{1}{3}$ ≈ 33.3%

The graph shows the percent of people in Gambia who
belong to various ethnic groups.

Ethnic Groups in Gambia

☐ Mandinka
☐ Fula
▨ Wolof
☐ Jola
▧ Serahuli
■ Other

5%
9%
10%
16%
18%
42%

7. Two Gambians are chosen at random. What is
   the probability that both are Fulas?

   3.24%

8. The 1994 population of Gambia was about
   960,000. Estimate the number of Jolas.   **About 96,000**

9. If you know that a Gambian is not Mandinka,
   what is the probability that he or she is Fula? **About 31%**

10. The table shows how many people live in each
    area of Smalltown, U.S.A. What is the probability
    that a randomly chosen small town resident:

	West of Broadway	East of Broadway
North of Main St.	106	243
South of Main St.	158	174

    a. Lives north of Main St.? **About 51.2%**

    b. Lives east of Broadway, if you already know
       that the resident lives south of Main Street?

    About 52.4%

Dependent and Independent Events

State whether each pair of events is independent or dependent.

1. You roll a 6 on a number cube and then flip a coin that
   comes up heads.   **Independent**

2. A person was born in winter and born in February.   **Dependent**

3. You get an A in science and an A in math.   **Independent**

4. A man is 42 years old and his phone number begins with
   the digits 4 and 2.   **Independent**

5. You draw a red marble from a bag, and then another red
   marble (without replacing the first marble).   **Dependent**

Suppose that two tiles are drawn from the collection shown
at the right. The first tile is replaced before the second is
drawn. Find each probability.

6. P(A, A) $\frac{4}{225}$ 7. P(R, C) $\frac{2}{25}$ 8. P(E, not E) $\frac{44}{225}$

9. P(vowel, vowel) $\frac{4}{25}$ 10. P(vowel, not R) $\frac{6}{25}$ 11. P(consonant, vowel) $\frac{6}{25}$

Suppose that two tiles are drawn from the collection shown above. The
first tile is *not* replaced before the second is drawn. Find each probability.

12. P(A, A) $\frac{1}{105}$ 13. P(R, C) $\frac{3}{35}$ 14. P(E, not E) $\frac{22}{105}$

15. P(vowel, vowel) $\frac{1}{7}$ 16. P(vowel, not R) $\frac{8}{35}$ 17. P(consonant, vowel) $\frac{9}{35}$

Suppose you're new in town and you do not
know your way around, so you choose your path
randomly. Assume that you always travel in a
northbound direction.

18. If you take path 1, what is the probability
    that you end up at Karl's house? $\frac{1}{2}$

19. If you take path 2, what is the probability
    that you end up at Leo's house? $\frac{2}{3}$

20. Find the probability that you end up at:

    Jane's house $\frac{1}{6}$ Karl's house $\frac{5}{18}$ Leo's house $\frac{7}{18}$ Mary's house $\frac{1}{6}$

Section 12B Review

1. Identify the sample space for the experiment of randomly choosing a letter from the word C O M P U T E R. Find the number of outcomes in each event, and find the probability of each event.

Sample space: **C, O, M, P, U, T, E, R**

Events: **a.** Choosing R **b.** Choosing a vowel   **c.** Not choosing P

Number of outcomes: **1**   **3**   **7**

Probability: $\dfrac{1}{8}$ $\dfrac{3}{8}$ $\dfrac{7}{8}$

2. If you toss two number cubes, what are the following probabilities?

   a. P(sum of 10) $\dfrac{1}{12}$ **b.** P(sum < 7) $\dfrac{5}{12}$ **c.** P(sum of 8, 9, or 12) $\dfrac{5}{18}$

3. You draw two chips from a bag containing 2 white, 3 red, and 5 blue chips. Find each probability if the first chip is replaced. Then find each probability if it is not replaced.

       a. P(blue then blue)   **b.** P(white then red)   **c.** P(red then *not* red)

If replaced: $\dfrac{1}{4}$ $\dfrac{3}{50}$ $\dfrac{21}{100}$

If not replaced: $\dfrac{2}{9}$ $\dfrac{1}{15}$ $\dfrac{7}{30}$

4. What is the probability of spinning orange? $\dfrac{1}{3}$

5. If you don't spin pink, what is the probability of spinning brown? $\dfrac{3}{5}$

6. If you spin the spinner twice, what is the probability of spinning orange then brown? $\dfrac{1}{6}$

7. If the first spin lands on brown, what is the probability that both spins land on brown? $\dfrac{1}{2}$

(Spinner sectors: Brown, Pink, Orange, Brown, Brown, Orange)

8. A living room on a floor plan is 4 in. by $5\frac{1}{2}$ in. If the scale factor is 36, what are the perimeter and area of the living room? *[Lesson 9-2]*

Perimeter: **684 in.**   Area: **28,512 in²**

9. The top of the Commerzbank Tower in Frankfurt, Germany, forms a 71° angle with a point 89.2 m from the tower's base. How tall is the Commerzbank Tower? *[Lesson 11-4]*   **About 259 m**

Cumulative Review Chapters 1–12

Find the surface area of each figure. *[Lesson 9-4]*

1. **1734 in²** (17 in., 17 in., 17 in.)
2. **209.88 cm²** (8.5 cm, 9.2 cm, 7.7 cm, 3.6 cm)
3. **1347 ft²** (12 ft, $15\frac{1}{4}$ ft, 18 ft)

Multiply. *[Lesson 10-8]*

4. $(3x^2)(4x^5)$ **$12x^7$**
5. $2p(p^2 - 3p + 5)$ **$2p^3 - 6p^2 + 10p$**
6. $-t^3(t^3 - 8t)$ **$-t^6 + 8t^4$**
7. $3u^2(u^4 - 5u^2 + 7)$ **$3u^6 - 15u^4 + 21u^2$**
8. $\frac{2}{3}c(12c^2 - 18)$ **$8c^3 - 12c$**
9. $8d(3d^2 - 4d - 11)$ **$24d^3 - 32d^2 - 88d$**

Tell what transformation of the left figure in each pair produces the right one. *[Lesson 11-6]*

10. **Rotation**
11. **Translation**
12. **Reflection**

How many ways can the letters of each of these words be arranged? (No letter is used twice.) The letters do not have to form a word. *[Lesson 12-2]*

13. MYOPIA   **720**
14. BARN   **24**
15. MONKEYS   **5,040**
16. FORMALITY   **362,880**
17. DINOSAUR   **40,320**
18. POWER   **120**

Express the probability as a fraction, decimal, and percent. *[Lesson 12-4]*

19. Rolling a 3 or 5 on a single roll of a number cube $\dfrac{1}{3}$; ≈0.333; ≈33.3%

20. Drawing a rectangle that is also a pentagon   0; 0.0; 0%

21. Selecting a purple marble from a bag that contains 8 purple and 22 red marbles $\dfrac{4}{15}$; ≈0.267; ≈26.7%

22. A randomly chosen person being born on a Saturday or Sunday $\dfrac{2}{7}$; ≈0.286; ≈28.6%